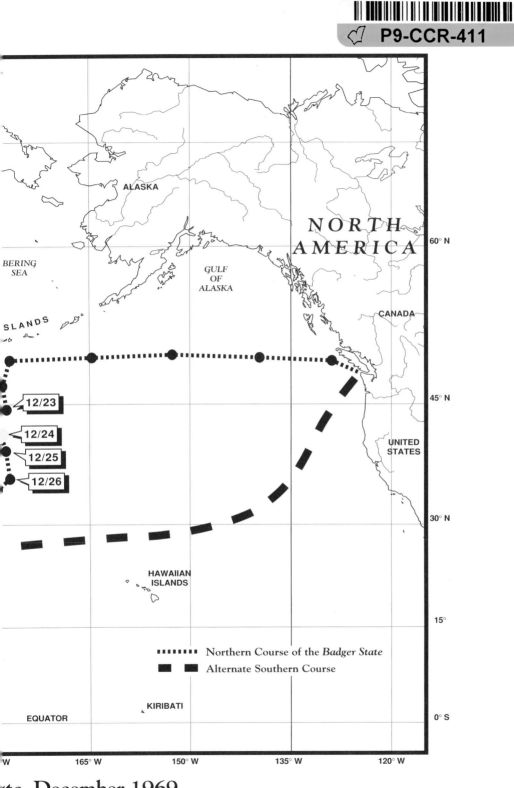

ALASKA

NORTH
AMERICA

60° N

BERING
SEA

GULF
OF
ALASKA

CANADA

SLANDS

45° N

12/23

12/24

12/25

UNITED
STATES

12/26

30° N

HAWAIIAN
ISLANDS

15°

▪▪▪▪▪▪▪ Northern Course of the *Badger State*
■■ ■■ Alternate Southern Course

KIRIBATI

EQUATOR

0° S

W   165° W   150° W   135° W   120° W

te, December 1969

Sailing into the Abyss

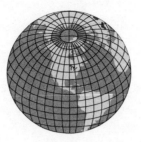

Sailing into the Abyss

*A True Story of Extreme Heroism
on the High Seas*

William R. Benedetto

CITADEL PRESS
Kensington Publishing Corporation
www.kensingtonbooks.com

CITADEL PRESS books are published by

Kensington Publishing Corp.
850 Third Avenue
New York, NY 10022

All Kensington titles, imprints, and distributed lines are available at special quantity discounts for bulk purchases for sales promotions, premiums, fund-raising, educational, or institutional use. Special book excerpts or customized printings can also be created to fit specific needs. For details, write or phone the office of the Kensington special sales manager: Kensington Publishing Corp., 850 Third Avenue, New York, NY 10022, attn: Special Sales Department; phone 1-800-221-2647.

CITADEL PRESS and the Citadel logo are Reg. U.S. Pat. & TM Off.

First printing: March 2005

10 9 8 7 6 5 4 3 2 1

Printed in the United States of America

Library of Congress Control Number: 2004110748

ISBN 0-8065-2634-3

To

Captain Charles T. Wilson
and the
Brave Crew of the
SS *Badger State*

AND TO

Their Brother Seafarers
of the U.S. Merchant Marine,
who served their Country
Honorably and Heroically
in War and Peace

I have fought a good fight,
I have finished my course,
I have kept the faith.
—*The Epistle of Paul to Titus 1:15*

———⊱◦⊰———

IN MEMORIAM

Michael Joseph Schiro
Captain, U.S. Coast Guard (Retired)
Died July 14, 2000

Contents

Foreword

The death-defying challenges confronting the captain and crew of a ship under assault by the twin elements of hurricane-force winds and towering seas are the stuff of maritime legend. In earlier eras, wooden ships, their sails rendered into useless, flapping rags by perverse winds, ofttimes found themselves driven onto the rocks of a lee shore. Today's iron ships, despite modern technology and improved weather predictions, also encounter great dangers on the high seas. Given the isolation of ship from shore, the battle inevitably becomes the classic age-old contest of man against the sea.

The 1969 voyage of the SS *Badger State* dramatically exemplifies that battle in the extreme when the ship confronted not only the elements in all their fury, but also contained a deadly enemy within its hull—a cargo of 500-, 750-, and 2,000-pound blockbuster bombs breaking loose in the ship's holds. The night-and-day battle by captain and crew to deal with this peril is brought to life by William Benedetto's *Sailing into the Abyss*. His book may most properly be included among the elite sagas of man against the sea, even if based only on his superbly written chronicle of the SS *Badger State* and its final voyage in the Pacific Ocean, bound for the war in Vietnam with its dangerous cargo of bombs and other munitions.

But the author provides much more than a spellbinding tale of a doomed ship. While the reader becomes quickly engrossed in the evolving story of the *Badger State*, Benedetto manages to intersperse some history of the United States merchant marine and its invaluable contribution to the nation's defense and general welfare. In addition, the author reminds us of such horrific disasters as the *Titanic*, *Port Chicago*, and *Texas City*, and also describes the loneliness felt by sailors far from home, during the Christmas holiday. And he does it all so smoothly; you won't begrudge the minor interruptions in this masterfully written account.

To most landlubbers (in my view, one who has never experienced a few weeks at a time on an ocean out of sight of land), the idea of a stormy sea is usually the result of watching an epic film or, for a few, a mental image created during the reading of one or more stories of great adventures at sea. Whether it is a Hollywood production such as *The Perfect Storm*, or a book by an author like C. S. Forester, the fact remains that the image is formed while sitting in a rock-steady seat or chair. To those who *have* seen a wall of foaming, wind-whipped water, forty or fifty feet high, or even higher, rise up to challenge the strength of the ship and the skill of the helmsman, to be followed by another and yet another mountainous wave in an unending line, this is a story you will "live" as you read it. And, as you are forming your own mental images of these events, I am confident you will not only feel strong admiration for the valiant battle fought by the captain and crew of the *Badger State*, but will be left with the feeling "I'm really glad I wasn't there!"

—Howard B. Thorsen
Vice-Admiral, U.S. Coast Guard (Retired)
April 2004

Acknowledgments

This book would not have been possible without the enormous help of a number of talented people. First and foremost, I am indebted to Captain Charles T. Wilson of the SS *Badger State* for sharing with me intimate details of his life as well as his experiences and emotions during his ship's tragic voyage. Without doubt, recalling the memories of those December 1969 days and nights had to be a painful ordeal for him. And yet he gave me his wholehearted cooperation in every aspect of writing this story.

Others intimately connected with the *Badger State*, who offered to share their memories and recollections with me, included Nancy Keys and Jennifer Miller, wife and daughter of Bosun Richard Hughes; Violet Woods and Theresa Anderson, wife and daughter of Third Engineer Kinnie Woods; Lyle Rilling, brother of Able Seaman Floyd Rilling; and Elvis McLure, a surviving crewmember then known as James McLure. I am indebted to these good people.

Several retired Coast Guard captains came aboard to help this mission along. In particular, I appreciate the assistance and encouragement of John F. Mundy, a close friend, for his critique, timely suggestions, and boundless enthusiasm; the encouragement of another very good friend, Michael J. Schiro, now deceased; and the assistance of Captain Albert L. Olsen, Jr., a member of the Coast Guard Board of Investigation, for his help in obtaining copies of records.

Many others contributed their time and efforts. I thank the following persons, listed in no particular order, for their work on my behalf: author Peter Maas and publisher Bob Follett for their suggestions and encouragement early on; Charles E. Cardinell, Ph.D., librarian Robert Waldt, historian and merchant marine Captains Niels Nielsen and Gene Harrower, all serving at the Portland Maritime Museum; Captain John McDonnell for sharing his experiences aboard the SS *American Robin*; seafarer Randy G. Brandon for updating me on life aboard ship; Emile Dreuil, former Shipping Commissioner, New Orleans, Louisiana, for a favorite recollection; Gibson Bell Smith at the National Archives for help with research above and beyond the call of duty; Marco Cannistraro, editor of the Marine Engineers' Beneficial Association's *The Marine Officer*; Talmage Simpkins, Executive Director, AFL–CIO; Professor Douglas K. Fleming, University of Washington; the Reverend Dan Adams for inspirational guidance; Chuck Koepnick for unraveling the mysterious workings of my computer; Heidi Sue, librarian at Kalispell, Montana, for magically finding an obscure record; Walter Willigan for a helping hand; Ron Laliberte, Mary Wilson, Emily Buckberry, Evelyn Mundy, and a host of good friends too numerous to mention for their constant encouragement and good wishes.

Most beginning writers need the help of a dedicated and persistent agent. I was fortunate to find one in the person of Agnes Birnbaum of Bleecker Street Associates. Agnes, a remarkable lady, showered me with encouragement and ideas and eventually connected me with Kensington Publishing Corporation. There, senior editor Michaela Hamilton took over, helping me to broaden the scope of the book to include a brief history of the merchant marine. Her patience and understanding in dealing with a novice writer sailing his first voyage through the rocks and shoals of the publishing world was truly commendable.

Finally, a work of this nature with its demands of time and energy requires the help, encouragement, and cooperation of family. I have had that in full measure from my children: Cher Pataki, Lee Martin, Val Koepnick, and Bill, Jr. And, finally, and not the least for the fact that it is last, I acknowledge the greatest debt to my wife Barbara, a truly remarkable lady who has been my strongest source of encouragement, no matter what uncharted waters I decided to sail on throughout the more than fifty happy years we have spent together.

Prologue

In the annals of maritime history, one finds no parallel to the odyssey of the SS *Badger State*. No other ship has ever been held hostage by a cargo of bombs, 500- to 2,000-pound blockbusters, roaming free in the hull of the ship—"a big pit of deadly, dangerous snakes," as one crewmember described it.

The ship, bound for Vietnam in the winter of 1969, encountered violent storms in the north Pacific Ocean. Pallets holding the bombs captive began to break down. A night-and-day battle ensued between crew and cargo, exacerbated by two unpredicted and violent storms that hammered the ship over the Christmas holiday. An explosion followed; the ship radioed an SOS; and the crew abandoned ship.

Then followed a series of unusual events that again have no equal in maritime history—strange, inexplicable phenomena that befell the crew as though some mystical, malevolent spirit would bar their escape. And, in fact, most did not escape.

Small wonder that the tragedy snared my attention. I was then a Coast Guard shipping commissioner, work concerned with the rights of merchant seamen. I began to collect records over the next thirty years, perhaps amassing the most extensive library anywhere on the *Badger State*. This book is the result.

Early on, I decided to stick to the facts of the case and, insofar as possible, tell the story through the eyes of Captain Charles T. Wilson, the skipper of the ship. To do so, I largely relied on the written record of the Coast Guard Marine Board of Investigation, 372 pages of which were devoted to Captain Wilson. To insure accuracy, I periodically furnished him chapters of the book for review. In addition, I maintained close—at times almost daily—contact with him throughout the several years I devoted to writing the story.

On occasions when Wilson was not present, statements attributed to crewmembers in quotations have been taken from their testimony before the Board. Radio messages received and sent by the ship, shown in capital letters, were part of the eighty-eight exhibits attached to the Board's record. In both instances, only minor changes were made for clarity.

My initial focus centered on the tragedy of the *Badger State*. My editor, Michaela Hamilton, suggested that I include a brief history of the U.S. merchant marine—a term that describes *civilian* merchant seamen and, typically, privately owned ships to transport goods from port to port. An excellent suggestion, as it turned out. However, time and space limited me to highlighting dramatic moments of that history. A more comprehensive review may be found in the books listed in the bibliography.

Much of the information about seamen, ships, and sailing comes from personal experience dealing with hundreds of thousands of merchant seamen while I was a shipping commissioner in the ports of San Pedro, New Orleans, Port Arthur, and Portland (Oregon). Sailing aboard Coast Guard cutters involved in search and rescue, buoy-tending, and ocean station patrol added to that background. Finally, my work as a lawyer for the past twenty years proved helpful in researching laws relating to merchant seamen.

I decided to avoid cluttering the book with footnotes. However, for the reader who wishes to pursue certain matters further, the bibliography furnishes the sources that I referred to in writing this story. I am indebted to the authors of those works. For those readers who have more than a casual interest in the merchant marine, I strongly recommend the following authors and their works: *The U.S. Merchant Marine at War, 1775–1945*, edited by Bruce L. Felknor, a first-rate collection of stories about the merchant marine; *The Abandoned Ocean, A History of United States Maritime Policy* by Andrew Gibson and Arthur Donovan, an invaluable source of information on the political and economic concerns of the merchant marine; *Ships of the Esso Fleet in World War II*, published by Standard Oil Company (New Jersey), valuable because of the recollections of survivors compiled by the company (out of print but possibly available used on the Web); and a technical book, *The Law of Seamen* by Martin J. Norris, one oriented toward lawyers but still a "good read" to anyone interested in the lives of seafarers in earlier times.

And so we begin at the beginning. . . .

The Crew of the SS *Badger State*

Master Charles T. Wilson

Chief Mate Leonard Cobbs

Second Mate Robert A. Ziehm

Third Mate Willie L. Burnette

Third Mate Sam A. Bondy, Jr.

Radio Officer William K. LaFayette

Bosun Richard D. Hughes

Deck Utility Lawrence O. McHugh

Able Seaman Joseph Candos

Able Seaman Nelson Fabre

Able Seaman George Henderson

Able Seaman Edward C. Hottendorf

Able Seaman Floyd K. Rilling

Ordinary Seaman James McLure

Ordinary Seaman Richard C. Murray

Ordinary Seaman John S. Kaleiwahea

Chief Engineer Gilbert F. Baker

First Assistant Engineer Steven Bordash

Second Assistant Engineer Raymond W. Reiche

Third Assistant Engineer Richard Pattershall

Third Assistant Engineer Kinnie Woods

Cadet Engineer Neal Kirkwood

Electrician Konstantinos Mpountalis

Second Electrician Jose A. Rodriguez

Oiler Francisco C. Nunez

Oiler Calvin R. Smith

Oiler Nick Barbieri

Fireman-Watertender James H. Beatty

Fireman-Watertender Samuel Kaneao

Fireman-Watertender Leonard J. Scypion

Wiper Mohamed T. Al-Muwallad

Wiper Florencio Serafino

Steward Bennie L. Brown

Cook/Baker Naji S. Saiban

Third Cook Donald D. Byrd

Messman Charles E. Coe

Messman Ali A. Gazaly

Messman Edwin L. Jones

Messman Charles McCullar

Galleyman John H. Jenkins

Sailing into the Abyss

CHAPTER 1

Under Way

**And darkness covered the abyss, while
a mighty wind swept over the waters.**

—Genesis 1:2, New American Bible

The Pacific Ocean, the desolate graveyard of dead sailors and wrecked ships, is a colossus. Eleven thousand miles across at the equator, it plunges downward an average of two miles to the ocean floor. Over eons, it has swallowed whole enormous mountain ranges and ridges and valleys. Even so, all the world's continents, and all its unwilling inhabitants, would still fit nicely in its belly with room to spare.

But there is more to this ocean than its size. Possessed of a savage temper and a capacity for random violence, it is a breeding ground for disaster. Giant typhoons routinely spawn in its equatorial regions; tidal disturbances spring up from the nearly three-hundred active volcanoes on its rim; and wintry hurricane and gale-force winds drive huge waves to distant shores, disrupting the temper and schedules of countless numbers of seamen and their ships. Mariners venturing forth on this sea do so at their peril.

In one corner of this turbulent ocean, at a point south of Alaska and west of Seattle, Washington, sailed one such challenger. Shrouded in mottled gray paint, rust streaks bleeding down her hull like blood from a mortal wound, she looked the part of the tramp she was. The letters branded on her stern, still visible after years of ocean abuse, spelled out the name SS *Badger State*. A United States merchant vessel owned by States Marine Lines, the ship sailed in pursuit of her country's business. In the winter of 1969, that business meant carrying rockets and bombs urgently needed by American troops fighting the war in Vietnam.

High up on the exposed bridge deck, extending from the wheel-house, crouched a lone figure, Captain Charles Wilson. Strong winds sweeping across the open deck billowed out the back of a loose-fitting foul-weather jacket he wore—like the main sail of a small boat scudding before a nor'easter. Matching trousers helped protect a six-foot muscular frame from cold winds and wet spray. He wrapped his bare hands tightly around an ice-cold metal railing.

The Old Man, as the crew privately referred to him in their kinder moments, was in his late thirties. Dark, penetrating eyes dominated an even-featured face, unremarkable save for a pointed tuff of whiskers covering a prominent chin—admiration for a cousin fighting in Vietnam inspired the last. There was a sort of weary, hard-bitten look about him that sometimes sets apart young men dealing with difficult decisions

As maritime skippers go, Wilson was young for the challenge of commanding the ship. The job demanded that he nursemaid, counsel, and oversee the welfare of the thirty-nine men plying the decks below, as well as be accountable for the safety of cargo and ship. In addition, countless other intricate details calling for diplomacy, delicacy, and determination, which could make or break the ship and its owner, awaited his call. But experience and training trumped youth in placing him on the bridge of the *Badger State* at this moment in history.

Wilson shivered uncontrollably. The cold air had a sharp edge to it, honed by the frigid watery spray drifting up from the gray-green waves rampaging over the ship's bow. He hunched up his shoulders, trying to withdraw within himself for warmth. He could not stop the shaking, or the chattering of his teeth, as he automatically braced himself to keep his balance on the steel deck that rocked beneath his rubber-soled shoes. "To hell with this," he muttered, fumbling with cold fingers to unfasten the latch to the wheelhouse door, held tightly shut by the sheer force of the winds battering the ship.

Like all other compartments on the *Badger State*, the wheelhouse was short on space and long on equipment. The ship's nerve center, it featured the latest technology that 1969 had to offer. Morse code, and voice radio for close-in talk, provided the critical and fragile link between sea and shore. Radar—short powerful radio pulses bouncing off solid objects in the surrounding ocean area and showing up as blips of light on a dark screen—tracked intruders in the surrounding area. Within arm's reach of the watch officer stood a Radio Direction Finder, a device capable of homing in on radio waves sent by stations located along the shores of most maritime nations. A ship within roughly 150 miles of shore could nail down its position by intersecting signals transmitted by two or more of those stations.

Standing conspicuously near the center of the wheelhouse, within a tarnished brass case, stood the engine room telegraph. Linking wheelhouse and engine room, it resembled a circular two-sided clock with glass dials on each side, stenciled with standard engine orders relating to speed. A duplicate in the engine room mocked whatever speed was selected in the wheelhouse. It was generally used in port, orders at sea being given by telephone.

Dominating the wheelhouse, and almost as ancient as sailing itself, stood the helm of the ship: a large-spoked oak wheel made lustrous by the caressing of the calloused hands of scores of seamen over the years. Near the helm, partly enclosed in a brass cage, a gyrocompass—a mechanical compass not subject to the meanderings of a magnetic compass with its attraction to the iron and steel of the ship—reached to chest level for easy reference by the helmsman. Close by, a sheaf of well-thumbed navigation charts showing the ship's track and position lay scattered across a scarred metal table bolted to the ship's deck.

Wilson secured the door. The idle chatter of the men in the wheelhouse subsided into a familiar silence at the sight of the Old Man. Acting unconcerned, he automatically checked the radar screen. Another ship in the area was highly unlikely given the vastness of the ocean and the relatively few ships sailing on its broad expanse.

Third Mate Willie Burnette was the watch officer on duty. Thickly built, crew-cut, he had the look of a sailor comfortable with his calling, one who fancied ships over a wife and home ashore. A veteran of World War II, he had also sailed on vessels carrying bombs to American military forces during the Korean War. The experience would stand him in good stead during this voyage. One of his major jobs on the *Badger State* was to con the ship—see to her navigation. He was preoccupied with a set of parallel rulers marking off the ship's course on the navigation chart.

At the helm stood Ed Hottendorf, a soft-spoken seaman out of Oregon, another longtime sailor, hard working, and well liked by the officers and deck crew.

With Wilson peering at the chart over his shoulder, Burnette said, "It's impossible to keep our heading, Cap'n. These damn waves are just too—"

"I know, Mr. Burnette, I know," Wilson interrupted, addressing him with the formality he favored while on duty. "Just do the best you can. We'll get through this somehow."

But Wilson had cause to worry. Barely out of sight of land, they were already being slammed by a continuous string of storms, one strong blow after another without letup. He held fast to the brass rail below the porthole, a slight shiver stirring through him as he braced his feet against the steel deck. It was the sailor's subconscious reaction to the ship's synchronous rolling, the deck angling steeply first to one side, then to the other. To Wilson, the ship seemed to be rolling at an increasingly steeper angle.

He glanced at the inclinometer, a curving glass tube with a bubble measuring the ship's angle of roll. The gauge was recording rolls of thirty to thirty-five degrees, which, although uncomfortable, would hardly test the sea legs of any sailor worth his salt. Still, it might make a seaman grip his coffee cup to keep it from sliding off a table. At forty-five degrees, however, it would be time for all hands to hang on to something bolted down. Beyond that angle, even the permanent fixtures aboard ship might break loose and run free across the deck. A 441-foot cargo vessel like the *Badger State* could theoretically roll to an angle steep enough to turn the ship keel side up. But that was highly unlikely for a relatively modern ship, absent some other critical factor such as faulty design or water breaching the ship's watertight compartments. Given this lopsided work platform, small wonder then that a sailor ashore walks with a rolling gait, each foot looking for an uneven surface.

Wilson stared out through the water-streaked glass as the storm continued descending in sheets from a shadowy and sullen sky. Reaching the deck, the rain reunited with the seas, tumbling endlessly over the ship's bow to splash across the main deck. There was not much more to be done. He had already radioed the Navy for permission to temporarily divert to a more southerly route. Such a course might lead the ship to calmer waters and bring it closer to the ports of Pearl Harbor and Midway, both possible sanctuaries if needed.

The Navy okayed the diversion. However, Wilson soon discovered that sailing a southerly course exposed the ship to swells both off its side and stern quarters. The force of those waves caused the ship to roll even more steeply, up to forty-five degrees on occasion. As a result, he was forced to alternate between staying the northerly track and diverting south, as wind and waves allowed.

There were two possible sailing routes from the Seattle area to Vietnam. The northern route lies northwest of the Seattle area; west to roughly mid-Pacific—a point about a hundred miles south of Attu at the end of the Aleutian Islands—diagonally down to the south of the north Pacific Ocean; and then across to the Philippines and on to Vietnam. A ship sailing the southern route would proceed roughly southwest and then west to Hawaii, taking advantage of the Pacific trade winds blowing westward, and then on to Vietnam. Weather projections determined the best route to sail.

With the experts initially predicting foul weather on the southern course—strong head winds and crossing swells were expected—the Navy routed the *Badger State* on a northerly track. But the experts seemed to be dead wrong. Sailing not far off the cold Gulf of Alaska seemed to account for much of the ship's troubles.

Wilson had eighteen years of sailing under his belt, and the sea conditions were beginning to approach some of the worst he had ever dealt with. He tried to gauge the direction the waves were coming from—heading the bow directly into oncoming swells was one way to cut the ship's roll. Unfortunately, the *Badger State* was facing confused swells, long waves flowing in multiple directions. The combination was creating a short-and-tight stiff roll, jockeying the ship from side to side. A jerky snap roll could exert unusually heavy pressure on the ship's cargo. And it was the nature of the cargo that was driving Wilson's concerns.

A grab-bag collection of claymore mines, detonators, small arms ammo, and, in particular, bombs weighing from 500 to 2,000 pounds were stuffed into the ship's holds. The bombs were packaged in pallets, framed with steel for the blockbuster bombs, wood for the 500- and 750-pounders. The belly of the bombs rested within elliptical cuts inside the frames. Metal straps tied the whole of it, frame and bombs, together. Each pallet held multiple bombs: six 500-pound bombs, for example, or two 2,000-pound bombs.

The pallets were stowed in the cargo holds in rows running fore and aft (bow to stern), side to side, or a combination of the two. Additional rows of bombs, or related hardware such as bomb fins, were sometimes piled on top of that bottom layer.

One hundred pallets containing 2,000-pound blockbuster bombs, for example, were stowed in a single layer in No. 5 hold, located near the stern of the ship. The layers were arranged in rows that stretched from side to side, interrupted in the centerline of the ship where two rows were stowed fore and aft. Some of the bombs were loaded nose to nose. Thirty-three pallets of bomb fins and couplers were crammed on top of rows at one end of the hold.

With this pattern of loading, the sides of the ship were used as fixed boundaries—similar to bookends on a library shelf—holding the pallets against each other. Wooden blocking was installed at each "bookend" where the straight side of the last pallet of each row met the curving hull of the ship.

Packaging bombs in pallets was a relatively new scheme. Roughly eighteen months earlier, 2,000-pound bombs were laboriously loaded one by one into a ship's holds, laid down like cordwood with bracing to hold them in place. Changing to the pallet system may have been done for practical reasons—pallets were easier and quicker to winch aboard ship and into the holds; once inside, they were much simpler to deal with using forklift trucks. Still, the use of pallets presented potential problems not present with the old method of simply laying the bombs down in the hold like logs in a woodbin.

To simplify, visualize a single row of fifteen pallets, each three feet wide, laid flat on a horizontal surface, exactly as some of the pallets of bombs were loaded aboard the ship. Assume there are no pallets piled above this row. Obviously, the weight on each pallet is minimal, merely the weight of the pallet itself. Then take this flat surface and tilt it over at a forty-five-degree angle, one which the *Badger State* rolled to on many occasions. Suddenly, the dynamics have changed dramatically—one side of the ship has become the "top," and the other side the "bottom." That bottom pallet is suddenly bearing the cumulative weight of the fourteen pallets above it. The steeper the roll of the ship, the heavier the weight bearing on the bottom pallets. This was one potential problem confronting the *Badger State*.

A second aggravating factor could also prove pivotal. With the ship snap-rolling from side to side, a pendulum-like shift in weight occurs, exerting pressure first in one direction, then the other. This constant jockeying back and forth—like jimmying loose a rock in a hard place—could conceivably break down the frames of the pallets and the metal straps holding bombs and pallets together. Once a single pallet caved in, adjoining containers would have more space in which to move about. That extra leeway would then, in a chain of events, tend to create still more stress on other pallets, eventually leading to a breakdown of more containers. In the worst-case scenario setting, bombs could break out of the pallets and roam loose in the holds.

If the pallets began to break apart, the first logical step would be to cut out the splintered, cracked, and broken frame, and then jury-rig a new pallet. Alternatively, if the shoring gave way, loose pallets could be braced in by hammering wooden supports between them, or between the end pallets and the sides of the ship. This would be tough work ashore in the best of circumstances and, even then, a job best reserved for professional longshoremen. On a rolling platform of a ship at sea, in the tight, confined spaces of the holds with makeshift lighting, inadequate tools, and inexperienced hands to wield them, the work would present a challenge that could be met only by an enormous effort by the captain and crew.

Those concerns were never far from Wilson's mind, particularly when the ship's rolling intensified. Sensing a change, he glanced at the inclinometer. It registered forty degrees. He turned to the watch officer. "Mr. Burnette, see what you can do to head the ship into these confused swells."

"That'll take us off our heading, sir."

"Don't worry about that," Wilson said sharply. "We need to cut the ship's roll a bit. I don't like the pressure these steep angles are putting on the cargo." The words were no sooner spoken when the two men were interrupted by Chief Mate Cobbs entering the wheelhouse, breathing heavily.

Cobbs was the second-most senior man on the ship, and in line to assume command. He was an old salt who, as scuttlebutt would have it, actually served on ships that depended on sails and wind to get from one port to another. Of course he was hardly that old. It was just that with his rolling gait and a wind-blown face bearing a few navigational lines, it seemed like he must have sailed before the mast in more storied times.

Water streamed down the mate's face. Wiry wisps of gray hair stood at attention on his scalp despite all attempts by wind and water to lay waste to them. He looked up at Wilson, agitation plainly visible in the furrowed lines crisscrossing his brow.

"We got trouble, Captain, serious trouble; we got cargo loose—."
The mate paused to catch his breath.

Wilson groaned. "Where?"

"In the tween decks, sir!"

"Number?"

"No. 3, lower, amidship, Captain."

"Dammit to hell!" Wilson exploded, then paused briefly to rein in his
emotions. He took a deep breath, pausing, and then spoke in a quieter
tone. "Okay, mate, okay. Let's take a look at it."

The *Badger State* took on her cargo of bombs at the Bangor Naval
Ammunition Depot in Washington State in mid-December of 1969.
Spread-eagled across seven-thousand acres west of Seattle, the Bangor
Depot was the primary military base on the west coast charged with sup-
plying the explosives needed by American troops in Vietnam.

The military had an insatiable need for such explosives. A single
Boeing B-52G Stratofortress routinely carried dozens of 2,000-pound
blockbuster bombs within its belly. And there were scores of such planes,
all engaged in repeated air strikes in Vietnam. U.S. Navy planes alone
dropped over 700,000 tons of bombs on enemy targets in one three-year
period.

Given that huge volume, there was only one practical way to get adequate supplies of explosives to Southeast Asia in the 1960s: cargo-carrying
merchant ships sailing the wide-open spaces of the ocean. It was up to the
Navy, operating through its Military Sea Transportation Service, to find
those ships and to develop the 10,000-mile lifeline needed to do the job.

While the Navy had scores of government-owned World War II–
vintage merchant ships rusting away in National Reserve Defense Fleet
anchorages around the country, those were not nearly enough to carry
the volume of supplies needed in Vietnam. The solution was to charter
ships engaged in the commercial trade—ones that carried refrigerators
and iron ore and sewing machines from port to port in peacetime—to
transport the troops and guns and bombs needed in time of war.

Such a fleet was available and ready to sail in the form of the U.S.

merchant marine. The name—not to be confused with the U.S. Marines— refers collectively to ships primarily engaged in commercial trade (as distinguished from naval warships) and the thousands of civilian mariners who man them.

Historically, when war beckoned, nations relied on such merchant shipping. In earlier years, and extending up to the mid-nineteenth century, these civilian ships actually sailed out to wage war against the enemy—in effect, serving as a country's "navy." They did so under authority of government-issued letters of marque and reprisal which authorized them to place cannons aboard for that purpose. The lure of riches drew these privateers—ship owners, captains (usually part-owners in earlier times), and crew split the value of the goods captured from enemy forces. Time and technology eventually ended privateering, with merchant ships returning to their primary role of transporting goods during times of war.

The First and Second World Wars, in particular, dramatized the use of the merchant marine for that purpose. And for those civilian seafarers manning those ships, it proved to be a dangerous business. A ship loaded to the gunnels with guns and bombs in her cargo holds, but having relatively little on deck with which to defend herself, was a prime target of enemy subs, surface raiders, and torpedo bombers. By every account, however, the merchant marine rose admirably to the challenge.

Given this intimate relationship between the military and the merchant marine, one wonders why a more formal connection between that civilian service and the U.S. government was not established. Militarizing the merchant marine was seriously considered during World War II, but objections by various parties shot the idea down. In its place, Congress established a military link to the merchant marine by moving regulations and oversight—including licensing, ship inspections, shipment and discharge of seamen—from a civilian bureau to a military organization, the U.S. Coast Guard.

What has slowly evolved over the years is an alliance, uneasy at times, between the United States and its civilian merchant marine.

Mutual needs drive the relationship, with the government taking the lead in most cases. During World War I, for example, recognizing the importance of merchant marine shipping to the nation, a congressionally-created shipping board established a standard design for merchant ships to be used in times of war and peace. The hope was that a single simplified design would lead to mass production by private companies at large savings in time, money, and materiel. The design proved popular and 122 ships of that class were built at the Hog Island shipyard near Philadelphia.

Based on that favorable experience, the U.S. followed suit with another set of standard designs in the late thirties: the C-1, C-2, and C-3 vessels. The *Badger State* was a C-2. Its design called for five cargo holds, three forward and two aft. To load and unload the ship, fourteen 5-ton cargo booms and two 30-ton booms were positioned near the cargo holds. All crew and officer spaces—sleeping quarters, galley, mess hall—were situated amidships, an improvement over earlier designs which squeezed the crew's quarters forward of the ship. At a higher level of the ship, the bridge deck, could be found the captain's offices, wheelhouse, chartroom, gyro, and radio rooms.

In addition, the interior of the ship was split up into eight watertight compartments. Sealing off sections of a ship from each other with steel walls—"bulkheads" in sailor talk—keeps a ship afloat after her hull has been holed. With a damaged compartment walled off, there is theoretically enough buoyancy remaining in the undamaged sections to keep a ship from sinking.

Building a double hull, an inner and outer shell enclosing an air space of several feet, is another technique used to keep a ship afloat. Theoretically, a ship would still float even if that external hull was torn open. Like all such "unsinkable" ships, the unforeseen vagaries of wind and waves, not to mention human error, take their toll.

Titanic remains the classic example of an "unsinkable" ship sinking. Built in a British shipyard to a "two compartment standard"—theoretically, the ship would remain afloat even if two of her sixteen watertight compartments were holed—she departed Southampton on her ill-fated maiden voyage April 10, 1912, bound for New York. Seeking the publicity an early arrival would generate, her captain ordered the ship's steam engines cranked up to maximum power.

Cruising along at full speed in the dark, and in waters home to floating icebergs—a blind person running on a congested highway—the ship encountered immortality. A lookout in the crow's nest suddenly spotted a giant iceberg directly in front of the ship, immediately struck a warning bell three times, and phoned the bridge. Reacting promptly, the watch officer ordered the helm to starboard, reversed engines, and electrically closed all watertight doors. Lookout and watch officer performed flawlessly, but fate intervened as the ship smashed into the iceberg, ripping open at least five of the ship's watertight compartments. *Titanic* and 1,517 passengers went down to an icy grave off the Grand Banks of the north Atlantic Ocean. The disaster generated a storm of second-guessing "ifs"—*if* the berg had been spotted moments sooner; *if* the SOS signal had gone through; *if* the ship had been built with an inner skin, she might have stayed afloat, and so on.

Given their experience with the "unsinkable" *Titanic*, its ship owners, White Star Lines, decided to make its sister ship, the *Britannic*, truly unsinkable. It retrofitted the ship with more safety features, including the massive undertaking of adding an extra inner hull. This double hull, it was thought, would surely prevent the ship from suffering the same fate as the *Titanic*. Ironically, the ship struck a mine (torpedoes have not been completely ruled out) instead of an iceberg and went down even faster. Experts theorize that the ship took on "unsymmetrical flooding," incoming water concentrated on one side of the ship. Once that happened, there was no way to counterbalance the list of the ship. In addition, and perhaps a much more serious factor, the crew decided to crank open the ship's portholes—some located less than five feet from the waterline—to air out the interior of the ship. That act proved fatal once the ship began to list to starboard. Entering water breached the ship's watertight integrity and took her down 400 feet in less than an hour.

Of course, passenger ships do have a unique characteristic not shared by other commercial vessels: freely circulating "cargo." Passengers move about, up and down stairways, port to starboard and back on the whim of the moment. Such movements affect a ship's stability in the water, and may cause it to list. Ballast tanks—a series of compartments within the ship that can be rapidly flooded or emptied—help to keep the ship in trim. A ship listing to starboard (to the right), for example, can be brought upright to an even keel by pumping water from starboard to port tanks. However, prematurely emptying the ballast tanks can also create problems.

The Italian passenger ship *Andrea Doria*, bound for New York in 1956, discovered that the hard way. As the ship burned fuel on its transatlantic crossing, it filled the empty tanks with seawater, a standard practice, to keep the ship's huge hull in balance. Reaching the U.S. coast off Nantucket, the ship's fuel tanks were full of this oily seawater that would normally be offloaded after docking in New York. To save a few bucks, the ship pumped the water into the open ocean before entering the harbor, effectively shifting the ship's weight from the bottom to the top.

While the top-heavy *Andrea Doria* was inbound, the passenger ship *Stockholm* had cast off her lines ashore and was proceeding outbound. The ships first encountered each other on radar and later confirmed it visually. It was the classic head-on, Alphonse and Gaston meeting situation— You first? No, no, you first?—on a wide-open expanse of ocean between strangers whose intentions could not easily be discerned. The rules are explicit in such a meeting: change course to the right, to starboard.

Unfortunately, the parties misconstrued each other's locations and intentions. *Stockholm* sliced into the *Andrea Doria*, ripping open seven of her eleven decks. The *Andrea Doria* began to take on water and, with her fuel tanks empty, almost immediately began to list to starboard. Eventually, the ship capsized, taking 54 of the 1,600 people on board down with her.

Cargo ships, the blue-collar workers of the commercial trade, have no need to cater to the whims of high-paying passengers. Hundreds of the C-2 ships were built and sailed during World War II and for many years afterwards. The *Badger State*, like many others, became a tramp ship—one without an established route and available to carry any type of cargo, anywhere, anytime, for the right price. The Navy had chartered the ship earlier, and by the winter of 1969 Wilson had already finished one successful voyage, carrying bombs to Danang. Preparations were under way for a second voyage back to the war zone.

At the Bangor Naval Depot, countless details had to be attended to. Tramp ships are typically the senior citizens of the seagoing fleet, subject to the aches and pains of old age. Since breakdowns at sea are potentially disastrous, radios, radar equipment, steering engines, and other critical equipment have to be checked and possibly repaired, adjusted, or replaced before sailing. And then there is the inevitable wearing down of other odds and ends from the hammering a ship takes daily at sea almost as a matter of course. Coast Guard hull and boiler inspectors board the ship to ferret out problems spelled out in the law as relating to everything: "boats, pumps, life preservers, floats, anchors, cables, and other things" to make sure ship and crew are relatively safe during the voyage.

In addition, sailors on the previous voyage were eager to collect their hard-earned wages, and replacements had to be signed on for the new voyage. That could be a time-consuming chore—total crew wages for a run-of-the-mill voyage of several months might run to six figures. An armored truck is sometimes needed. Quite possibly an armed guard as well, depending on the port involved. And, complicating matters further, wages have to be paid in cash. Seamen prefer the look of bills and the jingle of coins in their pockets. A more practical reason is that banks do not look kindly on cashing checks issued to men with no permanent address.

On December 9, 1969, G. E. Howe boarded the *Badger State* at the Bangor Depot. A shipping commissioner for the port of Seattle, he was there to oversee the payoff of the ship's old crew, and the signing on of a new crew.

Howe first checked out the ship's official log book—every American ship has one. He skimmed through it, looking for troublemakers: those given to disobeying orders, fighting, stealing, and other undesirable shipboard behavior. For these offenses, a seaman's document—his meal ticket—could be temporarily or permanently taken away.

The *Badger State*'s new voyage to Danang was targeted for not more than a year, although everyone knew it would last only a few months at best. The voyage description would be a tongue-twister known as tramp Articles, the wording favored by the Navy because of the leeway it allowed in setting the ship's agenda. While everyone knew the ship was headed for Vietnam and then back to the U.S., the new Articles provided for an alternative: everywhere! The new crew would be signing on for a voyage from Bangor

> on a tramp freighter voyage, either direct or via one or more coast-wise ports, to one or more U.S. Atlantic, Pacific, Gulf or Great Lakes Coast, and/or to one or more ports in the Caribbean Sea and/or South America and/or Europe and/or Africa and/or Far East and/or Near East and/or Australia, and such other ports and places in any part of the world as the Master may direct, and back to a final port of discharge in the Continental United States, excluding Alaska and Hawaii, for a term not exceeding twelve calendar months.

Captain and crew might conceivably find themselves sampling the delights of Cape Town, or even Djibouti, the only limitation to tramp Articles being that the ship must return to a continental U. S. port within twelve months for discharge.

Preliminaries finished, both captain and commissioner set up shop on adjoining tables in the crew's mess deck. Old and new crews mingled in line, talking about the ship, the Old Man, and women, real and imagined. What distinguished old from new was the gleam in the eyes of the seafarers receiving their wages. For them, beards had succumbed to razors; hair grown long was carefully slicked back with Brylcreem; and the men sported their best dress canvas: gleaming leather street shoes, topped off with wrinkled shirts, trousers, and jackets rescued from under mattresses.

One by one, the men appeared, flashed their Z-Cards—seaman's ID card showing qualifications—and put their signature to the Articles, releasing the ship and Master from all claims during the voyage. Each man then meandered to an adjoining table, eyes as bright as brass on a Navy ship as the cash was counted out, dollar by dollar. Satisfied, the seafarer would stuff the whole wad in his pocket with a flourish and leave with a hearty wave of his hand to the shipmates left behind.

Waiting to greet the seaman at the head of the gangway would be wife and kids—hugs and kisses followed later by the battle to set up new territorial rights in a family grown independent. For other hungry seafarers, it might be shapely ladies who had earlier boned up on "Dear Abby," Ann Landers, and the really important news in the Seattle papers: ship arrivals and departures, with close attention focused on American-flag ships. That's where the money was. Recognizing that seamen deprived of womanly comforts need help, these lovely ladies could be counted on to be at the pier when the ship docked. There, with chests puffed out and eyes demurely cast down, they awaited Jack Tar as he swaggered down the gangway, a lifeboat full of cash weighing his trousers down.

Old crewmembers, electing to stay aboard for the new voyage, signed new shipping Articles as well. The new guys came from the maritime unions. The union hiring hall marked a major turning point for seafarers and their unions.

Earlier, within living memory, seamen were hired directly by the master of a ship right off the dock, lining up in what was then known as a shape-up. The practical result was that the lowest bidder got the job, and everyone else got shafted with low wages. A series of waterfront strikes brought change. Instead of hiring seamen directly, ships like the *Badger State* notified unions of the ratings needed for the voyage. Unions then assigned most jobs based on seniority—a seaman with the longest time ashore got the first job posted on the board for his rating.

That didn't mean Wilson couldn't help his own cause. He wanted a topnotch crew aboard, and he encouraged the good men he had sailed with in the past to rejoin the ship. He even made his way to First Avenue in Seattle, wall-to-wall with bars and sailors and good-time ladies, to do some recruiting on his own.

Some of the guys knew him from previous voyages. "Have a good trip, Cap," they would say.

"How come you're not back with us?"

"We thought you didn't want us back," they might say with a wink and a nod.

"You're damned right I do. I need a crew!" Wilson would roar.

More likely than not, the guys would go through their union and show up aboard ship soon after, none the worse for the whiskey they had washed down the previous evening. And probably pleased that the captain had personally asked them aboard.

All these chores ate up a valuable commodity in the trade: time. The skipper had to keep an eye out for the bottom line, and that meant the ship had to take on her cargo and move out as quickly as possible.

That concern was foremost in Wilson's mind as he met with Navy Lieutenant Commander John Brennan, the ordnance officer at the Bangor Ammunition Depot. Brennan bossed a staff of roughly 600 workers engaged in receiving, stowing, and issuing ammo at the station. He briefed Wilson on Bangor's procedures in receiving ammo and loading it aboard ships. Wilson had attended Navy briefings before and was familiar with its methods.

Once there was some inkling of the ammunition needed—and that info came directly from the individual military branches—the Navy scrambled to find the right ship to carry the load. Capacity, number of available holds, stability, and other factors weighed in. The munitions scheduled for the *Badger State* were ordered by the Air Force. Given the basic data, Bangor Depot diagrammed a stowage plan.

After all the ammunition was loaded, the Depot prepared a second plan. This final diagram identified where the explosives were stowed, the number of pallets loaded, the tonnage, and other information.

Loading a ship with ammo called for special preparation. A small detachment of blockers and bracers, marine cargo specialists, leader snappers, and other esoteric specialties were hired by the Depot to deal with such problems. They attached wood sheathing to the inner metal skin of the *Badger State*—a precaution to deal with condensation. Wooden bulkheads, or walls, were built to square off the spaces in the ship's holds. This required the curving metal skin of the ship to be boxed in with 4-by-4 and 2-by-12-inch lumber.

Trucks and railroad cars carried the explosives to Bangor where they were routed to the shipping dock for direct loading aboard the *Badger State*. That process would take roughly five days, an average loading time for the amount and type of cargo to be carried.

In addition to these procedures, there was the somewhat delicate nature of the cargo to be carried to Danang. As William Burwell, a naval engineer knowledgeable about the ammo being shipped, explained, the explosives consisted of tritonal, a combination of 80 percent TNT and 20 percent aluminum. That combination was optimum, according to the military experts. The aluminum burned at a rapid clip and that meant a quicker release of explosive energy, a blast wave traveling at the speed of sound knocking down whatever was in its path—like a string of dominoes toppling over. TNT—trinitrotoluene—being relatively stable and adaptable to long-term storage, was the explosive of choice for military shells, bombs, and grenades.

In 1969, bombs were classified as general purpose, penetration, fragmentation, and cluster types. The weight of the explosives to the weight of the whole of the bomb determined its class. General purpose bombs—one type carried by the ship, for example—had roughly half their weight in explosives. The explosive itself caused blast damage—tremendous pressures which caved in roofs, and leveled buildings, walls, people, and whatever else was in its path. Detonation broke the metal casing into hundreds of pieces and spun them off at velocities of 3,000 to 11,000 feet per second. The resulting fragments tore holes in troops, planes, vehicles, and anything else within firing range. At the other end of the spectrum, penetration bombs had slightly more than one fourth of their weight as explosives. Such bombs were designed to break through hardened bunkers before exploding.

Free-fall or "dumb bombs" needed a fuze (sometimes spelled "fuse") in the nose or rear of the bomb set to a desired timing, and tail fins to stabilize the flight of the bomb through the air. Fuzes detonated the bomb at a predetermined moment and could be activated in many ways ranging from the bomb hitting the target; a small prop turning a specific number of revolutions; at a certain height or distance from a target (proximity fuzes); or abrupt changes in the speed of the bomb in flight. The specific type of fuze used depends on the objective. A delayed detonation might be needed for the destruction of a building, while a proximity fuze might be most effective against troops and vehicles.

The explosive energy of these bombs is difficult for a layperson to grasp. Burwell points out that such energy "is in the form of heat when it burns. When this heat is confined, it will result in a pressure rise sufficient to push things away. This is similar to burning of propellants in gun barrels and dynamite underground where, when it is confined, it will do a tremendous amount of work. And when it is not confined, it just makes a little noise—flash."

The *Badger State* had carried similar bombs on its last voyage. The ship had received general instructions from the Navy on handling ammunition, but Burwell was the expert on explosives. In terms of a ship taking precautions during a voyage, Burwell noted that the behavior of explosives is not entirely predictable. There had been tests trying to detonate a bomb, minus a fuze, with a bullet fired from a high-powered rifle. Surprisingly, a bomb might go off once in fifty tries. In similar fashion, dropping bombs without fuzes from aircraft led to high-order explosions roughly four percent of the time. So it was unlikely that there would be much of a risk for a ship carrying the bombs, but the potential for explosion was always there.

Anyone visiting Bangor could see that the Depot took that potential seriously, and acted to lower the risk. Matches and smoking were strictly off-limits; the workers wore special clothing and used tools designed to ward off static electricity; and a lightning tower loomed over the docks, designed to carry any lightning strikes safely to ground. Even the Depot's location was a factor—it was located well away from populated areas.

That lesson was learned well from waterfront explosions that had decimated other communities. Halifax, Nova Scotia, was one such, and probably the granddaddy of all munition ship explosions, a blast so horrendous that it almost destroyed the entire city.

Europe was at war in December of 1917, and Halifax was ideally located for ships to assemble in convoy for the voyage across the ocean. The French SS *Mont-Blanc* was one such ship, bound for a European port. It carried a chemical cocktail of explosives: 2,300 tons of picric acid (used in the manufacture of artillery shells), 200 tons of TNT; and 35 tons of benzol, an explosive mixture. Entering the harbor on the morning of December 6, the *Mont-Blanc* collided with the outgoing Norwegian ship *IMO*, bound for New York to pick up relief supplies for Belgium.

Fire broke out aboard the *Mont-Blanc*. Her captain, fearing an explosion, ordered the crew to abandon ship. The blazing ship, a massive bomb left to fend for itself, drifted erratically in the harbor until it smashed into Pier 6, the busy end of the harbor. The fire drew a crowd of curious spectators unaware of the danger of the ship's cargo.

A thunderous explosion followed shortly afterwards, leaving almost no recognizable parts of the ship, or nearby spectators, anywhere. The blast leveled most of an immediate square-mile area, and rained down tons of shrapnel and debris on the city. Water pushed out of the harbor by the tremendous power of the blast returned in force, sweeping in to capsize tugs and small crafts, washing away whatever lay in its path. Finally, fire destroyed what was left of the harbor and surrounding areas.

The losses were staggering: more than 1,900 dead, and countless others seriously injured; 1,630 houses leveled, and 12,000 others damaged. It was one of the largest non-nuclear explosions ever witnessed. Ironically, the captain and crew of the *Mont-Blanc* survived. Help poured in from all over the world, most notably Boston which sent a train carrying supplies and medics. The occasion is remembered in Boston every year by a brightly lit Christmas tree, an annual gift from the grateful townspeople of Halifax.

On board the *Badger State*, in the face of possible metal-to-metal contact in the hold, the immediate problem faced by Wilson was to avoid sparking in the vicinity of the bombs. As the Navy bluntly put it in a directive dated November 10, 1966:

> One of the major fears of mariners is having blocking carry away and cargo go adrift in rough seas. This is especially hazardous if the vessel is carrying explosives. Ammunition is sensitive to friction, shock, sparks, or heat. Immediate action must be taken to secure explosives, or cargo stored with explosives, that shifts or goes adrift while in transit. The first and most important thing to do is to stop all movement of cargo within the holds as rapidly as possible.

The Navy did not say what would happen if their instructions were not followed. The unspoken assumption was that the bombs would blow sky-high.

Chief Mate Cobbs and Captain Wilson climbed quickly down the ladder, hand over hand, into No. 3 hold. The confined space made it awkward going. Wilson, on hands and knees, clutched a flashlight, his body braced against the incessant rolling of the ship. He shot the beam of light across the forward end of the hatch. The light landed on a row of pallets containing 500-pound bombs. The pallets seemed to have shifted all the way from one side of the ship to the other. Wood on the end pallet and the wooden sheathing covering the skin of the ship had splintered. The damaged wood allowed enough slack for one of the bombs to move out of the confines of its container.

Wilson felt the short hairs on the back of his neck rise as the light reached the pallet at the end of the row. It had jammed into one of the steel ribs of the ship.

"There's metal-to-metal contact!" Wilson said, eyeing the exposed metal nose of a bomb that lay tight up against the metal skin of the ship. As the two men braced themselves, the tier of pallets swayed away from the frame in the direction of the ship's roll. Transfixed, they watched as the ship began to roll in the opposite direction, the tier swaying back and again bringing the nose of one of the bombs into contact with the metal skin of the ship.

Wilson focused the light on the splintered wood. "We need to get this tier braced down one way or another," he ordered the Mate. "Get a few men down here on the double and let's see about securing this mess. Get the bosun going on it. And keep me updated."

"Aye, aye, sir," Cobbs replied, as he quickly left the hold.

Wilson returned to the wheelhouse and instructed Burnette to try to cut the ship's roll.

"Continue directing the bow into the swells," he ordered. "Don't worry about the heading."

The Captain then turned his attention to the waves that continued to flow in a confused pattern. Despite the warmth of the room, he shivered. *If there was a problem in one of the holds*, he thought grimly, *there was the possibility of problems in the other holds as well.*

Dimly, in the sky ahead obscured by wind and spray, a suggestion of movement caught his eye. It was the great seabirds in flight. They glided smoothly on wind currents, hundreds of miles from any land, circling. Occasionally, they dropped down, a flurry of motion delicately and gracefully settling on some errant wave. Wings folded, the seabirds floated serenely, oblivious of the chaos of the sea that surrounded them. *These birds were in no danger*, Wilson reflected with some envy; *the sea was their natural environment.*

He drew a deep breath. There was one other matter to be handled. He braced himself against the chart table and wrote out the following message to U.S. Naval Headquarters:

CARGO NO. THREE LOWER TWEEN DECK FORWARD SHIFTED. SHEATHING AND SHORING SPLINTERED. CARGO IN ONE CASE STEEL TO STEEL WITH SHIP. CAUSED DURING HEAVY ROLLING. PROCEEDING ON ASSIGNED MISSION. CARGO BEING RESECURED BY SHIP'S CREW. USING SPARE SHORES LEFT ABOARD IN LOADING PORT. COMPLETION TIME 180200Z.

CHAPTER 2

Driving Off the Spleen

Charlie Wilson had always felt the pull of the sea. Even as a young lad, the lore of ancient ships and rough and ready sailors fascinated him. His own family history—perhaps more fancy than fact—told of how his great-great-grandfather, a renowned Glasgow shipbuilder, had joined forces with another family, the Dunbars, to build a ship on which they sailed to the great North American continent.

Reaching the coast was not nearly enough for these hardy sailors. They wanted to get as far inside this "America" as they possibly could. And so they sailed inland, through a series of rivers and past a host of landmark communities until they plumb ran out of water and went fast aground. The spot where this occurred was memorialized in family lore as Wilson's Landing. Settling down, the two clans intermarried to such an extent that it was hard to tell where one family began and the other left off. And so it was no surprise when Wilson's Landing metamorphosed into Dunbar, Nebraska. Charlie Wilson was born in a nearby town in the early 1930s.

The sea beckoned early to Wilson. While working on his baby teeth, and with his mother's help—a job awaited her overseas—he signed on as a passenger of a ship and sailed to the Philippines by way of Hong Kong and Shanghai, eventually returning to the States the same way.

Hard times were everywhere then. The Great Depression had savaged the country: jobs were scarce; people hit the road looking for work; young adults returned home to live with their parents. The Wilson family fared no better, relocating to Springfield, Missouri. Wilson doesn't

recall whether he enjoyed life there or not, but one of his earliest childhood memories was trying to run away at the age of four. His maternal
grandmother, Jo (tougher than dirt, he remembers) sent her German
shepherd, Spike, to track him down. Spike collared young Wilson near
the train depot, glommed onto his sleeve, and towed him home to a worried family.

It was a tough, hardscrabble life for the Wilson family. And when
Charlie bothered to complain—about new schools, finding new friends,
settling down in different homes—his Dad had only one answer: "You
carry your weight in life, son, and you do what you have to do." Those
words of parental wisdom stayed with Wilson for the rest of his days.

Graduating from high school, he applied to the Merchant Marine
Academy at Kings Point, New York, for admission. Kings Point was
pure happenstance for Wilson, one of those fateful moments in life that
started with a chance conversation with a close friend.

"Hey, Charlie," his pal had said, "take a gander at this," shoving a
colorful catalog at Wilson. It was a brochure from Kings Point. "You get
to become a ship's officer, and sail on passenger ships with all the good-
looking babes!"

That sounded exciting, Wilson remembered, particularly the reference to babes. All that, and an education too, seemed hard to beat.
Wilson applied to the school, and ranked fourteenth nationally in the
entrance exam. The campus became his home for the next four years.

The school—established by the United States during World War II
and structured like the Navy, Army, Air Force, and Coast Guard acad-
emies—became a favorite training ground for the new kind of educated
skippers favored by shipping companies. Coming up through the hawse
pipe—practical, nuts-and-bolts, on-the-job training—was a practice
fading fast in the early fifties. Formal book learning was replacing that
ancient route from the foc'sle to the wardroom.

Kings Point is the best-known school for the training of merchant
marine officers. But it's not the only one. Congress earlier authorized the
Navy to lend ships to states wishing to set up their own nautical schools.

New York jumped at the offer, and the naval sloop-of-war *St. Mary* became the classroom, dormitory, and recreation room for young New York students. Rules for admission were minimal—one notable prohibition: no one could be compelled by any court to attend the Academy as a means of punishment.

Pennsylvania, Massachusetts, and Maine eventually followed New York's lead and set up their own nautical schools. Texas, California, and the Michigan-based Great Lakes Maritime Academy followed later. Virginia considered establishing an academy, but apparently only in connection with another "school up in the mountains," a condition which Virginia Congressman Schuyler O. Bland characterized as "the most absurd thing I ever saw". The difficulty of navigating ships at such a high level apparently scuttled any such ambitious plan.

Kings Point challenged Wilson, and the next four years were filled with studies, drills, and discipline. Included in the curriculum was a "sea year," firsthand experience sailing on a merchant ship, and eagerly anticipated by every student. Wilson's turn came in 1951. The school slated him for a berth as deck cadet aboard the SS *Magnolia State*, a ship then owned by States Marine Lines.

Wilson, bubbling with excitement and accompanied by his dad, drove to the pier at Terminal Island, next to Long Beach, California. Waved in by the guard, the two found a parking spot and then looked around for a relatively new vessel. None of the spruced-up and squared-away ships had the name he was looking for. About to give up, father and son noticed an old rustbucket off to one side, obviously hard used, and badly in need of a paint job. High tide had come in and the ship, riding higher in the water than usual, displayed more of its battered hull than would normally be the case. It was the *Magnolia State*.

Wilson's heart sunk. *Maybe the ship's condition had to do with the war*, he thought gamely, trying to reassure himself. He gathered himself together, forced a smile to go with a stiff upper lip, and father and son boarded the ship where they met the mate, Warren Wagonseal. After exchanging pleasantries and seeing his dad off the ship, Wagonseal turned Wilson and fellow cadet Walter Bradley over to the bosun. That crusty old seafarer showed the two newcomers around the ship and then directed them to clean out the "rose boxes."

"What are those?" the two cadets asked in all innocence.

"Well," the bosun said, "you know what they call the part of the ship where the sides and the bottom meet?"

"The bilges?"

"Right!" the bosun exclaimed, sounding like the cadets had just passed a major exam. "Well," he continued, "the rose boxes are the small square boxes with little holes in them that protect the bilge suctions from plugging up with scale and rust and rubble in general. We need to get them little holes cleaned up."

"Oh," the two men exclaimed in unison, as they departed to receive their baptism in the waste and oil-soaked bilges of the ship that was to be their first seagoing home. Another crew member was detailed to supervise the cleanup—Wilson sensed he must have been there to ensure that he and his new friend didn't pass away unnoticed in the bowels of the ship. The cadets survived this greenhorn indoctrination without complaining, the experience later providing Wilson with grounds for bragging that he had learned the shipping business from the bottom up.

Notwithstanding its blue-collar appearance, the *Magnolia State* proved to be a great learning experience for Wilson. Since he was being schooled to be a deck officer, standing bridge watches—fixing the ship's position by bearings, conning the ship, seeing that the course was being steered properly—proved exciting. Then came seaman's work under the watchful eye of the bosun which Wilson remembered as fun work: splicing mooring lines and wire rope; rigging bosun chairs and going aloft; painting the stack and kingposts; stopping off topping lift wires; and attending to the countless other details that keep a seaman busy on deck.

It was not all work and training for the cadets, however. When the ship hit port, learning continued at local "houses of joy" where the two students took leave of their innocence. The old timers saw to that.

Following the voyage of the *Magnolia State*, and a second one aboard the Grace Lines SS *Santa Juana*, Wilson returned to Kings Point, where he graduated in the top third of his class.

The Navy beckoned shortly after graduation—the Korean War had come to a close, and officers were needed to man naval ships. Wilson answered the call and signed on as an ensign for a two-year hitch. He spent most of his tour of duty aboard the USS *Tortoga*, LSD-26—essentially a seagoing dry dock—assigned to a fleet of ships engaged in minesweeping operations off the Korean coast.

The ship carried helicopters to search out minefields, and three 45- to 60-foot-long wooden boats on its well deck to sweep for the mines. Once a minefield was spotted, the ship would anchor in a safe position, flood the well deck, and launch the boats into open water. The mines, contact and magnetic, were typically sewn under water. The boats used either paravanes to cut the mooring lines holding the mines in place, or a heavy metal towline to attract the mines to the surface. The mother ship's job was to vector the small boats in a grid search of the area for the mines.

Wilson tended to business and was eventually promoted to lieutenant. Upon release from the Navy, he set his sights on becoming the skipper of an American merchant ship. Eleven years later, after serving aboard ships as third mate, second, and then chief mate, he became the master of the SS *Steel Rover*, a cargo ship. Then in his mid-thirties, he was one of the youngest skippers on the company's roster.

For a merchant marine officer, the impressions of a first command are indelible. And Wilson remembered the excitement and the feelings that came with it. He had walked the pier at the Portland, Oregon, docks, with its perspiring longshoremen and giant cranes, whining and groaning under the weight of huge cargo pallets swinging overhead.

And then it came into view, *his* ship, the *Steel Rover*, tied to the dock with huge hawsers rapped around steel bollards at the pier's edge. Coated with blotched gray paint streaked with rust, it was, like many merchant ships, hard used. But that didn't matter at the time. It was a *first* and, more important, it was visible evidence of the company's confidence in him.

He clambered up the long, arching, metal gangway leading to the main deck. "I'm Captain Wilson," he had said to the night mate on duty, savoring the sound of the words.

"Welcome aboard, Captain," the officer replied, raising his hand in a casual salute.

Wilson had then walked quickly across the gray paint-scarred deck, entering the passageway leading to his new quarters and the culmination of a dream. It was a moment not to be forgotten.

States Marine Lines owned the ship. Wilson had tied his fortunes to the company ever since his cadet days aboard the *Magnolia State*. A rough-cut, first-rate outfit, States Marine enjoyed a good reputation and Wilson liked their style. For one reason, not every shipping company could boast of being able to deliver a vessel anywhere in the world on twenty-four hours' notice. States Marine could walk the talk—everybody knew the outfit was that good.

The company was probably the largest cargo ship operator in the world in the late 1950s, according to a study by Douglas Fleming, a University of Washington professor. It got its start in the early 1930s, chartering ships to carry cotton, steel, tobacco, and other goods from U.S. ports to Europe and Japan. The trade proved profitable and company execs began to spread their sails. They bought a few Hog Islanders before World War II, and a fleet of C2s, Liberties, and Victories from the government at the end of it. Its ships operated in a tough, competitive environment, and it did so without federal construction or operating subsidies. But it helped to get government business: the U. S. military became a favorite customer, probably because the company could make its ships available on a moment's notice.

States Marine ships were easily identifiable since the company tagged them with the nicknames of states. Wisconsin gave its name to the *Badger State*; New York, the *Empire State*; and Texas, the *Lone Star State*. But beyond the unique names, there was also a certain flamboyant, don't-give-a-damn, get-the-job-done attitude, a feeling that the company could do absolutely anything it set its mind to. States Marine was the kind of company Wilson favored, figuring that he might spend his younger years sailing as skipper of her ships, and his later years at the top.

After finishing his tour on the *Steel Rover*, Wilson continued sailing as captain of several other ships. Finally, States Marine assigned him as master of the SS *Gopher State*. And in October of 1969, the company gave him command of the *Badger State*, then involved in carrying bombs to the Vietnam war zone.

Wilson was no stranger to that far-flung country. From January through October 1966, he was assigned to Saigon as a local representative for States Marine. There he met all company ships docking at Danang, Cam Rahn Bay, and other Vietnamese ports; helped the ships to enter and clear port; and handled billings for company ships. Dengue fever cut his tour of duty short and he then returned to the States.

The voyage of the *Badger State* was, in a sense, one in a long string of voyages for Wilson. Part and parcel of life at sea were loneliness, strange ports, one-night stands, and the inevitable hard drinking while ashore. But there was also a certain pleasure in simply getting away from it all— the hassle and hurly-burly of life—and becoming involved in the set of challenges that came with every new voyage. Most seamen, if put to it, understood that feeling completely. However, no one quite ever articulated the sentiment with such passion as Melville in his classic, *Moby-Dick*:

> Some years ago—never mind how long precisely—having little or no money in my purse, and nothing particular to interest me on shore, I thought I would sail about a little and see the watery part of the world. It is a way I have of driving off the spleen, and regulating the circulation. Whenever I find myself growing grim about the mouth; whenever it is a damp, drizzly November in my soul; whenever I find myself involuntarily pausing before coffin warehouses, and bringing up the rear of every funeral I meet; and especially whenever my hypos get such an upper hand of me, that it requires a strong moral principle to prevent me from deliberately stepping into the street, and methodically knocking people's hats off—then I account it high time to get to sea as soon as I can. This is my

substitute for pistol and ball. . . . If they but knew it, almost all men in their degree, some time or other, cherish very nearly the same feelings towards the ocean with me.

That seagoing lifestyle demanded a price, however. For Wilson, and for many other sailors, relationships with women were deliberately casual. As a practical matter, a sailor's life had little room for excess cargo or lasting entanglements.

Wilson had, however, met one young woman who had put him to the test, a trim, dark-haired beauty by the name of Mary. On their last date together he had splurged on a first-rate restaurant overlooking downtown Portland, a view of twinkling city lights stretching to the endless night horizon. They sat side by side, shoulders and knees touching. And, naturally, he tried to put the make on her.

She didn't mince words. "You know, Charlie," she said, laughing softly, "I'm no sailor's fancy. Never have been, and," she stared hard into his eyes, "never will be."

And that was that for Wilson, since he wasn't about to drop anchor anywhere. The arguments against long-term relationships were all around him, in the men he sailed with. On the *Badger State*, fully half of the crew claimed a mother or sister as next-of-kin. It could hardly be otherwise, given the faithfulness a marriage required, particularly in the face of the many long separations caused by a seafarer's life.

The irony of it was that legend, amplified by Hollywood, gave to Wilson, as master of a merchant ship, the authority to legalize the marriage of others at sea. Maybe. However, it is not certain that he has any more authority to unite anyone in marriage than does the ship's chief cook.

Federal law requires a captain to log "every marriage taking place on board, with the names and ages of the parties." Emile Dreuil, a shipping commissioner in the port of New Orleans long enough to recall when the standard uniform was a full-dress, cotton seersucker suit, remembered one voyage where the master had performed a marriage at sea.

The ship had sailed to a South American port where one of the crew-members became enamored of a local beauty and wanted to marry her. Accordingly, the captain embarked the young lady and then sailed outside the territorial limits where he united the couple in "the bonds of holy matrimony." He entered the marriage in the ship's official log.

Later, it was Dreuil's sad duty to inform the seaman that he may or may not have a *wife*, this iffy situation resulting from a case involving Bud Fisher, creator of the one-time popular comic strip, *Mutt and Jeff*. Fisher had persuaded the captain of the passenger ship *Leviathan* to marry him and his lady at sea. The captain obliged; the two were "married"; the relationship subsequently soured, and when Mrs. Fisher brought suit for a legal separation, Mr. Fisher denied the existence of any marriage whatsoever.

The New York Court of Appeals stated that Congress, in requiring the log's entry, implicitly recognized common-law marriages. However, "if the federal statute cannot thus be interpreted," the court said somewhat hesitantly, then the law of the state where the owner of the ship resided—in this case, the District of Columbia—would prevail. The District recognized common-law marriages. The court then held that the Fishers, having publicly held each other as husband and wife, enjoyed a valid marriage.

However, notwithstanding that decision, some skippers argue that federal and state laws are irrelevant. A skipper has the inherent authority to perform marriages at sea, they claim. It's just that the marriages have a relatively short lifespan: the duration of the voyage.

For Wilson, there were a host of other activities ashore that didn't fit the pattern of a seagoing life—music, for one. He had developed a yen for it, but cargo ships don't carry pianos on board. He had also occasionally thought of buying a Harley and hitting the open road between ships. And he sometimes toyed with the idea of splurging on an airplane. He could always get a pilot's license. But, given his heavy schedule at sea, none of it made much sense. Time enough for that when sailing days became sweet memories, he figured.

*   *   *

At the Bangor Depot, the sailing board was posted conspicuously at the gangway of the *Badger State*—"Departure scheduled for 1700 hours, December 14."

With time running short, the inevitable rush of last-minute details had to be dealt with: meetings with Navy and Coast Guard officers to insure that the cargo was properly loaded and the ship ready to sail; stragglers to be signed on; clearance from customs officials, the final stamp of approval that all was in order. No problem there; carrying rockets and bombs to the war zone in the winter of 1969 cut through bureaucratic red tape quickly.

Wilson made his own last-minute inspection. He met with his department heads—the chief mate, chief engineer, and the steward—to ensure that their areas were squared away and ready for sea. Then he climbed to the wheelhouse to check the radio and radar equipment. Bob Ziehm was there, busy plotting the ship's course on a navigation chart. An enormous man pushing fifty, Ziehm stood out wherever he happened to be. He had signed on as second mate and served as the ship's navigation officer. The two had sailed together on several ships and became good friends. Wilson admired Ziehm's professional competence and thought him the absolute best at dead-reckoning—keeping track of the ship's course when sightings could not be taken due to bad weather.

The two men exchanged small talk, moving out to the open wing of the bridge, a vantage point for keeping tabs on the cargo being loaded aboard.

The dock was strewn with a few pallets loaded with bombs, dunnage for bracing and blocking in the holds, lines, cables, stores and equipment for the ship and her crew, along with the tools and bits and pieces which define a workingman's space. The sound of the ship's booms, creaking and whining under their load of tons of explosives, swinging cradle-like back and forth between dock and ship, and the intermittent sounds of the workers themselves—sound bites of yesterday's memories amid curses hurled halfheartedly at today's frustrations—drifted to the upper deck. Below decks, forklift trucks scurried around, stowing the pallets in the holds under the Navy's pre-stow plan.

The cargo holds—huge box-like compartments within the *Badger State*, the very reason for the ship's existence—were numbered one to five, proceeding from bow to stern. Most of the holds contained three separate compartments: upper tween deck, lower tween deck, and the lowest space that bottomed out near the ship's keel. "Tween deck" was a contraction of "between deck"—sailor talk referring to the space between deck levels. No. 3 upper tween deck hold, for example, refers to the space in the hold between the main deck and the second deck level below it. No. 3 lower tween deck hold is the cargo space between the second and third deck levels.

The main deck of the *Badger State*, as the term implies, was the deck visible to an onlooker ashore. It extended from the bow to the stern. Rising above this deck were, in order, the cabin deck, boat deck, and bridge deck at the wheelhouse level. The top of the wheelhouse was referred to as the flying bridge. In descending order from the main deck was the second deck, followed by the third deck.

A World War II veteran, the ship carried the decorations to show it: a splash of red, white, and blue campaign ribbons boldly outlined on a sign above the main deck level. That record was a source of pride for Wilson. The ship, built by the North Carolina Shipbuilding Company in 1944 and christened as the SS *Starlight*, hit the water about the time the Navy desperately needed ships to carry American soldiers and sailors from one battle zone to another. The Navy took over the ship and converted her cargo holds into living quarters to ferry troops to the Mariana Islands, Leyte, the Philippines, and Okinawa. Her crew was credited with shooting down four enemy planes, earning an equal number of battle stars in the process. Following the war, *Starlight* reverted to the commercial trade where she eventually got a new owner and a new name to go with it.

The two men talked over the *Badger State*'s previous voyage, when they also transported bombs to Danang. The weather had been rough then, and strange sounds had been heard coming from one of the cargo holds. There was a vaguely uncomfortable feeling that some bombs might have come loose in lower No. 4 hold, but there was no way to get into it. Bangor had loaded the lower cargo hold to the top, and then floored the opening over. The possibility of loose bombs that might explode proved nerveracking to officers and seamen alike. Rather than take such a chance, Wilson made an unscheduled stop at Pearl Harbor Navy Base.

Navy hands unscrambled the cargo but could find nothing amiss. As a precaution, extra dunnage, blocking and the like, was added to the cargo hold. While it was a relief to the captain to know that the bombs were not loose, the wasted effort disturbed him. It was an experience he did not aim to go through again.

Satisfied that the ship was on schedule in being readied for sea, Wilson returned to his cabin. Bearing in mind the *Badger State*'s previous experience with explosive cargo, Wilson met with Depot officials for a final conference before the ship's departure.

We don't want to sail light on cargo, he told them. The jerky rolling of the ship was hard on the crew and probably on the cargo as well.

Sorry, he was told, but there was no other cargo available for the *Badger State*. The Depot had been short-changed on the cargo, and the bombs loaded aboard the ship were all that the Air Force had targeted for shipment. There was nothing Bangor could do about it.

Sailing light troubled Wilson. It meant they would probably have to again deal with the same hard jerky roll that made the previous voyage miserable. The only way to ease that was to distribute the load better, move some cargo from the lower holds to higher ones. Doing so, Wilson figured, would spread the ship's weight more evenly throughout and per-haps ease the snap rolling the ship had previously experienced.

Bangor agreed to the change and then briefed Wilson on the heavier bombs loaded aboard ship. The 500- and 750-pound bombs were loaded in the ship's lower holds; and two hundred of the 2,000-pound bombs were loaded in No. 5 upper tween deck, the hold closest to the stern of the ship. These blockbuster bombs were loaded two to a pallet, stretching in a single layer across the bottom of the hold. Small arms ammo, mines, rocket fins, and similar materiel were also loaded, most of it stacked on top of the rows of bombs.

I want all hatches tommed down, Wilson told the men. Tomming—bracing from the top of the hold down to the cargo—would, he thought, keep the cargo from rising up in the holds.

Loren Mathis, a general foreman, explained that tomming down was a practice followed when they used to load ammo in loose form, a precaution no longer necessary with the use of pallets. Loaded, the pallets weighed anywhere between 2,000 and 4,000 pounds, he explained. Those weights made it doubtful that any cargo could move up in the holds, an assessment that made sense to the captain.

Wilson's last concern came out of the experience of the previous voyage. He insisted on access to every hold, as far as could be done. Some bottom holds were loaded, and then covered at the second hatch level. Cargo was then placed over this second level, preventing access to the lower hold. Bangor was able to bend on this issue and worked to clear access to all the holds except lower No. 3 hold. There was no help for that particular hold.

Having raised as much hell as he could, Wilson resigned himself to the inevitable. He had transported cargo for the Navy before and the scenario was all too familiar: they took the ship from his hands, opened the hatches, loaded her up, and then handed it back to him to be sailed to wherever. There were no ifs, ands, or buts with the Navy. He was satisfied that he had done all that was possible.

Casting off her lines ahead of schedule, the *Badger State* shifted over to anchorage at Thorndyke Bay in the Hood Canal to finish her final repairs. The ship's radar needed to be worked over, and Navy regulation banned the use of radar at the Depot out of safety concerns.

At departure, the ship was loaded with 5,336 long tons of bombs and accessories, 10,640 barrels of heavy fuel oil for the steam turbine's boilers, 600 tons of water, and over 10,000 pounds of chicken, steak, milk, beans, and dozens of other items, including the Christmas holiday fixings.

Forty-one seamen signed on for the voyage. Four of them could not make the trip; two replacements walked aboard at the last moment.

The ship's destination, in Danang, was an elaborate complex containing Navy-built ammunition and bomb-storage structures, fuel-storage tanks, observation towers, crew quarters, aircraft runways, and other facilities. The voyage from Bangor to Danang would take roughly twenty days, weather permitting.

The Navy, through its weather and fleet-routing office in Alameda, laid down the preferred sailing route—nothing unusual, as the Navy typically provided routing services for all chartered vessels operating in the Pacific. The route selected was the northern route.

As a general rule, according to George Hammond who supervised the Navy's ship routing department, climate in wintertime favors the southern route. However, as Hammond explained, "the expectation of headwind and seas with crossing swell on the initial part of any potential southerly route was considered bad enough that the ship should not sail on any southerly route at this time."

Several other ships were also scheduled to sail from the West Coast around the same time as the *Badger State* and to proceed to Vietnam by the northern route: the cargo ships *Empire State*, *Sunshine State*, and the *Steel Director*. Delaying departure in the hope of better weather was not an option simply because the northern track was considered not only acceptable, but the best possible route.

The *Badger State* weighed anchor late on the evening of December 14th, and proceeded north, threading its ways through the Hood Canal, Admiralty Inlet, and out the Strait of Juan de Fuca to the Pacific. Wilson could only hope that this voyage would meet with greater success than did the Strait's namesake who, in 1592, sought a water passage from the Pacific to the Atlantic Ocean, and went to his grave thinking he had found it.

The following morning, the *Badger State* encountered a west-to-southwest swell and tough sailing conditions. Two days later, Wilson requested permission to divert from his route to seek calmer waters. At the time, the winds near the ship were from the east at 30 knots (slightly

over 34 land miles per hour). Winds were creating 12-foot high waves—
measured from the crest, or highest point, to the trough, the lowest point.
And the ship was encountering long swells flowing from more than one
direction. The confused swells were causing the ship to roll up to forty
degrees during a period of eleven seconds.

Weather and sea conditions continued strong on December 17, with
the ship experiencing rolls of as much as 45 degrees. It was the steep angle
of the rolls that seemingly caused bombs in No. 3 hold to break out.

CHAPTER 3

Below Deck

Below officer's country, down where the orders are carried out, work the deck hands and their counterparts in the engine room and steward's department. Separating the officers from the unlicensed ratings is the bosun, short for *boatswain*. Any extra work on deck or in the ship's holds comes under his control. And he gets his orders, in the rough hierarchy of command at sea, primarily from the chief mate.

Dick Hughes, a ruggedly handsome, curly headed man in his mid-thirties, who had sailed on merchant ships most of his adult life, had signed on as the ship's bosun. The voyage of the *Badger State* would be his last—he had promised as much to his wife, Nancy, after she pleaded with him to stay home through the holidays. Their only child, Jennie, had celebrated her third birthday shortly before the ship sailed, and Christmas seemed tailor-made for three-year-old toddlers. But then a money shortage popped up, and sailing always seemed like an easy way to make a pile of cash in a relatively short period of time.

That was the big lure for most seamen. "I'll ship out for a couple of months," they might brag. "Make a bundle; pay off the bills and get a new car, and then take it easy. A little trip to Vegas maybe. Hey, the life of Riley!" But the reality often differed. The seaman who bounded off the ship at the end of a voyage with a fat bankroll in his jeans all too often opened bloodshot eyes two days later wondering where it all went. But for Dick and Nancy Hughes, a final-voyage payoff did seem like the answer to their financial worries.

Cobbs, the chief mate, tracked Hughes down, as he later told the Captain, and the two of them climbed down to No. 3 lower tween deck hold, located roughly amidship, immediately in front of the superstructure. Like each of the ship's other holds, it resembled a three-layer cake. The lower tween deck hold was the middle layer.

Access to all the holds for loading and unloading in port was through a large opening cut into the main deck. Huge steel covers, called pontoons, sealed the opening after loading was finished. There was only one means of entry at sea and that was through the mast house (sometimes called the escape hatch), a slender opening off to one side of the hold big enough for a ladder and a body to climb down to each of the three sections of the hold.

Once in the tween decks, Cobbs shot the beam of his flashlight across the stack of pallets, letting it rest on the end pallet. We need to secure that whole row somehow, he told the bosun. Take every available hand you need to do the job and get it squared away now!

The bosun at once headed for the one spot where the crew typically hung out, the mess deck. With its tables and benches and coffeepot perking, it was every man's gathering place when off duty, between watches, or just plain killing time. There, gripes and groans about everything from the chow to the Old Man melded nicely with the latest scuttlebutt or rumors from the wheelhouse.

Part of the popularity of hanging out in the mess hall was its relatively large size and location. It formed a central part of the crew's living spaces located in the superstructure, the part of the ship that stands conspicuously above the main deck. Layers of compartments there corresponded roughly with rank and authority. The unlicensed crew's spaces—sleeping quarters, the main galley, heads (toilets), showers, and the mess hall itself—were at the main deck level; deck and engineering officers quarters rose one deck above at the cabin deck; the Captain's quarters rose still higher at the third boat deck level.

Sleeping and eating amidship was a major improvement in living accommodations for seafarers. From the earliest days of sailing, and extending well beyond the transition to steel and steam, the biggest and best spaces aboard ship were reserved for cargo. The seamen got the left-over spaces, oftentimes cramped, ill-smelling, and even dangerous spaces in the foc'sle (forecastle), the forward part of the ship. Andrew Furuseth, the first national leader of a seaman's union, captured the image of the foc'sle in his capsule description of it as "too large for a coffin and too small for a grave."

In that earlier era, laborers ashore also worked under deplorable conditions. However, they were able to go home at the end of their shift. For the seamen aboard ship, their workplace *was* their home. Collective bargaining through the maritime unions eventually evened the score; the *Badger State*'s C-2 design was one of the first attempts to provide more comfortable quarters for seafarers.

Inside the mess hall, men sprawled on well-worn, linoleum-topped, twin-bed sized tables surrounded by benches and chairs anchored to the deck. An inch-high wooden border edged the tables to keep dishes and utensils from running loose in rough weather. A wet cloth placed beneath plates and saucers sometimes helped keep place settings from going adrift.

Most of the seafarers sported beards and moustaches, razors having been put aside for the duration. There was no set uniform of the day—merchant seamen lead a more casual life aboard ship than Navy sailors do—and denim trousers paired with chambray shirts, turtlenecks, and flannel shirts predominated. Rubber soles were a must on steel decks, and sneakers were favored.

The men gulped down cups of black coffee, and then headed back to the communal pot for refills. A few shots of whiskey might have tasted better, but federal law banned its presence. The Shipping Articles specifically prohibit DANGEROUS WEAPONS OR GROG on board ship.

No grog was a quantum leap from the early days of the British fleet when it was a seaman's sacred right to demand his daily ration of booze. Beer was initially preferred. With the conquest of Jamaica, rum replaced beer, a half-pint being considered the equal of a gallon of beer. Liquor inevitably led to drunkenness and a breakdown in discipline. The solution, according to British Admiral Edward Vernon, was to dilute the rum with a quart of water. Disgusted sailors derisively called this weakened mixture "grog," shorthand for the grogram cloak commonly worn by the admiral.

That didn't necessarily mean there was no hard liquor on board, but there would be little evidence of it. It could cost a man his seaman's document—his Z-card, as seamen call it, from the letter that precedes the serial number of the card. Losing your Z-card means losing one's livelihood. No one could sail aboard an American merchant ship without a valid seaman's document issued by the U. S. Coast Guard

In between nips of black coffee, the men puffed Luckies, Camels, and Chesterfields—*coffin nails*, they called them—blowing smoke in each other's faces. The talk was sailor talk: short sentences, mainly about long-legged ladies in horizontal positions with their skivvies half-masted—Did you see the babe I was hitting on, just laying there at that bar in San Pedro? No, no, she sure as hell was not short and squat; she had boobs out to here. And the seaman extends his hands wide, as though measuring the fish that got away.

The subject of wives and sisters occasionally enters the conversation. Not surprisingly, to hear men talk about it, these creatures were of a different species altogether—circumspect, virtuous, and invariably vertical, with a secret longing to become nuns in a convent far removed from the depraved temptations of the life the sailors swore by.

Able Seaman George Henderson and Larry McHugh, a deck maintenance man, were in the middle of it. Both were veteran sailors. Henderson, a handsome man in his thirties, had sailed earlier on an ammo ship, a fact that gave him bragging rights whenever an apprentice brought up the topic of the *Badger State*'s cargo.

Rounding out the group were Able Seaman Ed Hottendorf, Fireman-Watertender James Beatty (who had sailed on the *Badger State*'s last voyage), Ordinary Seaman Jim McLure, making his first trip ever on a merchant ship, Able Seaman Floyd Rilling and Fireman-Watertender

Sam Kaneao, the ultimate plank owner on the ship, having signed back on the ship for a fourth voyage.

All the seamen aboard the *Badger State* were certified by the Coast Guard as qualified to do the work of the ratings they signed on for. Certification was based on experience, a minimum time in grade in a lower rating, and knowledge as determined by an exam. The Coast Guard also set minimum manning scales for merchant ships. For the *Badger State*, that meant carrying six able-bodied seamen and three ordinary seamen on deck; as well as three oilers and the same number of firemen-watertenders in the engine room. Setting the minimums ensured that qualified men were standing round-the-clock watches to see the ship on its course. In addition, all the officers and a majority of the unlicensed men had to be U.S. citizens. Eighty-two percent of the *Badger State*'s crew qualified in that respect.

Federal concerns in setting manning scales and in establishing minimum requirements for safety equipment related primarily to safety of life at sea, and stemmed from such disasters as the *Titanic*, whose lifeboats had space for only 1,178 of the 2,206 persons on board. Other provisions stemmed from the fire that destroyed the passenger ship *Morro Castle*, one of the worst maritime disasters ever experienced by a U.S. flag vessel.

The *Morro Castle* sailed from Havana in September 1934, bound for a return voyage to New York City. Save for the fact that it was a major tragedy, the cast of characters and the events that transpired aboard might well qualify the voyage as a classic Hollywood B-movie.

Shipping lines were experiencing hard times then, and the *Morro Castle* tried to cut corners. Reportedly, it carried secret arms packed in crates marked SPORTING GOODS destined for the dictator of Cuba. On its return voyage to the States, it took on a cargo of stinking salted animal hides. To keep the odor away from passenger quarters, the ventilation system was disconnected, and this unfortunately, also disconnected the smoke detection system.

The skipper, Captain Robert Wilmott, had years of experience behind him, but he did have his suspicions: he thought one radio operator was a "communist" and the senior operator a "very bad, bad man"; about his chief mate, the man who would succeed to command, he voiced an opinion that "he don't know his mind from one minute to another"; and he suspected someone had added poison to a fish dinner that made him violently ill.

Within a day's reach of New York, Captain Wilmott did not appear at his table for dinner. A search of the ship located him in his bathtub, dead, apparently of a heart attack—a cause that has been disputed. The Chief Mate succeeded to command. Shortly afterwards, when fire broke out in the ship's "writing room," the new skipper, the one who didn't know his mind from one minute to another, delayed sending out an SOS for more than half an hour because he could not personally see any fire from the bridge—he was unaware that the smoke detection system had been disconnected. Meanwhile, ships miles away spotted the flames quite clearly.

With fire hoses located too far away to have any effect, the blaze quickly spread to another deck. Smoke, rather than an alarm, awoke passengers. Officers and an untrained crew were totally unprepared to deal with the flames—one crewmember likened the efforts to "a village volunteer fire department trying to put out a fire in a skyscraper."

With fire spreading rapidly, members of the crew fled, leaving hapless passengers to fend for themselves. The chief engineer, in full dress whites and gold-braided cap, led the stampede, commandeering one of two motor-propelled boats for himself and other crew members. The boats, which could have accommodated sixty-three persons carried the Chief, twenty-seven crew members, and three passengers to safety. Those less fortunate jumped into the sea in a vain attempt to swim to the shore, some distance away.

The *Morro Castle* went aground off Asbury Park, New Jersey. Although the how and the why of the disaster may never be known (although theories abound), the drama did not end with the grounding of the ship. The *Morro Castle*'s chief radio operator traveled the vaudeville

circuit to recount his role in sending out the SOS, and was later con-
victed of two separate charges having nothing to do with the ship:
murder and attempted murder.

Lessons learned from the disaster led to better qualified and trained
merchant seamen—such as those who had signed on the *Badger State*—
as well as changes in firefighting methods and equipment on passenger
ships.

Aboard the *Badger* (as Captain and crew often referred to the ship),
Henderson and his shipmates had already gotten wind of the loose bomb
in No. 3 hold. Secrecy aboard ship was nonexistent, the inevitable consequence of men in close contact, isolated from any real contact with the
outside world. No doubt, a watch stander in the wheelhouse had become
privy to the juicy report of the loose bomb. And that inside knowledge
precipitated a need for him to void his bladder, the universally accepted
excuse for relief while on watch. He would then race to the mess deck to
broadcast the news to wide-eyed shipmates.

I need a hand in No. 3, the bosun told them. Henderson, Hottendorf, and a handful of others quickly followed him down the ladder in
the mast house.

In the ship's hold, flashlight in hand, Hughes braced himself against
the roll of the vessel. The beam of light skipped across the top of the
cargo in the dim light, dancing along row after row of gun-metal gray
bombs, six each cradled in wooden pallets, the bombs held in place by
parallel metal bands. And then, as Henderson recalled, "we could see
where the bombs had moved away from the side of the ship and they
had been moving back and forth. The bombs broke out of the sweatbat-
tens, and we had one case of bombs right up on a rib of the ship."

It was a fearsome sight, but Henderson was not surprised. It seemed
to jibe with his recollection of watching the longshoremen at Bangor load
the bombs. They didn't appear to be as efficient as workers at other ports
and, to his way of thinking, spent a lot of time skylarking: "just playing
around; running around in the holds; dropping wedges on each other;
throwing wedges around; acting in a way that you don't normally expect
from longshoremen."

Such playful behavior probably would not have been of any immediate concern to the crew at the time of loading. More mundane matters would have intruded—the date the ship was leaving port; where she was headed; and the ports they would hit between the two. However, in the hold, in uncomfortably close proximity, the explosive nature of the cargo must have weighed heavily on the minds of these seafarers.

The Bosun asked whether anyone had any first-hand experience with this stuff before. "I was on two other ships which carried bombs," Henderson told him, "the USS *Mate* which loaded at Bangor and the SS *Gainsville* which loaded at Port Chicago."

The mention of Port Chicago, a much-celebrated name in maritime and ammunition-loading circles, must have triggered a few unpleasant memories about the volatility of explosives similar to those carried aboard the *Badger*. During World War II, the Navy built an ammunition depot at Port Chicago, located thirty miles northeast of San Francisco. Like the Bangor depot, it supplied explosives to American troops fighting in the Pacific—at that time, against Japan.

In July 1944, two horrific explosions occurred at the Port Chicago ammunition dock where two ships, the SS *E. A. Bryant* and the SS *Quinalt Victory* were being simultaneously loaded. The blast resulted in the total destruction of the two vessels and a Coast Guard fire barge, as well as a 1,200-foot wooden pier, a railroad locomotive and boxcars, and most of the buildings at the depot. No recognizable pieces of the *E. A. Bryant* were ever found, while only bits and pieces of the *Quinalt Victory* surfaced. The force of the explosion, rivaling the magnitude of the atomic bomb dropped on Hiroshima in World War II, triggered seismographs miles away at the Berkeley campus of the University of California. Over 300 men died instantly; a larger number suffered serious injuries.

The bombs being loaded aboard the ships included depth charges, and 2,000-pound blockbuster bombs similar to those loaded aboard the *Badger State* at Bangor. However, the manner of transferring explosives from dock to ship at Port Chicago differed substantially. The explosives were laboriously transported by hand, one person to another, or on pushcarts. Larger bombs were simply rolled down a ramp from the boxcars (positioned on tracks next to the ships) and wrestled into netting spread on the pier. Ship's booms then hoisted the net, and jerked it over and down into the ship's cargo holds. Workers there stowed the bombs—again by hand, layer upon layer, and all secured in some fashion with scrap wood.

A Naval Court of Inquiry could not pinpoint the cause of the explosions—surviving eyewitnesses were few. However, the Court believed that detonation occurred either during loading operations or from "rough or careless handling." It defined such handling as that "which would subject a component or its container to a severe blow or cause deformation of the case or container by the application of a concentrated stress. Examples of this would be a bomb which is allowed to roll against and strike another bomb."

An even bigger catastrophe involving an explosive occurred in Texas City in 1947. Fire broke out aboard the French ship *Grand Camp*, loaded with ammonium nitrate fertilizer—the same substance used in 1995 to destroy the Murrah Federal Building in Oklahoma City—while moored to a city pier. The Texas City fire department responded to fight the flames, drawing a large crowd on shore to watch. Shortly afterwards, the ship disintegrated in a massive explosion, leveling the entire dock area, including the nearby Monsanto Chemical Plant, as well as a number of oil and chemical storage tanks and grain warehouses. The blast scattered chunks of metal, cargo, and machinery throughout Texas City, setting off numerous fires in the process. A miniature tidal wave, spawned by the huge explosion, flowed out of the harbor and then returned with renewed energy to batter the shore, destroying everything in its path. Rescue and fire fighting continued past midnight of that first day.

As if that wasn't enough, a second freighter, the *High Flyer*, also loaded with ammonium nitrate, appeared to be in danger. Harbor tugs tried, but were unable to tow the ship to the open sea. In the early morning hours of the following day, a second massive explosion erupted, destroying the *High Flyer*, and finishing off whatever the *Grand Camp* had missed.

Out of a population of 16,000, roughly 600 people died—ship's crews, firemen, spectators, workers—and several thousand others suffered serious injury An estimated thousand residences and other buildings were destroyed or damaged by the explosions. Property losses exceeded 67 million dollars. It was a human tragedy dramatically measured by statistics, the most telling of which being the 4,000 volunteers who manned hospitals, morgues, and makeshift shelters.

Despite those disasters, the crew of the *Badger State* received no direct instruction on the dangers posed by the bombs, presumably because no direct contact between crew and bombs was expected. What little knowledge the crew had could be summed up in the signs posted about the ship: NO SMOKING, and NO FIRE OR SPARKS IN THE HOLDS. However, it was precisely the latter danger the crew now faced in the metal-to-metal contact between bomb and hull.

Recollecting, perhaps, the earlier Port Chicago and Texas City disasters, the men talked over ways to deal with the wayward bomb. It would have to be hauled out of the crate it shared with five others, that much was clear. A block and pulley was needed, but there was not enough elbow room in the crowded space of the hold to hook it up.

Maybe we can wrestle that one baby away from the side, someone suggested. The moniker stuck. From then on, throughout the ship, this one bomb became known as the *baby*.

"We need to lift the bomb out and lay it in a cradle," Henderson recalled saying. "We can then band the bomb to the cradle and move it out of the area."

That seemed like a workable plan and the bosun huddled with the mate and Captain Wilson. It would be tough work in a restricted space, but the Bosun was confident they had the muscle to do the job.

Wilson told the bosun to go ahead with the work and to take every available man needed to do the job. To help ease the work, Wilson planned to change the ship's heading, as necessary, to keep the ship's rolling to a minimum.

The bosun set about organizing the work. A power saw to cut

lumber up on deck, well away from the explosives, as well as handsaws and other tools, would be needed to do the job. Bangor had left some lumber on board—not nearly enough, some thought—and that would be used to rebuild and shore in the pallets.

Lighting was poor in the hold, but was improved through a little ingenuity. As Henderson described it, "We had to take cargo lights down and rig those, and we had a little trouble with the marine switches on the forward end of Number 3. We ran some of the lights from the after end of Number 2 over the mast house and then down into the hold. We had lights on almost every level—always had two or three lights in every area that we were working."

With the preliminaries over, the hard work began. The pallets loaded with bombs resembled a triple-decker sandwich, the "bread" being the wooden frames and the "filling" being the bombs. Each pallet, measuring roughly three feet wide by four feet long, and two and a half feet high, contained from top to bottom: a wooden frame; a layer of three bombs (each one measuring approximately 61 inches long and 10 inches across); a wooden frame in the middle; a second layer of three bombs; and a wooden frame at the bottom.

Elliptical cuts in the wooden frames encircled the upper and lower part of each bomb in a snug fit, separating the bombs from each other. Metal bands, two lengthwise and four crosswise, held the sandwich snugly together. The actual weight of each bomb was 493 pounds; the total weight of six bombs and a pallet was 3,100 pounds.

The top frame on an end pallet had splintered, allowing enough slack for one bomb to contact the metal hull.

"We were working on top of the row of bombs," Henderson said. "The one that was up against the rib, we just took the saw and cut the bands, cut right down through the plywood—there was a plywood sheet on top—and cut through the four-by-four-inch frame. We then turned this section over and this left us with a cradle to work with. We took this and secured it to two-by-twelve-inch pieces of wood, and made a larger footing for it. We then lifted the bomb out and laid it in this cradle. We had banding material and banders aboard, and we banded the bomb to the new cradle and moved it out of the area. Where we took the bomb out, we replaced it—shored that area with four by fours back to the next bomb. The bomb below it was almost up against the rib, and we drove wedges between it and the steel of the ship."

This would be a hard job in the best of conditions. With the ship snap-rolling back and forth, it was made even more difficult and awkward. But the men did the work. Once the pallet was sawed through, there remained the formidable job of wrestling the 500-pound bomb out of the old cradle and into the new one they had built.

As Henderson recalled, that was the major problem. There was no way to work out the weight of the bomb—they guessed it might tip the scales at around 250 pounds. A tag was attached to the pallet, but they could not see it clearly. Henderson felt he was good for 200 pounds all by himself, and so it didn't seem like too much of a haul. The only way they would find out would be to lift it.

In the cramped space, two men would try to lift the bomb, Henderson and Hughes. The bosun wrapped his arms around one end of the bomb while Henderson did the same on the other end. The men tentatively applied pressure to the bomb casing, testing it. But it did not budge. They heaved again. "We thought at first [it] was wedged in," Henderson recalled, "but it was just heavier than we thought it was." The bomb moved slightly. Encouraged, they intensified their efforts, and then the bosun hurt his back—he had apparently pulled or strained a muscle. The men were undoubtedly concerned, but he assured them that he was okay. They continued to struggle with the bomb and, with help, finally managed to work it out of its nesting place and on top of the tier. Pushing and shoving, they gradually slid the bomb into its new cradle. With the bomb out of the pallet, the men were finally able to read the tag and discovered that they had lifted not a 250-pounder, but a 500-pound bomb! The bosun seemed to pay little attention to his injury, although most believed it to be a serious one that might hamper him for the rest of the voyage.

The men nailed the wood down in the new cradle, banded the bomb tightly inside, then shoved and pulled bomb and cradle to a new area where they braced it with lumber discarded in the holds at Bangor. The rest of the work—shoring the tier of pallets with lumber, bracing, and then tomming—went quickly.

Wrestling dangerous cargo was not the kind of work crewmembers bargained for when they signed on. However, on voyages carrying other kinds of cargo, most seamen looked forward to being called out by the bosun to do routine work about the ship. It meant extra pay.

Keeping the ship operating and on course to her destination has top priority. That's where watchstanders come in, four hours on and eight off, around the clock, everyday. Able seamen and ordinary seamen take their turn at the helm or stand lookout under the watchful eyes of one of the mates, while oilers and firemen-watertenders work the engine room supervised by an engineering officer. Other non-watch business about the ship is handled by the day workers—maintenance men, electricians, and others primarily in the steward's department.

For these labors, a typical merchant seaman in the late 1960s earned a monthly wage of several hundred dollars plus board and keep. A few perks came with that, the primary one being maintenance and cure—a catchall term for board, room, and medical attention when ailing. Taxes took a chunk out of the monthly wage. In addition, most of the men set aside part of their wages to be sent to their grandparents, parents, wife, sister, or children. Notably omitted from this list were brothers who, by law, were not entitled to receive any part of a seaman's wages—males continued to carry the onus left over from the days of crimps and boardinghouse keepers.

Despite these debits, the average sailor could still look forward to pocketing several thousand dollars in hard cash at the end of a relatively short three-month trip. True, the math doesn't compute. That's because we haven't added in the magic of overtime. The notion that seamen should work more than eight hours a day without extra pay went out sometime after the maritime unions came in.

Work involved in departing port, arriving port, chipping, painting, securing cargo, you name it, usually spells O/T. It's extra cash for other work done about the ship. Better still is penalty overtime—overtime pay for no work at all. Such pay might kick in when the men can't eat because of work that spills over into chow time. Or it might occur when the men are called out on standby and, for whatever reason, there is no work to be done, or the work might be unusually hard and filthy—tank cleaning, for example. There is also an extra premium paid to crewmembers for serving on a ship carrying hazardous cargo, for which the men of the *Badger State* qualified.

Finishing the job in No. 3 hold, the men were tired, but satisfied that they had done a solid job of securing the bomb in the hold. Scooping up saws, hammers, nails, and other loose gear, they climbed back up the access hole to the main deck where they were greeted by the mate.

We took care of the bomb, the bosun told him, explaining how they had done so, and that was good news to Cobbs, but he had bad news to tell the men in return. Checking all the holds, he unexpectedly found cargo loose in Nos. 1, 4, 5 upper tween deck, and No. 4 lower tween deck.

This cluster of simultaneous breakdowns in the holds marked the beginning of a battle aboard the *Badger State* that was to continue almost without letup throughout the holiday season. Now the problems were coming in bunches, and it seemed to suggest that it was not just a single flaw in the loading of one hold, but rather a common loading problem affecting most of them.

Work in multiple places called for organization and the bosun saw to the details of it. All the holds had to be inspected, and a system of priorities set up to deal with the worst cases first. He split the crew into separate work groups so that work could proceed in more than one compartment at a time.

Always, above the ship, a familiar companion, a winged form glided effortlessly on wind currents. Hazy and obscure in the perpetual wind and rain, hanging as though by a thread, gently moving one way and then another before disappearing, swallowed up in the wind spray whipping across the turbulent sea.

An albatross, the largest of all flying creatures, plays out its destiny in the wide expanse of the ocean, returning to land only to breed. The birds, gliding on wind currents with their six-to-eight-foot wingspread—the species called the wandering albatross can spread eleven feet of wing—thrived in the same stormy conditions that threatened to overwhelm the *Badger State*. These giant birds tended to be associated with bad luck. And seamen were inclined to believe that killing one, as related by Coleridge in "The Rime of the Ancient Mariner," would bring a curse on all of them. The superstition seemed to apply equally to other large seabirds.

Survivors of the U.S. Army Transport *Jack* had occasion to test that belief in May 1942. The ship, bound for New Orleans, took a direct hit from torpedoes and went down within minutes. Seamen able to do so jumped overboard. Ten of them managed to board a raft that had floated loose from the ship. Thus began an odyssey that was to cover a distance of roughly five hundred miles over a period of thirty days.

During the course of the voyage, a seafarer managed to grab ahold of the legs of a good-sized dinner—one of the large seabirds tracking the raft. Then followed a spirited debate by the half-starved men over whether to eat it. Superstition won out over hunger. As one of the men said, "We let it go. We were afraid it might be bad luck, and we didn't need any more bad luck!"

Those sentiments might have found favor with the seamen of the *Badger State*. But their concerns were focused inward, on the need to get the bombs back in their cages and get on with the ship's voyage.

Continuing on the voyage was officially beyond doubt. In the wheelhouse, Radio Officer Bill LaFayette, a forty-four-year-old sailor out of Oakland responsible for all the ship's communications with the outside world, handed Wilson a message from Naval Headquarters:

REQUEST POSIT, COURSE AND SPEED. REQUEST KEEP ALL CONCERNED INFORMED OF STATUS. CONTINUE ON ASSIGNED MISSION.

CHAPTER 4

Wards of the Admiralty

A man—a human being, made in God's
likeness—fastened up and flogged like
a beast . . .

—Richard Henry Dana,
Two Years Before the Mast

typical seaman during the era of the *Badger State* displayed a certain brashness, a two-fisted willingness to stand up for what he perceived to be his rights. First Engineer Steven Bordash, when asked whether anyone had "talked" him into making the ship's voyage, stated it bluntly this way: "I was never *forced* to sail on the ship; I was *asked* to make the trip. In the merchant marine, nobody forces you to do anything. You do it of your own volition." To better understand that attitude, and a seaman's drive to unite and deal with ship owners collectively, one need only look to his past.

Author Richard Henry Dana gives us a glimpse of that past, and a taste of life at sea in the early 1800s. He sailed aboard the merchant ship *Alert*, bound from the east coast of North America to the west coast, and later wrote a first-hand account of his experiences in *Two Years Before the Mast*. One passage, in particular, resonated loudly with readers:

When he was made fast, he turned to the captain, who stood rolling
up his sleeves, getting ready for the blow, and asked him what he
was to be flogged for. "Have I ever refused my duty, sir? Have you
ever known me to hang back or to be insolent, or not to know my
work?"

"No," said the captain, "it is not that that I flog you for; I flog
you for interference, for asking questions . . . nobody shall open his
mouth aboard this vessel but myself;" and he began laying the blows
upon his back, swinging half round between each blow, to give it
full effect. . . .

The man writhed under the pain until he could endure it no
longer, when he called out. . . . "O Jesus Christ! O Jesus Christ!"

"Don't call on Jesus Christ," shouted the captain; "He can't help
you. Call on Frank Thompson! He's the man! He can help you!
Jesus Christ can't help you now!"

One might fault the temper of the times that allowed a man to be put
to the whip for merely asking questions. However, sixty years later, in
1890, a master could whack a seaman over the head with a stick, breaking the stick in the process, and causing the man to suffer a sore neck for
four or five days. According to the judge hearing that case, bouncing a
stick off a seaman's skull did not constitute unusual punishment, adding
that "interference by the court in a case of this kind by way of damages
would lead to unfortunate consequences."

Using a stick is one thing; using a gun seems a substantial escalation.
For being disorderly and insubordinate—but not mutinous—a skipper
shot at one of his crewmembers several times with a pistol, and then
dumped him in solitary confinement to subsist on bread and water for
fifteen days. He deserved it, the judge said.

No one believed a seaman over the master. In relatively recent
times—1924—a seaman signed aboard the merchant ship *Polybius* as a
"work-away" at a penny a month. It was a penny hard earned: cleaning,
painting, lifting heavy boards, and carrying buckets of suds during which
he developed a hernia. Despite the injury, he was ordered to clean the
ship's smokestack in a storm. He declined to do so. That was too much

for the captain who had the poor man confined in chains—manacled at the wrists and fastened to a brass ring a few inches above the deck. At court, the seaman so testified, his words being corroborated by the ship's bosun and the captain's waiter. Nevertheless, the district court refused to believe the unfortunate fellow had been shackled in this fashion.

Given the harshness of life at sea, what redress did a seaman have in a foreign port? He (as well as the master) could complain to a U.S. consul about ill treatment or behavior aboard ship. Consular officials, appointed in most maritime ports of the world, were charged with safeguarding the rights and interests of both American merchant seamen and owners of ships and cargo. The consul's response sometimes depended on who lodged the complaint, master or seaman.

In 1856 several seamen signed aboard the *Anna Kimbal* in Calcutta for a voyage to Boston. Leaking badly, the ship put into Mauritius. Certain members of the crew sought pay-off there due to, among other matters, ill treatment by the mate, who had beaten several of them, one with "ratline stuff," another with a belaying pin. The master refused to discharge the men and, when they refused duty, sought consular help. That official had the men thrown into prison straightaway and they remained there for thirty-three days. When the men finally returned to the ship, the mate attempted to put them in irons. Perhaps feeling that they had already paid a sufficient penalty, the seamen rebelled.

The supposedly impartial U.S. consul boarded the ship and, along with the master and several others, armed himself with a pistol, a move akin to a judge holstering a six-shooter and going on patrol with a posse. A minor struggle ensued, whereupon the armed men took aim and fired at the hapless seamen (the consul proved to be a poor shot, inadvertently putting a bullet into the mate). The seamen, having survived the shooting, were severely beaten and then confined in irons.

An American court later ordered money damages, the judge observing that "the consul sometimes permits himself to be made use of, as an instrument of oppression, instead of extending to the seamen that protection which they had a right to demand from his official character."

The consul's problem lay in determining the truth. American author

Nathaniel Hawthorne served as U.S. consul at Liverpool, England, from 1853 to 1857. He later wrote a lively sketch entitled "Consular Experiences" and, in prose that sparkles, gives us some insight into the problems arising from complaints lodged by seamen against their officers:

> Scarcely a morning passed, but that some sailor came to show the marks of his ill usage on shipboard. Often it was a whole crew of them, each with his broken head or livid bruise, and all testifying with one voice to a constant series of savage outrages during the voyage. . . .
>
> Taking the seamen's view of the case, you would suppose that the gibbet was hungry for the murderers. Listening to the captain's defence, you would seem to discover that he and his officers were the humanest of mortals, but were driven to a wholesome severity by the mutinous conduct of the crew. . . .
>
> The consul could do little, except to take depositions, hold forth the greasy Testament to be profaned anew with perjured kisses, and, in a few instances of murder or manslaughter, carry the case before an English magistrate, who generally decided that the evidence was too contradictory to authorize the transmission of the accused for trial in America.

Faced with a hell within the ship and indifferent, if not hostile, officials ashore, a seaman had few options. He could, of course, walk off the gangplank at the end of a voyage, putting behind him the master's lash and the terrible hardships of the maritime life. Unfortunately, the perils faced by the sailor ashore were every bit as fearsome as those he faced at sea. Once on land, seamen were everywhere set upon by crimps and boardinghouse keepers, the vulturous scavengers of the waterfront.

Crimps, the employment agencies of the time, furnished seamen to ships in need of a crew. They worked in tandem with boardinghouse keepers, the bed-and-board purveyors of the waterfront. The keepers provided certain necessities and niceties to the seamen to entice them to drop anchor.

As a consequence of this unholy alliance, the iron men in the era of wooden ships fared badly. Happily leaving a vessel after a long miserable voyage, an uneducated Jack Tar was usually taken in tow by the crimps and delivered into the clutches of the boardinghouse keepers. The keepers provided board and bed and other attractions, all exorbitantly priced. After the seaman's pockets were picked clean by practiced fingers, a feat done in a remarkably quick time, services were extended on the cuff. Ultimately, the debt had to be repaid with the only asset owned by the sailor, his labors. To that end, he was delivered to a ship, forcibly if necessary. There, he was forced to sign Articles and an allotment of his wages to the keeper to pay off the debts previously incurred, a practice keeping a seaman in bondage from voyage to voyage.

Of course, the nineteenth century was an era scarcely removed from slavery on cotton plantations. And such practices were not illegal—crimps and keepers were described as providing needed services to both shipmasters and seamen. Maybe, but that could not be said of the fairly common practice of shanghaiing seamen. Disabled by drugs and alcohol, the men were delivered to ships in need of a crew. Awakening, often to the blows of the mate, the unfortunate seaman found himself aboard an alien ship in the middle of the ocean bound for an uncertain destination. Most of the time, it was aboard a ship bound for the Orient, hence the term *shanghai*.

As the passage of time seems to have brought improved living and working conditions for seamen, one might reasonably conclude that regressing to earlier times would show even more extreme cruelty towards seafarers. However, that was not the usual case. One ancient maritime law, for example, provided that if a seaman became sick in the service of his ship and could not do his work, "the master ought to put him ashore, and seek a lodging for him, and furnish him tallow or a candle, and supply him with one of the ship's boys to tend to him, or hire a woman to nurse him."

On the other hand, one of the laws provided that if "the master strikes one of his mariners, the mariner ought to abide the first blow whether it be of the fist or the palm of the hand; if the master strikes him again he may defend himself. If a mariner strikes the master first he ought to lose a hundred shillings, or his fist, at the choice of the mariner." Loss of a hand seems harsh, but it was a punishment not infrequently meted out during the Middle Ages.

Changing times and attitudes eventually brought legislative relief for American seamen. Such prominent spokesmen as Dana and Hawthorne, joined by various humanitarian groups, threw light on the issue in public forums. A more sensitized attitude followed, as did a revulsion toward the cruelty visited upon men at sea. Congress responded by passing the Shipping Commissioners Act of 1872, a law that still governs the treatment of merchant seamen today. The Act required the protective presence of a government official, the shipping commissioner, in most matters arising between master and crew, particularly in signing on or discharging seamen. Commissioners were also given the power to arbitrate "any question whatsoever" between master and crew.

Badger State crewmembers signed Shipping Articles before the shipping commissioner for the port of Seattle, binding themselves to the ship for the duration of the voyage. Nevertheless, four seamen missed the sailing of the ship: three for medical reasons; one for "failure to join." Wilson could have logged the last one as a "deserter" if he believed the man had no intention of returning to the ship.

That fate happened to four sailors who signed aboard the ship *Arago*, bound from San Francisco to Chile in the 1890s. The men left the ship in a U.S. port. The captain decided to make an example of them, charging them with desertion. He had the men arrested and placed in jail for leaving their job. That seems tough, but ancient maritime laws were tougher still—one imposed a punishment of a year on bread and water; another provided that a deserter "shall be stigmatized in the face with the first letter of the name of the town to which he belongs." That's as tough as it gets.

In the case of the sailors from the *Arago*, the U.S. Supreme Court sided with the master, holding that a seaman in signing the unique contract contained in Shipping Articles was, in effect, surrendering his personal liberty, and could be imprisoned for deserting his ship. That decision smacked of military law, and the 1915 Seamen's Act cancelled the effect of the *Arago* decision, leaving the penalty for desertion as forfeiture of pay and effects left on board the ship.

In the hostile world of the seafarer, the one branch of government seemingly the most sensitive to his plight—notwithstanding some harsh decisions—was the judicial branch. An American court, as early as 1823, in an era when flogging a seaman was done as a matter of course, ruling for a seaman who became ill during the course of a voyage, laid out a unique role for the nation's courts:

> Every court should watch with jealousy an encroachment upon the rights of seamen, because they are unprotected and need counsel; because they are thoughtless and require indulgence; because they are credulous and complying; and are easily overreached. But courts of maritime law have been in the constant habit of extending toward them a peculiar protecting favor and guardianship. They are emphatically the wards of the admiralty.

Despite that privileged status, the courts were distant, and only consulted after a great deal of time had elapsed and a large sum of money spent to reach their docket. Improvident seamen could afford neither.

In the face of these problems, and the outright hostility sometimes arrayed against them, it remained for the seamen themselves to bootstrap changes in living conditions, pay, and benefits. This they have done, acting collectively through their unions. The master and crew of the *Badger State* were well represented in that process by the International Association of Masters, Mates, and Pilots; the Marine Engineers Beneficial Association; and, most importantly for the unlicensed crew of the ship, the National Maritime Union of America.

Unfortunately, some other countries continue to lag behind. The International Commission on Shipping—initially funded by the International

Transport Workers Federation, but now reportedly independent—conducted a yearlong study of international shipping. Its findings, released in 2001, showed that thousands of seafarers, in 10 to 15 percent of ships all over the world, work in conditions reminiscent of those that prevailed in the United States two centuries ago: long hours at low or no pay; inadequate food; beatings; men disappearing after complaints to officers; and employer blacklisting.

Today's brash descendants of yesterday's much maligned seafarers may not be fully aware of the writings of Dana and Hawthorne, but most seamen, if put to the test, would acknowledge with pride that they occupy a unique position in American jurisprudence as the "wards of the Admiralty."

CHAPTER 5

A Fragile Ship

O nly a few days had passed by since the *Badger State* set her sea watches. Hardly enough time to wash away city dust from the ship's deck, or to get away from the roar of auto traffic. Even her sailors, staggering about in search of their sea legs, still reeked of the cloying scent of aftershave lotions and sticky deodorants. At this early stage and still a thousand leagues away from Vietnam, bombs had broken out of their restraints in five separate holds of the ship.

All hands pitched in to deal with the danger. Without regard for departmental hierarchy, galley cooks and messmen labored alongside engine room wipers and oilers, and these sailors coupled their efforts with ordinary and able seamen from the deck department.

The bosun, the key man on deck, cobbled the work gangs together and then hurried them on their way to work in the holds. Wilson, responsible for ship and crew by virtue of command, drafted the plan of attack from topside. The wheelhouse became the command post where he also backstopped the efforts of the watch officers in maneuvering the huge ship. As second in command, Chief Mate Cobbs linked captain and bosun together, conveying orders from the one to the other. In addition to working alongside the bosun and his crew, he shepherded, inspected, and reported the results back to the captain.

It was in this capacity that Cobbs scrambled the bosun and his men to secure the pallets that had broken down in the several holds. Following up, he checked out the work that the crew had done earlier in No. 3 hold and climbed to the wheelhouse to meet with Wilson.

No. 3 hold was located just forward of the wheelhouse and Wilson had kept an eye on the men working on deck. They scurried about, gathering large pieces of four-by-four and two-by-twelve lumber, stick-like figures in the watery haze of wind and sea, tilting back and forth as they adjusted to the shifting platform of the deck. Occasionally a seaman caught his eye. A glimpse of grim smiles exchanged, and then they returned to the work at hand. The use of the power saw on the rolling deck called for manual dexterity and patience. The crew displayed both, rough-cutting sections to order with a power saw, and then dropping the pieces down to the men working below decks.

The metal-to-metal contact of bomb and hull in No. 3 worried Wilson. Cobbs reassured him, describing how the men had to wrestle the troublesome 500-pound bomb out of its crate before they could hog-tie it into a new cradle to hold it down. The bosun and his men did a first-rate job, he told Wilson.

Captain and mate realized that the heavy rolling of the ship was creating the major problem in the ship's holds, and that the breakdowns so far had followed periods of severe ship's rolling. But curing that problem was out of their hands. It arose in the first place when they were routed onto the rampaging waters in which they now found themselves—an area of frigid seas and cold winds that packed a wallop in the wide open spaces of the North Pacific.

And yet, paradoxically, it also seemed that the wiser course might have been to route the ship even *farther* north—up through the fan-shaped swath of ocean framed by the Soviet Union and Alaska, threading their way through the Aleutian Islands at Unimak Pass, sailing across the Bering Sea, and then south to Danang. With the help of hindsight, confirmed by recent weather broadcasts, such a route probably would have avoided the worst of the storms then battering the ship.

But sailing farther north wasn't a practical alternative. The United States did not want to provoke the Soviet Union with the presence of American ships or planes—particularly those carrying bombs—anywhere near the borders of that country. In the chess game of the cold war, the

Soviets might well view unkindly such an incursion close to their shores, as they were actively aiding North Vietnam in their own fashion.

The ship was then rolling to 35 degrees-plus in the span of eleven-to-twelve seconds—timed as the ship jerked from one side to the other and then back again—about the same length of time it takes to hoist a cup of coffee to your lips, take a few sips, and then put it down. The principles that underlie this rolling, as well as the behavior of a ship in the ocean, are now well understood.

Place any object on water, whether it is an oceangoing ship or a cup in the kitchen sink. Either object will displace a volume of water exactly equal to its own weight—Archimedes discovered that concept more than two thousand years ago. A cubic foot of salt water weighs sixty-four pounds. A cubic foot of any object weighing less will float; if it weighs the same, its top will be at water level; and if it weighs more, it will sink to the bottom. Try pitching a metal carjack into the water—excess concentrated weight will quickly escort it to the bottom.

A second important consideration is a ship's stability or trim—a quality that ensures that it squats in the water evenly balanced on all sides. The shape of the hull and distribution of weight in it are the critical factors considered by engineers in designing a ship. Once built to specs and placed in service, the captain must see to the proper loading of cargo to make sure the ship stays in trim. If weight is concentrated too high, the ship may be unstable, even to the point of capsizing. The cure is to redistribute the weight of the cargo. If concentrated too much in any one direction, it may list to the heavier side, or be heavy in the stern or bow. That's where ballast tanks come in to help correct those problems.

Once launched from dry dock into water, a ship is affected by two contravening forces that keep it floating right side up. One is the same force which keeps us from drifting into outer space and which works to press a ship down into the water: gravity. Working against that pressure is the force of buoyancy, which tends to push the ship up out of the water. The interaction of these two forces largely determines whether a rolling ship will return to its original position or capsize.

In the case of the C-2 *Badger State*, design and cargo loading were intended to avoid that unhappy fate in most circumstances. However, mountainous waves or hurricane-force winds, in tandem with other factors, might conceivably cause a roll of a magnitude that would push the ship completely over, ending belly side up. It would be highly unlikely, the odds being astronomical, for any ship to capsize in a *calm* sea. But that ignominious fate did overtake the passenger ship *Eastland* in 1915 when the ship improbably rolled over on its side while still moored to a Chicago dock. Despite being steps away from safety, 844 passengers drowned in twenty feet of water alongside the pier.

The *Eastland* seemed jury-rigged from day one. Its owners wanted a fast ship, but also one that could be operated in the shallow waters of the Great Lakes. Consequently, it was built with a narrow beam and a shallow draft—no keel of any consequence. As designed, the ship would have been too long for its intended service, and sixty feet of length was chopped off, further decreasing ship's buoyancy.

Changes made over the years didn't help: extensive and heavy air-conditioning equipment installed; between 30 and 57 tons of concrete spread across the dining room and a large area of the main deck; and more lifeboats and rafts added on the top hurricane deck. Increasing life-saving equipment allowed the ship to boost its passenger limit under anticipated new Federal laws calling for tougher passenger ship standards. The unintended consequence was that the additional boats and rafts added substantial weight to an already top-heavy ship.

The *Eastland*—the first and only passenger ship ever built by the Jenks Ship Building Company—measured 265 feet from stem to stern, 38 feet across her main deck, and rose four decks high. Five gangways provided access from the dock to the ship, the lowest being a mere 12 to 18 inches above the water when the ship was fully loaded. Half-doors closed off the passenger gangway entrance to the ship, the top usually being left open—a list of only 15 degrees would invariably bring water over these half-doors into the ship.

Small wonder that the ship quickly developed a reputation for being "cranky" and somewhat temperamental in her handling. She "behaved like a bicycle," one observer noted, being unstable when taking on or discharging passengers, but stable once under way.

Thus, "ready for sea," the ship ran true to form when excited passengers, many of them Western Electric employees on a summer outing, began boarding the ship early on the morning of July 24. Passengers also ran true to form, either going to the cabins below, or milling around on deck, meandering from side to side. *Eastland* responded by listing first to one side and then the other.

The crew closed down the gangway shortly after 7:00 A.M. (departure was scheduled for 7:30 A.M.). By that time, the ship was doing a slow dance, moving from port to starboard and back. Ballast tanks to trim the ship, pumping the water from side to side, failed to do the job they were intended to do.

The ship's listing grew increasingly more precarious. Few passengers, however, seemed aware of the peril confronting them. Some appeared to look at the ship's behavior as something of a joke. The festive occasion probably contributed to that mood, and some passengers may have experienced *Eastland*'s "crankiness" during a previous voyage. At 7:15, the ship listed 10 to 15 degrees to port, away from the wharf, righted itself, and then began listing to port once again.

Water began to enter through the port gangways onto the main deck. Passengers topside reportedly began to swarm over to the opposite side of the listing ship. Line handlers cast off the stern line, but the ship remained attached to the dock by the forward lines.

In minutes, the port list increased to 25 to 30 degrees. Dishes clattered to the floor in the dining room; a piano rolled across the deck; and a large refrigerator keeled over and slid past the eyes of the amazed, and now panicking, passengers.

The ship struggled to right itself, but the insults accumulated over the years proved too much to overcome. The ship continued rolling to an angle of 45 degrees, stopped only by her mooring lines. An avalanche of screaming passengers lost their footing and began to slide across the deck toward the port side. The concentrated weight broke some of the remaining mooring hawsers and the ship continued her death roll. A mass of screaming humanity struggled to escape but it was too late. Scores drowned in the water; hundreds of others were trapped inside the ship's hull.

A board of inquiry convened in 1915 took years to arrive at its finding, lending credence to the notion that if you want an embarrassing matter to disappear, appoint a committee to stall for time. The board did relieve the captain and crew of responsibility for the disaster. Even the ship was exonerated, the board concluding that it was "seaworthy."

The *Eastland*'s capsizing had nothing to do with waves and everything to do with her lack of stability, a failing made worse by improvident changes over the years. Still, a ship going belly up while tied to a pier seems to defy understanding—the "unsinkable" mentality transferred to another arena. However, it did happen again in a case having nothing to do with design, or mountainous seas, or shifting cargo. Mindful that the road to hell is paved with it, one ship capsized largely because of the best intentions of those trying to save it.

The French passenger liner *Normandie*, moored to a pier in New York City, was immobilized there when Germany occupied France in 1939. Entering the war two years later, the United States took over the ship with the idea of converting it to a troop carrier.

The Navy had overall charge of the project. Several successive groups—the *Normandie*'s original crew; a Coast Guard detachment; and, finally, contract workers and a new crew—saw to the care and upkeep of the ship during the years it was laid up. Inevitably, with so many hands involved and leadership diffused, certain matters of shipboard routine went by the wayside. Firefighting was one: fire alarms to shore were disconnected; a fire detection system did not work; fire guards lacked training; French-language instructions remained on empty fire extinguishers; hoses had incompatible connections—all in all, a catastrophe waiting to happen.

It did when hot work ignited a stock of highly flammable kapok life preservers aboard the ship in February 1942. Fire spread quickly and workers on board couldn't handle it. Outside help came on scene and, in a burst of zeal to save the stricken vessel, destroyed it. The fire fighters poured in so much water that the ship, still tied to the dock, reached what is graphically known as an upsetting moment and capsized. A red-faced Navy, also upset, no doubt took out its frustration on a lifeboat full of captains and commanders. The *Normandie* remained tied to the New York City dock for the duration of the war, a rusting reminder of the proverb that too many cooks spoil the broth.

Aside from these unlikely events, a capsizing is still usually associated in the public mind when a ship is under way and subject to severe rolling. And the reality is that if storm-driven waves become severe enough, the results can be devastating. This is what happened to the U.S. Navy in the Philippine Sea in December 1944.

An armada of naval ships, operating against the Japanese, encountered a series of enormous waves generated by a typhoon. Little warning of the storm's approach had reached the fleet. Hurricane-force winds and extreme seas hammered the ships, particularly those near the storm's center. Monumental damage ensued: three destroyers capsized and sunk with all hands; a cruiser, five aircraft carriers, and three destroyers massively damaged; 146 planes destroyed; and, not the least, roughly 790 sailors lost or killed and many others seriously injured. It was one of the worst disasters the Navy ever suffered.

On a less serious level, excessive rolling jump-starts other problems: increased wear and tear on the ship's hull, deck, and superstructure; sickness and general misery for the crew trying to eat, sleep, work, and carry on the semblance of a normal seagoing life; and, for Navy warships, difficulty in aiming and firing its guns. For those reasons, naval architects and engineers have worked hard to find a way to cut down the agitation that a ship experiences in rough waters.

Several methods evolved to deal with the problem of excessive rolling and pitching, particularly on passenger ships where creature comforts dictate the bottom line: computer-controlled fins that automatically take into account wave motion; tanks of "sloshing fluid" set in motion by the ship's movements—the fluid moving against the roll of the ship; and "spinning flywheels" designed to counteract the ship's movement. Simplest of all, and the most basic, is to install bilge keels—steel fins fitted externally on each side of the hull at the bottom of the ship. The *Badger State* had none of these gadgets to control its rolling. Its shipyard-installed bilge keels, standard equipment on merchant ships, had been removed for reasons unknown. And the ship responded accordingly.

The crew could deal with that. But they were also being called upon to do what they lacked training for: longshore work. That thought prompted questions about the loading done by the Navy at Bangor. How else could one account for the breakdowns that were occurring so soon after the ship's departure? And since it was the bracing and the pallets themselves that were giving way, it seemed logical that the problem had to be either in the type of pallets used, or the way in which Bangor loaded the bombs into the ship's cargo holds.

Reaching out for any possible avenue of relief, Wilson again asked the Navy for permission to take the ship on a southerly tack in an effort to lessen its heavy rolling. Points south were enjoying relatively good weather. The Navy again authorized the ship to divert. In what had become a fruitless maneuver, Wilson brought the ship about to a south-westerly heading and quickly found the ship near broadside to large swells. The rolling only intensified.

Sailing light some 2,000 tons of cargo may have proved critical. The extra weight would have helped the ship ride deeper in the water and perhaps dampen the severity of the rolling. Sailing partly empty in peacetime was a fate to be avoided at all costs. But war time had its own needs and priorities.

Below deck, Bosun Dick Hughes struggled to wrest order from chaos by securing bombs in four separate holds. Too many jobs demanded simultaneous attention from too few crewmen working with the tools that were available. Priorities had to be set. He scrambled to get a firsthand look in each of the holds and then conferred with Henderson and Hottendorf. There was an easygoing, backslapping camaraderie among the three men, a relationship that sometimes develops when men sail together and become comfortable with each other's abilities. In this case, hard work was the common denominator for all three.

Dividing up the work, the men started working the holds. As Henderson recounted it, the tasks became almost routine. "It just became a matter of going from one hold to the next and bringing material. We were what I thought fairly organized. Dick Hughes, the Bosun, had a good line of supply coming all the time. While we were working in the holds, all we had to do was call for whatever we needed. He had it there almost immediately. The gang worked very well together." Reflecting the confidence of the crew, he added, "We thought all the time we could overcome all of the shifting cargo."

Most likely, this optimism sprung from the success the men experienced in handling the loose bomb in No. 3 lower tween deck. With that behind them, the men probably felt that other breakdowns could be handled in the same fashion, and that a temporary fix would deal with the problems until the ship could reach a safe harbor.

Some common-sense steps were taken. Lifelines were strung on deck. With men active topside, there was the possibility a seaman could fall overboard. If that happened, the captain would have to try to bring the ship about, and such a maneuver might prove disastrous for ship and crew.

The talk on the bridge sometimes turned to the holiday. Sam Bondy, a young man from California who had signed on as third mate, was the watch officer. He told Wilson he would have preferred to stay home for the holiday, but needed the sea time to sit for his second mate's license. Wilson, fifteen years his senior, understood, recalling his own younger days when sea time and practical know-how were the steppingstones to higher ranks.

Christmas, and its celebration of love and family ties, seemed a world away from the tribulations now facing the crew of the *Badger State*. They were literally sitting on top of bombs, surrounded by them, and no way to escape them. And yet there seemed relatively little talk about the danger. Perhaps it was because no one aboard had ever experienced such a problem during their seagoing careers, or even read about it. Loose cargo perhaps, but not explosive cargo.

Apparently, neither had the Navy. Given his experience during the last voyage when sounds were heard coming from one of the ship's holds, Wilson had played the "what if" game with one of the Bangor officials. "What action should be taken if pallets ever broke down?" he asked. "Nothing to worry about since it ain't going to happen," the fellow had said, "but to set your mind at ease, we'll get you some written instructions on that anyway."

Wilson had carefully gone over those instructions, trying to see past the language of government doublespeak. It stated the obvious: ammo was sensitive to friction, shock, sparks, and heat, precisely the kind of hazards to which the bombs on the *Badger State* were being subjected. That was hardly reassuring. Neither was the warning that the first order of ship's business was to stop all movement of cargo as rapidly as possible. Obviously, the Navy had never experienced the problem of bombs breaking loose in a ship's hold, or had even imagined it.

Wilson's reverie was broken by the creaking of the door to the wheelhouse opening and slamming shut. He turned to see who had entered and was surprised to see Chief Engineer Gil Baker. Baker was a big, calm fellow in his middle years who was raised in the South, and still spoke with a slight drawl born of that heritage. He worked below deck, heading the engine room department.

A ship's engine room is a windowless space that deck officers and seamen rarely have occasion to enter. In fact, deck officers as well as deckhands, would not, under any circumstances, consider signing on for a job in the engine room. Perhaps it is the appearance and atmosphere of the place: huge white asbestos-covered pipes twisting Rube Goldberg-style every which way; a collection of gauges poking out of odd places;

lights blinking a secret code; assorted valves awaiting manipulation; narrow steel-grating walkways; and, underlying the whole of it, overwhelmingly massive pieces of machinery crowding the area, leaving little workspace or walking space for the engineers.

Aside from the convoluted machinery that fills every nook and cranny, there is the chorus of discordant chaotic sounds. Machine talk: the creaking, groaning, and shrieking, that drives the ship forward. Sound waves ricochet around the compartment like billiard balls on a pool table, battering the ears of those unaccustomed to pandemonium. And then, a final touch: shimmering waves of hot air that float up from the depths, carrying the nauseating smell of oil fumes to the higher decks. Claustrophobic and seasick-prone seamen find no relief in the engine room.

This assault on the senses may be one reason why early steam engines found no favor with sail enthusiasts who resisted the advent of steam for decades in the 1800s. For those seafarers, sailing meant the fresh air of the open sea, the visible comfort of the sun and stars, and the leaping dolphins that kept company with the ship. However, to Chief Baker and his men, the noise, heat, and fumes would merely be signs that all was right with the machinery working normally in the engine room.

A ship, a miniature self-contained city, needs this community of mechanical objects to function effectively. From them flows the necessities for life at sea: electrical power for lights, refrigerated food, electric stoves, and all the conveniences modern seafarers are used to. It furnishes water for drinking and a bit extra for "sea showers." Finally, and not the least, the ship must be propelled forward to its destination. Fulfilling those lofty objectives requires massive engineering.

A turbine steam engine powered the *Badger State*. Steam implies boilers—essentially, sophisticated pressure cookers. The earliest boiler didn't seem much more than that. It generated steam to move a piston inside a single cylinder. Robert Fulton took to the idea and incorporated such a design into the ship *Clermont*, built in 1807.

However, the engine was massive and required a good chunk of the ship just to store the coal needed to operate. In addition, it only produced twenty pounds of pressure per square inch—sea level pressure is fifteen pounds—and a good head of the steam went out the smokestack. Such waste tended to limit the engine's use to wooden ships still using sail. Worse, if the primitive pressure release failed, the boiler exploded, a common occurrence in the early age of steam. Such explosions ranged all the way from the relatively insignificant (albeit disturbing) to disasters of major proportions.

The three-year-old, 112-foot Connecticut liner *Oliver Ellsworth*, named after an early American patriot, fell into the first category. In 1827, while under way, her copper boiler exploded, injuring several people. A panic-stricken horseman galloped off to Hartford to carry the terrible news. Interrupting a meeting of the Connecticut legislature, he excitedly shouted the unforgettable spoonerism, "The *Eliver Ollsworth* biled her buster!" History does not record the puzzled response.

America's worst maritime disaster ever, surpassing even the death toll on the *Titanic*, occurred aboard the SS *Sultana*. The Civil War had just ended and Union soldiers, prisoners released by the Confederacy, had gathered at Vicksburg, Mississippi, eager to get home. Several ships, attracted by the government's offer of $5 per soldier, then a monumental sum, were there to cash in. The 260-foot-long *Sultana* was one of them.

More than 2,000 soldiers squeezed aboard, leaving no room to sit or lie down—its authorized carrying capacity greatly exceeded. A leak in one of the boilers threatened to delay sailing and stymie profits, as other ships were on hand to pick up the slack. At the behest of the master, workers jury-rigged a patch over the leak. The ship left port, bound for Cairo, Illinois, with a stop scheduled at Memphis to pick up coal.

It never got there. Shortly after midnight on April 27, one of the ship's boilers exploded, instantly killing hundreds of soldiers, and spreading fire amidship. In the ensuing conflagration, two smoke stacks toppled to the deck, crushing passengers and adding to the general panic. By the end of the day, more than 1,700 persons were counted dead. (The *Titanic* lost 1,517.) Such boiler explosions were the cost of doing business with greed in the early days of steam.

The explosions shed light on two major problems with these first boilers: better steel was needed to withstand higher steam pressures; and the need to ease the concerns of sailors, passengers, and shippers fearful of a fire, the bane of ships, inside the hull of a ship out of sight of land.

Metallurgical advances worked out the first problem. Engineers developed the more efficient compound engine—adding a second cylinder to take advantage of waste steam leaving the first one. Coal consumption dropped by half, leaving more space for cargo and passengers, and regular schedules of departures and arrivals could be maintained. Familiarity with safely run steam-engine ships gradually eased the fear of fire aboard them.

The addition of a third cylinder in 1881—the triple-expansion engine—upped a steam engine's efficiency even further and dramatically cut its cost. This advantage endured well into the 1950s, and beyond for less-developed areas of the world. These so-called "up and downers," favored by old-timers for their dependability and ease of repair, eventually doomed iron sailing ships in the cargo trade.

The turbine—high-pressure steam hitting a series of vanes on a rotating spindle—marked another watershed change. Coupled with double reduction gears—needed to reduce the speed to a level a ship's prop could handle—the turbine became the standard for American ships until the late 1970s, when diesel engines took over.

To keep everything running properly, Chief Baker relied on Steve Bordash, his first assistant engineer. Bordash had also sailed on the previous voyage of the *Badger State* and recalled his feelings about it. "When we got back to port from that first trip, I told the port engineer that I hadn't slept on the ship for almost two months because of the way she was working . . . the violence of her rolls. Nothing comfortable or easy about it, like a normal ship does. Very violent back and forth, back and forth. It had to be the way the cargo was loaded in the bottom holds. It was not being distributed throughout the vessel to give her good stability.

The ship rolled violently, and that meant getting little sleep and a whole lot of discomfort."

Given that mind-set, it took a lot of convincing by both the captain and the chief to wear Bordash down. He finally agreed to sail, but remained dubious. "I regretted the fact that I was making this last trip because I could see we would be sailing with slack holds," Bordash said. "I had previously told the Captain and the Chief Engineer that if they got orders to go back to Bangor, that I wanted to be relieved because I thought I would be putting my life in jeopardy. But they asked me to make one more trip and I signed on against my better judgment. As soon as we sailed and the ship began to work as badly as she had on the previous trip, I told the chief that if my seagoing career hinges on sailing out of Bangor, I'm through sailing. Under way, it was a winter sea, inconsistent. There wasn't a constant roll from one direction. It would be here and then it would be there. It was a very aggressive sea."

There were other men in the engine department. Neal Kirkwood, a nineteen-year-old cadet making the second voyage of his brief career, both of them aboard the *Badger State*. Older by a generation was Kinnie Woods, third assistant engineer, who had been sailing off and on for years and was known for his subtle sense of humor. With two daughters in their teens, he typified the hard-working sailor with a growing family and a yen to spend some time with them. Sailing was hard on family life, and he took a stab at logging in the woods of northern Montana until the jobs dried up. But he still had his engineer's license. With that to fall back on, he moved his family to the Seattle area where in 1969 shipping was booming. He signed up for the first ship posted on the board at the union hall, the *Badger State*.

The other licensed officers in the engine room were Richard Pattershall, a Down-Easter from Maine in his second year of sailing; and Raymond Reiche, who had signed on as second engineer. In addition, the department was served by a handful of unlicensed ratings: electricians, oilers, fireman-watertenders, and wipers, the titles describing the work each man did.

While deck people seldom entered the engine room, the engineers returned the favor by rarely entering the wheelhouse. That was deck officer's "country." There was an invisible line of demarcation between the two groups of officers, a holdover from the days when the only officers aboard were on deck. In a good-natured poke at both groups, an unknown author once described a captain as a man who knew a great deal about very little, and who went along knowing more and more about less and less, until finally he knew practically everything about nothing. An engineer, on the other hand, was a man who knew very little about a great deal and kept knowing less and less about more and more, until he knew practically nothing about everything. Finally, everyone else started out knowing everything about everything, but thanks to their association with captains and engineers, ended up knowing nothing about anything.

Consequently, the chief engineer entering the wheelhouse came as a surprise to Wilson. "A bit out of your territory, Chief?" he said, extending his hand.

"Yeah, a bit," Baker replied, grasping Wilson's hand.

"Everything okay below?"

"Yeah, yeah. Just a minor thing, there." Baker wasn't much for small talk.

"How minor?"

"Just a leak in the steering gear."

Wilson jerked his head forward at the news, straining to hear every word coming from Baker's mouth. Conning the vessel, steering it, was all that was keeping them from a total breakdown in the cargo holds. The only tool they had to dampen the roll of the ship was to head it into the swells. And that required maximum use of the steering engine.

Steering a ship with brute force by turning a wheel connected to a rudder with line and pulleys is a relic of early sailing days. A ship of the size and magnitude of the *Badger State* required a mechanism to magnify the motions of the helmsman turning the wheel, not unlike that of power steering in a car. A hydraulic connection between helm, steering engine, and rudder did the job, and it was this hydraulic link that had sprung a leak. A loss of fluid meant inaccurate steering and, in the event of a major leak, an inability to turn the ship's rudder at all, leaving the ship at the mercy of wind and waves. Although there were various ways to jury-rig a steering mechanism, none of them seemed workable to Wilson in the sea conditions now confronting him.

The two men discussed the options. Baker told Wilson that they were losing hydraulic fluid through the packing in one of the rams. It would have to be repacked, a job that would probably take an hour or two to do. For Wilson, that meant the ship would be without steering for up to two hours, possibly longer. He wanted to put that off as long as possible—until the end of the voyage, he hoped. That was one option, but the problem was that the leak might worsen, as Baker pointed out, and perhaps cause a complete loss of steering. And that could conceivably happen when wind and sea were far worse.

For Wilson, it was one more crisis to contend with. But it brought to mind the possibility of other problems awaiting the ship and her equipment. The *Badger* was, after all, hard used, and well along in years. Breakdowns were bound to occur. On the plus side, his concerns were eased somewhat by the confidence he had in his engine-room crew. He had sailed on the previous voyage of the ship with both the Chief and the First Engineer.

Wilson gave the go-ahead, but he wanted to do a test run first—to heave the ship to, bring her down to a stop, and then ride with the waves. The engines were stopped for ten to fifteen minutes. The ship drifted without a hand on her rudder, and the ship's motions seemed tolerable to Wilson.

But the maneuver was worrisome. Once the engineers began work on the steering gear, they were committed, and at the mercy of whatever might be out there. In the worst possible scenario, seas might worsen, and cause the ship to broach to—wallow like a pendulum in the trough of huge waves. Experience thus far told Wilson that severe rolling of that kind would hammer the pallets badly, probably leading to more serious breakdowns in the holds. If additional metal-on-metal contact between bombs occurred—the scariest scenario—what then? Quite possibly an explosion, judging from everything Wilson had been told about the explosives. But, still, there were no other options available. The repair had to be made, and reluctantly he gave the order to the engineers to proceed.

With the engines stopped, the ship slowed and began to move sideways in the direction of the swells. But then came a break, an unexpected letup in the storm. It was enough to ease Wilson's major concerns. Still, the ship did roll to 40 degrees several times before the job was finished an hour and a half later. Some cargo was reported adrift in several holds shortly afterward, so if there were any remaining doubt about the connection between heavy rolling and cargo coming adrift, that seemed to settle it.

That evening, the mate reported to Wilson that the crew was keeping ahead of the breakdowns in the various holds. Wilson's spirits rose upon hearing the news. Despite the potential for serious problems, the leaking ram in the steering engine had been repaired without mishap. Even more important, the crew was able to control the breakdowns of cargo in the holds. All seemed secure aboard the *Badger State*.

Nevertheless, Wilson realized it would be prudent to look for calmer waters and more favorable weather. That track lay south of the *Badger State*'s westerly heading. Wilson again sought authorization to divert from the ship's assigned route. On December 16, the Navy radioed Wilson to divert to the southwest; and, on December 18, told him to proceed due south.

Heading south was exactly the course Wilson wanted to take. Again, despite his best efforts, the ship could not hold to a course due south without rolling steeply side to side. Heavy rolling had already broken cargo loose in the holds; increased rolling could only make a bad situation worse. With that in mind, Wilson reported to the Navy that all cargo had been resecured, but that the ship could not divert due south.

Later, the mate came to the wheelhouse to report that supports were breaking down in other holds, and this was happening in some of the holds the men had already worked in. Get the bosun on it, Wilson told the mate, feeling somewhat dispirited. He directed the mate to step up the inspections in all the holds. Maybe then they could stay several steps ahead of any problems.

Shortly afterward, in the continuing radio dialogue between Wilson and naval headquarters, a new diversion order arrived. It directed the *Badger State* to continue westerly on course to a point thirty-five miles south of Adak, Alaska. At that point, the ship was to change course to a southerly heading. Adak, home to a naval station, was located near the end of the beckoning finger of the Aleutian Islands that cups the southern border of Alaska. Given the weather, it seemed unlikely that the Navy could offer any assistance there, but the notion seemed comforting.

On December 19, Wilson received another visit from Chief Baker. Wilson knew it had to mean more trouble.

"Sorry to have to report this, Cap'n," Baker drawled maddeningly, "but we have water coming into the ship—"

"For God's sake, where?"

"Shaft alley, Cap'n."

Deep within the ship, buried underneath the cargo holds, a tunnel stretched from the engine room amidships all the way back to the stern of the ship. Inside this alley, the propeller shaft, a series of steel sections as big around as a slender woman's waist spins endlessly as it carries power from the engine back to the ship's propeller.

"Well, let's check it out!" Wilson growled, feeling a pounding in his chest. It was one more hammer blow on top of everything else that had gone wrong during the voyage.

CHAPTER 6

Fateful Prophecy

C aptain Wilson and Chief Engineer Baker climbed down to the shaft alley in the heart of the ship. First Engineer Bordash—the man responsible for maintaining the aging ship's steam engine, boilers, condensers, and hull—joined them.

Bordash beamed a flashlight on a section of shell plating, an area about ten inches in diameter, revealing a crusted scab of cracked and peeling paint stained with rust. Water was steadily working its way inside the ship. Rust and corrosion, the curse of iron ships, was gradually eating its way through the Liberties, Victories, and C-2s like the *Badger State* and her sister ships left over from World War II.

Baker defined the problem. His men would have to rig a patch over the leaking area. But doing the job meant that the ship's speed would have to be cut back, probably for the rest of the voyage. A further delay, from Wilson's viewpoint, posed problems. The ship was already behind schedule, and he preferred to postpone repair until the ship could be dry-docked ashore. To do so would be taking a risk, Baker explained. The leak, which seemed relatively minor at the moment, could worsen in a very short period of time.

The chief may have had in mind the fact that untended large leaks of water have led to a number of ships going down, among them the *Badger State*'s sister ship, the *Panoceanic Faith,* built at the same time. The gradual entry of water into the forward part of that ship led to her sinking before any repairs could be made. And the evidence seemed to suggest that the ship went down before anyone aboard became fully aware of the seriousness of the problem.

More recently, an ore carrier, the British motor vessel *Derbyshire,* had mysteriously gone down with all hands when she encountered a typhoon off Okinawa. Subsequent underwater investigation showed that, apparently unbeknownst to captain and crew, enough water had entered the forward part of the ship through damaged air pipes to bring the bow lower in the water.

That reduction in bow height, according to the International Maritime Organization—a U.N. agency charged with promoting safety at sea—could lead to a hatch-breaking wave. And, in fact, hatch covers on the two forward cargo holds of the ship appeared to have failed, allowing water to enter. Once that happened, flooding apparently occurred so quickly that there was not enough time for the crew to take to the lifeboats.

Bordash estimated that repairing the leak would take roughly six hours. Wilson, recognizing that the potential for more urgent problems ahead drove the agenda, reluctantly told Bordash to go ahead with the work.

Wilson returned to the bridge and instructed the watch officer to reduce speed to the lowest level possible while still keeping headway. Doing so, it was hoped, would slow the rate of water entering the ship, thus making it possible for the engineers to repair the hull. He then sent the following message to the Navy: SHELL PLATING HOLED IN SHAFT ALLEY, PORT SIDE, FRAME 166. TAKING WATER MODERATELY. PUMPS HANDLING ALL RIGHT FOR NOW. NO PERSONNEL CASUALTIES. CAUSED BY APPARENT WASTAGE IN WAY OF FRAME 166. MAY HAVE TO REQUEST PORT OF REFUGE FOR DISCHARGE OF CARGO AND REPAIR. ATTEMPTING TO PLACE SOFT PATCH AND CEMENT BOX OVER AREA. ESTIMATED TIME OF TEMPORARY REPAIRS SIX HOURS.

Repairing a leak at sea is a chancy proposition, as the work must be done in the face of water entering the ship—like trying to fix a leaky kitchen faucet without completely turning off the tap.

Rigging a cofferdam is the usual method. Workers box in the damaged area with heavy wood, or steel plates, the whole of it shored up with supporting timbers or steel bars welded in place. The top is left open. Engineers then stuff materials readily available about the ship—bedding, clothing, mattresses—into the box to stop up the leak and keep water out long enough for the ship to be dry-docked at her destination. A difficult but more secure method is to dump concrete into the cofferdam.

Bordash chose the latter. As he later described it, "The leak in the shaft alley was in the third or fourth frame forward of the afterpeak bulkhead. We built a dam out of two-by-twelve-foot lumber and then forced another two-by-twelve across the opening, using wedges so that I could get to it to begin with. We then poured into that section three bags of concrete and nine bags of cement. It set up about three days later."

To prevent the patch from vibrating loose, Wilson had no choice but to cut the ship's speed back for the remainder of the voyage. Slowing the ship's progress compounded the problems faced by captain and crew, lengthening a tough voyage already too long.

With luck, Wilson conjectured, this would mark the end of their engine-room problems. That proved to be wishful thinking. The port boiler began leaking and seemed to be getting worse. With the ship running at reduced speed, Wilson decided to have the repair done before the situation got worse. The engineers shut the boiler down while one of the elements was re-welded by Bordash.

The problem seemed not so much with the equipment and materiel failures themselves—those came with any ship growing old. Rather, the uncontrolled heavy rolling of the ship while the repairs were being made remained the ongoing problem dogging the ship since her departure from Bangor.

The battle continued below deck. The men worked all day or stood their watches; wolfed down their chow, plates in hand, usually standing to get a better purchase on the heaving deck; laid below to saw, hammer, heave, and sweat the cargo; and then, tired to the bone, collapsed into bunks which telegraphed every steep roll, pitch, heave, and yaw of the ship as it sailed on its tortuous track across the north Pacific. And then, after being asleep all too briefly, the rough shove and the tough voice, "C'mon, get your ass on deck. There's work waiting for ya!" Stumbling out of bed, falling, fumbling with buttons, cursing, stumbling. Swinging by the mess deck to gulp down black coffee, grab a quick smoke. Rest for the weary came hard aboard the *Badger.*

Midnight—eight bells, the end of one watch and the beginning of another—would bring a new cycle of the same wear-and-tear physical violence. The mental stress of the possibility of bombs exploding diminished slightly as repetition set in. The question, in short order, became not *whether* cargo had gotten loose, but *where*. Once the location was pinpointed, crewmembers turned to, replacing splintered wood, hammering in wedges to hold the pallets in place, replacing metal banding which had snapped open, and working hard to tighten and shore up the whole of what had become a gigantic jury-rigged enterprise hesitantly sailing the vastness of the north Pacific.

Everybody aboard knew that Bosun Hughes had injured his back early on and was in considerable pain. But he complained little and continued to give orders, detailing the men to the various holds and supervising the work. He struggled alongside them in the crowded cargo holds, helped them wrestle awkwardly sized lumber in too-close quarters; endured the same stink of bilge water and leaked engine oil that saturated the air they breathed. And he shared the few bright moments, too, when they all thought the cargo had been finally put to rest. But invariably, new and urgent reports of a disaster in the making elsewhere would surface—usually by scuttlebutt, but sometimes "officially" from the mate through the bosun, or more often than not, by the clanging sounds of the bombs loose in the holds.

When a particular job was finally done and sleep beckoned, some of the crew may have been able to take advantage of it. However, little rest was to be had by the bosun in his quarters. First Engineer Bordash recalled him saying that "every time he sat down in his room, it sounded like a subway train was coming through. In fact, he was referring to his room as a train station after a while!"

As breakdowns increased, the crew began to anticipate trouble spots to try to get a jump on problem areas. "We started going through all the hatches," AB George Henderson said. "The mate would take a man with him, or two of us would go down and go through the hatches. We would take a light and go around the outer edges of each hatch and then check the center to see if anything was loose. If we found loose cargo, we would take our materials and go into that hold."

Once a problem area was located, the crew dealt with it. Florencio Serafino, a wiper in the engine room, unaccustomed to carpenter's work but game for it all the same, recalled what it was like: "In Number Four, I passed lumber from a higher to a lower level. Someone hollered that he wanted twenty-four inches of two-by-four, or forty inches of four-by-four, or something. I tried to measure it as best I could, and then cut it to size. I then passed it down to the next deck level. We had breaks in between; went up for a smoke or a cup of coffee. It was raining and wet, and it was cold, and we didn't work the whole way through, no."

The misery of working the cargo was made worse by the ship's jerky movements. "It was the tremendous rolls," Fireman-Watertender James Beatty said. "We had a lot more bad weather this time than we did the prior trip. And it was a little more vicious."

Third Cook Donald Byrd also recalled how rough it was on the ship: "We have a rack there in the galley where we have pots. The rack is about eight inches high. The pots were jumping out of there just like somebody was throwing them at us. And the knives were also jumping out of the rack. It got so rough in there, I just walked out of the galley, and to hell with cooking!"

When it came to assigning blame, Lawrence McHugh, the deck utility man, voiced the opinion of many aboard the ship. "As far as I'm concerned," he said, "it was just a darn poor job of longshoring." Nothing else seemed to make sense. The pallets did not appear strong enough to withstand the stress that resulted when the ship rolled to 35 and 40 degrees, an assessment that seemed to tie in with another factor: Bangor had moved the *Badger State* out quickly. "It usually takes seven to eight days to load at Bangor, and they ran us out in five days," McHugh recalled.

On December 22, the Navy sent a revised diversion order to the *Badger State*, based on new weather reports. It directed the ship to proceed west-southwest. Wilson acknowledged the order, but reported the ship as having been hove to on a westerly course for the preceding six hours due to extreme rolling to 35 degrees on any other course. A combination of breakdowns in hull and machinery and sheer ornery weather was blocking the ship's progress westward.

Diversion orders and weather reports came out of the same naval office, Fleet Weather Central in Alameda, California, which had responsibility for ships sailing the Pacific Ocean. The forecasters there in 1969 relied primarily upon synoptic weather charts—weather phenomena over a wide area—showing lows and highs and depressions and other happenings foreign to the average seaman. The crew's interest, on the other hand, focused only on what lay ahead for their ship, not the mystery of how those predictions were made. So far, Fleet Weather Central, despite its scientific method, seemed to be doing no better than old-fashioned forecasters who relied on good luck. Or maybe even the fishermen of yore who seemed to do well just sniffing the salt air. Fleet Weather Central's forecasts were driving the diversion orders.

On December 23, the *Badger State*, then some 315 miles from Adak, Alaska, received still another diversion order to proceed southwesterly and to adjust course to suit the needs of the ship. By this point, Wilson realized that he had to get south one way or another, and he was making every conceivable attempt to move the ship down. Complicating this effort was a stream of reports from officers and crew about conditions below deck. While cargo was being secured in certain holds, more cargo was being discovered adrift in others. And one of the reports was that bombs had again come loose in No. 4 hold.

No. 4 highlighted a critical problem: lumber needed to shore and block the pallets in was now in short supply. Once used up, the crew would be unable to resecure the cargo in any of the holds. Their only hope then would be gentle winds and calm seas, neither of which had been in evidence since the ship's departure from port.

Bangor had discarded some pieces of lumber in the holds, and had allowed the crew to keep some extra pieces aboard as a precaution. But not nearly enough. This proved to be a sore point with Captain and crew. "We asked just prior to sailing from Bangor if we could have the materials that they had aboard that they were taking off," Henderson said. "They had a number of four-by-fours by No. 5 hatch, and we were told they had to take these off the ship. There were two-by-twelves on the starboard side of the foredeck that they were stacking to take off the ship. The weather had gone bad in the afternoon and it was raining and so they left these on the deck. This was the material that we later took and stowed. It was fairly common practice to have some material aboard to use for various things. We asked for some nails and we appropriated those ourselves. They were going to take the four-by-fours off and one of the bosses there said, 'To hell with it; let them have it.' This was the material we used until we ran out."

There was no help for it. Wilson scribbled a message and handed it to his radio officer: UNABLE TO HOLD RECOMMENDED COURSE DUE HEAVY ROLLING TO 35 DEGREES CAUSING CARGO IN NO. 4 LOWER TWEEN DECK TO GO ADRIFT AGAIN. BEING RESECURED BY CREW. HAVE HAD TO RESECURE CARGO ALL HATCHES EVERY DAY SINCE DEPARTURE LOADING PORT AND AM RUNNING OUT OF SHORING MATERIAL. PRESENTLY USING SHEATHING. REQUEST URGENTLY THAT YOU GET ME SOUTH TO GOOD WEATHER AS SOON AS POSSIBLE.

Later, the mate came to the bridge on one of his many visits that day. "Managed to find enough shoring to get No. 4 hold squared away, but there's something strange going on in No. 3 lower hold. Loud banging noises, Cap'n," he said matter-of-factly.

It was the last trip all over again. There were three levels to No. 3 hold: upper tween, lower tween, and the space at the very bottom. To get to that bottom level where the strange sounds were coming from, other than by unloading the level directly above it, was an impossible job at sea. Captain and crew would have to grit their teeth until the ship hit port to discover the cause of the sounds. Ironically, the ship had experienced the same problem on its previous voyage to Vietnam, but in a separate bottom hold. Luck was with them and they were able to dock at Pearl and get some answers. Based on that unhappy experience, Wilson had urged the Bangor staff to provide access to all the holds. But that could not be done in No. 3.

With the continuing breakdown of the pallets holding the bombs, and the inevitable contact of metal on metal, the danger of an explosion would seem to escalate—the Navy said as much in the instructions given to every ship carrying ammo. And yet, for the crew of the *Badger State*, there was no escape from that potential disaster short of arrival at a safe harbor. That possibility seemed increasingly remote, given the problems that were multiplying with each passing day.

In many respects, the plight of the seamen aboard the *Badger State*—facing the uncertainty and the increasing possibility of a massive explosion below deck—closely resembled the danger faced by thousands of mariners in wartime from enemy submarines, particularly during World War II. Merchant marine ships carrying bombs, small ammo, high-octane aviation gas—the explosive paraphernalia of war—were prime targets. These ships had little with which to defend themselves. Later, special naval armed guards were assigned. Even then, the ships were lightly armed and hardly a match for a speeding torpedo.

A trio of Standard Oil of New Jersey tankers illustrates the point. The SS *M. F. Elliott* departed Newport News, Virginia, in May 1942, bound for a Venezuelan port. Her master, Captain Harold I. Cook, recalled what happened: "We had reached, on the afternoon of June 3,

1942, a point about 150 miles northwest of Trinidad. The weather was clear with blue sky, wind Force 3, sea choppy. The torpedo struck without warning at 3:58 P.M. on the starboard side aft, in way of the fire room and bunker space. When the explosion came I was on the point of leaving my quarters, located on the boat deck amidships, to go to the bridge. Proceeding there immediately, I tried to telegraph the engine room, but communication was broken. I told Radio Operator Edward M. Stetson to send an SOS and gave orders for all hands to lower the boats. It was evident almost at once that the ship had been mortally struck. She was settling rapidly by the stern, taking a starboard list at the same time."

The ship went down within six minutes of being hit. A well-trained crew had, in that brief time span, successfully launched three lifeboats. Unfortunately, the rapid sinking of the ship by the stern capsized the lifeboats, throwing all hands into the water in every direction. Four life rafts had also been launched, and thirty-two of the survivors were able to reach them. Thirteen men drowned.

Another Esso tanker, the *R. W. Gallagher*, loaded with a cargo of fuel oil, departed Baytown, Texas, bound for Port Everglades, Florida, in July 1942. Her master, Captain Aage Petersen, was on the bridge when two torpedoes hit in rapid succession, causing the ship to immediately list 30 degrees to starboard. Fire quickly broke out across the midship section of the tanker, igniting the oil that had surrounded the ship.

A badly injured Captain Petersen reported later, "I wanted to remain with my ship until the last to see if the fire would subside, and what could be done about helping injured members of the crew and bringing the vessel to port." But it was too late and all hands were left to abandon ship in whatever fashion they could. Quick action by the Coast Guard cutter *Boutwell* saved all but nine crew members.

The SS *Allen Jackson* suffered a similar fate when torpedoes torched the ship's cargo of oil. The ship was underway, bound for New York with a cargo of Columbian crude in January 1942. As stated by Captain Felix W. Kretchmer, "I was in my bed resting when, at 1:35 A.M., the ship was suddenly struck without warning by two torpedoes, amidships on the starboard side, resulting in two consecutive explosions. The first explosion was comparatively mild, but the second, which occurred almost immediately afterward, was very severe and threw me against the walls of my cabin. It broke the vessel apart and set her afire. After the second explosion, I found myself on the bathroom floor. Flames were coming into the bedroom through the portholes and doors. My only means of escape was the porthole in the bathroom. This I was able to get through and I landed on the port side of the boat deck, which was the lee side of the ship. Seeing no sign of the crew, I started up the ladder leading to the bridge. The decks and ladders were breaking up and the sea was rushing aboard. As the vessel sank amidships, the suction carried me away from the bridge ladder."

Miraculously, Captain Kretchmer was carried into open water, away from burning oil on the ocean surface. He saw no one from the ship, and managed to find two small boards, which he clung to until rescued some seven hours later. Twenty-two others were less fortunate.

On the same ship, Bosun Rolf Clausen reported, "When the torpedoes struck the ship, I was in the messroom on the port side aft, playing cards with several members of the crew. We rushed out on deck and made for the nearest lifeboat, Number Four, but we couldn't launch it because the wind was carrying the flames in that direction. With men who joined us, we all went over to the starboard lifeboat, Number Three, which we immediately started to launch. When the boat was in the water and held in place by the painter, we were three to four feet from the ship's side. Around us, within a short distance, were the flames of crude oil burning on the surface of the sea. What saved us was the strong discharge from the condenser pump. The outlet happened to be just ahead of the lifeboat. The force of the stream of water, combined with the motion of the ship, pushed the burning oil away to a few yards outboard of the boat. By the time I cut the lashings and the oars were manned, the boat was being sucked toward the propeller. The propeller blades hit the boat a number of times before we succeeded in clearing it by shoving with oars against the ship."

The primary difference between the *Badger State* and these tankers was that the danger in one was internal, whereas the threat in the other was external. Although the crews in both instances were dealing with the fear of imminent destruction, the response of the men was the same: to confront what had to be done, and to do it, often in heroic fashion and without complaint. Wilson took particular pride in the response of his men to the threat they faced. He recognized that his officers played a prominent role in that response.

Chief Mate Cobbs, for one, brought his years of experience to bear on the ship's problems. He was a strong presence on the ship and a man to be trusted, and Wilson had come to rely on him heavily. Paying him the ultimate compliment, he recommended to States Marine that he be assigned as master of one of their ships. Bob Ziehm, next in line after Cobbs, ran a close second, particularly in view of his navigation skills. Of the two third mates, Wilson found the veteran Burnette to be meticulous in his approach to his job, a man not easily shaken by events, and an officer who could be relied on in an emergency. His counterpart, Sam Bondy, young and relatively new to sailing, showed considerable promise. With a little more seasoning, Wilson believed, the youngster had the makings of a first-rate deck officer.

Those were the officers and men who had thus far kept the ship's cargo under a measure of control. But the problem in No. 3 was beyond everyone's ability to deal with. With that unsolvable problem pressing on him, Wilson directed his radio officer to send the following message to Naval Headquarters: CARGO NO. 4 RESHORED. CARGO NO. 3 LOWER HOLD SUSPECTED LOOSE DUE HEAVY BANGING NOISE WHEN ROLLING. UNABLE TO ENTER HOLD DUE [TO] NO ACCESS. RUNNING BEFORE SWELL. REQUEST DIVERSION ORDERS TO SAFE PORT FOR RESECURING. CARGO ALL HOLDS NEEDS RESHORING.

It was shortly after sending this message that Bill LaFayette, the radio officer, returned with a message in hand. "Good news, Captain!" he said, handing the paper to Wilson.

The unexpected words jolted Wilson. He grabbed the paper. It was from Fleet Weather Central with a forecast covering the weather

through Christmas Eve: 24-HOUR FORECAST. WIND SOUTHWEST
TO WEST-SOUTHWEST, 20 TO 30 KNOTS DECREASING TO 15
TO 25 KNOTS. SEAS WITH WIND 12 TO 16 FEET GRADUALLY
DECREASING TO 7 TO 11 FEET.

Finally, a break—favorable winds and calmer seas ahead. Wilson
took a deep breath, savoring the moment, the one bit of luck they had
been praying for. With good weather and smooth sailing, they wouldn't
have to worry about loose cargo and no shoring. They would be well on
their way to Pearl. They might even be able to head directly to Danang.

The watch officer jokingly asked for permission to pass the word to
the crew. "Yes," Wilson exclaimed, "you're damn right you can!"

Several hours later, the euphoria of the moment still with him,
Wilson sent the following message to the Navy: PRESENT SITUATION
UNDER CONTROL, BUT NEAR CONTINUOUS RESHORING BEING
DONE BY CREW IN ALL HATCHES. MOST DANGEROUS SITUA-
TION WHERE CARGO IS STEEL-TO-STEEL AGAINST SHIP AND
CANNOT MOVE. WHEN SHIP ROLLS 20 DEGREES OR MORE,
CARGO COMES ADRIFT. HAVE HAD TO HEAVE TO NUMEROUS
TIMES TO KEEP FROM ROLLING. ETA 28TH OR 29TH DEPENDING
ON WEATHER. DO NOT REQUIRE ESCORT AT PRESENT BUT
MAY IF SITUATION DETERIORATES. THANK YOU AND MERRY
CHRISTMAS.

It was a heartfelt Christmas greeting, brought on by the forecast of
changing weather. A broad smile lit up the tired features of the captain
of the *Badger State*.

CHAPTER 7

Toughness

The U.S. Coast Guard praised the seafarers of the *Badger State*, using such gold-plated expressions as "untiring efforts," "devotion to duty," "calmness," "in the best traditions of the sea." A blue-collar term, *toughness*—defined by Webster as characterized by severity or uncompromising determination, and capable of enduring strain, hardship, or severe labor—seems a much better fit. The crew of the *Badger State* displayed those extraordinary qualities in a voyage notable for its extraordinary danger. And that danger was unrelenting, taking the measure of every man aboard for the duration of the voyage.

No need to gild the lily here. These were cigarette-smoking, hard-drinking, hard-cursing seafarers who had, in their own way, achieved a certain dignity merely by reacting courageously to life-threatening events beyond anybody's control. In the words of Captain Wilson: "The bravery of my men individually, I can't describe. But overall, they were magnificent!" It was that collective spirit that best described merchant marine seafarers down through the years.

The daring men of the American lumber schooners *Unity* and *Polly* were also part of that magnificent group. Their moment of fame came during an early phase of the Revolutionary War, when British arrogance met American intransigence.

Realistically, the colonists had little chance of achieving independence. At best, the colonies' army was a grab bag collection of untrained troops, and it lacked any warships to fend off its counterpart in the

British Navy, then one of the most powerful forces on the high seas. There would seem little doubt about the outcome of the war. But that conclusion did not take into account two factors: a sort of reckless renegade quality that characterized many of the colonists, and the use of colonial merchant ships as its "navy."

The first incident happened in Machias, a secluded province of Massachusetts so far out of the mainstream that the settlers thought they were in part of Nova Scotia. Residents discovered their true allegiance only after they petitioned for a grant of land to form a township.

In 1775, the British warship *Margaretta* departed Boston to escort two merchant ships, the sloops *Unity* and *Polly,* to Machias. One of the sloops carried supplies to be exchanged for lumber that, as rumor had it, was needed to build barracks for British troops in Boston. Machias then, like most of the outlying colonial towns, was a small island of settlers surrounded by forest.

Upon arrival, James Moore, the young, impatient British commander, refused to land the supplies unless the inhabitants first agreed to remove a "liberty pole," a stripped-down pine tree which had come to symbolize colonial resistance to the Crown. Furthermore, he threatened to shell the town unless they agreed to his demands. The ultimatum stuck in the craw of these feisty down-easters who soon hatched a plot to arrest the ship's officers at church services, and then seize the guns of the *Margaretta* to defend the town against future British insults.

The officers got wind of the plot and beat a retreat. Shots were exchanged between ship's cannons and the muskets of the townspeople. The contentious Moore then threatened to burn the village down if either sloop under his protection was harmed in any way. This threat particularly riled some young hotheads who took up position on the banks overlooking the British ship and opened fire. The *Margaretta,* unable to raise her guns high enough to return fire, weighed anchor and sailed out of range downstream, suffering the loss of her mainmast in the process.

Feeling their oats, the town's firebrands paddled out in a rowboat and commandeered the *Unity*. Fired up by this initial success, and by a band of Irish brothers named O'Brien, the youths began to dream of capturing the big prize, the mighty British man-of-war itself. The *Unity*, crewed by thirty-five volunteers, including all five O'Brien brothers (the youngest aged sixteen), set out in pursuit of the dream. Jeremiah O'Brien was the skipper of this ragamuffin gang of townsfolk.

There appeared to be a mismatch between the two ships. The colonists were armed with fowling pieces and enough powder and ball for three rounds, thirteen pitchforks, axes, and a single long-barreled large-bore rifle. Arrayed against them was the British man-of-war, twice its size and fortified with eight six-pounders, twenty swivel guns firing one-pound balls, forty muskets, forty cutlasses, forty pikes, forty boarding axes, two boxes of hand grenades, ten pairs of pistols, and plenty of powder and ball.

For some inexplicable reason lost in history, the *Margaretta*, in a monumental identity crisis, chose to retreat. Although it could have easily reduced the population of Machias by some thirty-five of its most volatile citizens, one rumor had it that the young British commander must have been swayed by humane considerations.

In a highly improbable series of events, the *Margaretta*, pressing on all available sails and seemingly running scared—a shark running away from a tadpole—was overtaken by the lighter schooner. O'Brien, displaying a cheeky impudence when facing the larger British ship and its cannons, *demanded* the surrender of His Majesty's Ship. The ship, remembering that it was a powerful warship of the mighty British fleet, joined the battle by responding with a single cannon shot that killed two men aboard the *Unity*.

A marksman from the *Unity* replied in kind, killing the helmsman aboard the warship. The two ships came together briefly, long enough for John O'Brien to leap aboard the British ship. The ships parted and O'Brien, suddenly realizing he was badly outgunned, nimbly leaped over the side and swam back to the American ship.

The *Unity*, her boarding party consisting of villagers armed with pitchforks, closed with the larger ship. Gunfire continued between the two vessels during which the commander of the British ship was mortally wounded. Pitchforks at the ready, the Americans boarded the British ship and, after a scuffle, received the surrender of its leader-less crew. HMS *Margaretta* struck her colors to the *Unity*, the first British warship to surrender to an American ship in a battle at sea. The *Unity* was, in today's maritime talk, a merchant marine ship.

A pitifully undermanned, ill-equipped, and under-armed merchant ship capturing a powerful British warship proved to be a dramatic shot of adrenaline for the American patriots. The *Margaretta* and the two sloops were awarded as prizes to Jeremiah O'Brien and his valiant crew. O'Brien, having bigger things in mind, moved the guns of the warship to the *Unity,* renaming her the *Machias Liberty*.

This incident was apparently not a fluke. Another British Navy ship, the *Diligent,* along with her tender, the *Tapnaquish*, sailed to Machias. Confronted by Jeremiah O'Brien in the *Machias Liberty*—his reputation apparently had preceded him—the British ships meekly surrendered without firing a shot. Unexpectedly, the Massachusetts colony suddenly found itself with a "navy" consisting of two commandeered British ships, the *Diligent* and the *Machias Liberty*.

O'Brien unquestionably led a charmed life. The British captured him in a battle at sea. Imprisoned, he subsequently escaped and went on to command two other ships before the War of Independence ended. Small wonder then that the O'Brien name resonates in maritime circles, with several Navy and merchant ships proudly taking it on. One of them, the Liberty ship SS *Jeremiah O'Brien,* played an active role in the Normandy invasion during World War II. Today, one can walk her steel decks at pier 45, Fisherman's Wharf, San Francisco.

Not only the names, but also the spirit of these young men have echoed down through the centuries, inspiring other seafarers in the service of their country. That spirit finds common ground in another quintet of Irish lads, the five Sullivan brothers, who died as one when their Navy ship, the USS *Juneau*, was torpedoed during World War II.

The O'Briens of that earlier era shared in the value of prizes captured by their ships, a practice called Privateering—sometimes confused with piracy. Both privateers and pirates made their living by robbery on the high seas, the distinction between them being that the former was authorized by, and shared their booty with, a governing power, while the latter worked solely for themselves. Looked at another way, privateering mixed patriotism and profit, spiced with a bit of rum, as dramatized in this ad that reportedly ran in a Boston newspaper:

**An Invitation to all brave Seamen and Marines,
who have an inclination to serve their Country
and make their Fortunes.
The grand Privateer ship DEANE,**

commanded by ELISHA HINMAN, Esq; and prov'd to be a very capitol Sailor, will sail on a Cruise against the Enemies of the United States of America, by the 20th instant. The DEANE mounts thirty Carriage guns, and is excellently well calculated for Attacks, Defense and Pursuit — This therefore is to invite all those Jolly Fellows, who love their country, and want to make their fortunes at one Stroke, to repair immediately to the Rendezvous at the Head of his Excellency Governor Hancock's Wharf, where they will be received with a hearty Welcome by a Number of Brave Fellows there assembled, and treated with that excellent Liquor call'd GROG which is allow'd by all true Seamen, to be the LIQUOR OF LIFE.

Privateering finds its precedent in a maritime law known as the Judgments of Oleran (an island off the French coast). That ancient law allowed a sovereign to license a private ship's master to attack the king-dom's enemies, based on the idea that one injured could retaliate on the high seas. Merchant ships would thus be used to wage war rather than to transport goods.

The American colonies readily adopted the practice, issuing Letters of Marque and Reprisal—a formal grant of power to private persons authorizing them to arm their ships and then proceed to fight enemy vessels. Their specific mission was to seek out British merchant ships, capture passengers, crew, and cargo, and deliver the whole of it ashore. Master and crew then shared in the value of the ships and goods seized. For most crew members, the reward was substantial—a single prize might yield the average sailor the equivalent of a year's wages ashore.

This sort of free-enterprise way of waging war seemed to fit the colo-nials very well. By 1781, more than 400 American privateers had been enlisted to prey on British shipping. And they proved uncommonly suc-cessful, taking roughly 700 British ships as prizes. In addition, during the period 1775–83, privateers captured or sunk British ships at a rate triple that of the Continental Navy.

Notwithstanding that the colonies won the War of Independence, Britain continued to harass American shipping, seizing vessels accused of carrying the goods of nations Britain considered belligerents. And it also engaged in the impressment of colonial seamen—forcibly removing them to serve on British ships.

Impressments predated the Revolutionary War. A flagrant example involved the British warship *Maidstone*, which sailed into Narragansett Bay and forcibly removed colonial seamen from ships anchored there, including a crew just home from a long voyage to Africa. As John Spears wrote in 1910, in his *Story of the American Merchant Marine*:

> It seems impossible now that a naval officer should be guilty of such needless cruelty as taking men under such circumstances, but the truth is that the naval officers of that period found pleasure in cru-elty. It was because of inhumanity—the harshness with which men were treated in the navy—that impressment was necessary. The

friends and relatives of the impressed seamen were unable to obtain redress, but they expressed their feelings by burning one of the *Maidstone*'s small boats.

These practices began to accelerate after Britain defeated its historic rivals, France and Spain, at Trafalgar in 1805, and became the dominant force on the world's oceans. Displaying its power, and its arrogance, it stationed ships outside American harbors; stopped and checked the manifests of all ships leaving port; and seized many vessels, forcing them to sail to Halifax to be declared prizes. In addition, it stepped up the impressment of American seaman to meet a shortage of qualified seafarers to serve on British warships. At one point, U.S. records showed that more than 6,000 Americans were serving against their will on British ships. These men were, as one author put it, "as much slaves and prisoners aboard British men-of-war as if they had been made captives by the Dey of Algiers."

With Britain flexing its maritime muscle and America feeling its honor compromised, a U.S. declaration of war followed on June 1, 1812. However, not all areas of the country followed suit; the island of Nantucket, for one, declared its "neutrality," perhaps for very good reasons. Nantucket Island, isolated from the mainland, had little protection against sea raids, and its whaling ships were hard-put to compete against English imperial warships.

Given Britain's predominant maritime power and prowess, the prognosis did not bode well for the upstart United States. British ships roamed the seas, raiding and pillaging at will. Adding insult to its seagoing depredations, it brazenly put the torch to the new nation's capital, in Washington, D.C. The United States could do little to stop these attacks. Its Navy simply had too few ships to contend with the numerous British warships that blockaded harbors up and down the Atlantic Coast.

What the United States lacked in military power, however, was more than made up for by its fleet of merchant ships, estimated at some five hundred, sailing as privateers to seize British shipping. These ships proved uncommonly successful in that venture, capturing double their number as prizes.

And they did so with a certain flair reminiscent of their swashbuckling ways during the Revolutionary War. Not content with merely seizing British merchant ships on the high seas and out-of-the way harbors, these American privateers sailed their ships, stars and stripes unfurled at the mast, into the very sanctuary of the mighty British fleet, the English Channel, and other coastal waters. Mortified Glasgow merchants, fed up with such shenanigans, drafted a resolution in 1814, venting their embarrassment and outrage over the success achieved by these daring privateers:

> That the number of privateers with which our channels have been infested, the audacity with which they have approached our coasts, and the success with which their enterprise has been attended, have proved injurious to our commerce, humbling to our pride, and discreditable to the directors of the naval power of the British nation, whose flag, till of late, waved over every sea and triumphed over every rival. That there is reason to believe that in the short space of less than twenty-four months, above eight-hundred vessels have been captured by that power whose maritime strength we have hitherto impolitically held in contempt. That at a time when we are at peace with all the world, when the maintenance of our marine costs so large a sum to the country, when the mercantile and shipping interests pay a tax for protection under the form of convoy duty, and when, in the plentitude of our power, we have declared the whole American coast under blockade, it is equally distressing and mortifying that our ships cannot with safety traverse our own channels, that insurance cannot be effected but at an excessive premium, and that a horde of American cruisers should be allowed, unresisted and unmolested, to take, burn, or sink our own vessels in our own inlets, and almost in sight of our own harbors.

The Glasgow merchants might have been embarrassed by such daring tactics as those displayed by the *Governor Tompkins*, which, baiting the British lion in its den, torched fourteen English ships in succession. Another vessel, the *Harpy* of Baltimore, hovered off the Irish and

English coasts for three months, returning finally to Boston with spoils that included the generous sum of a half-million dollars.

Other ships flying the American flag cruised in the same areas for months at a time, making coastwise trade difficult for enemy shipping. The London *Morning Chronicle* was roused to complain "that the whole coast of Ireland from Wexford round by Cape Clear to Carrickfergus, should have been for above a month under the unresisted domination of a few petty fly-by-nights from the blockaded ports of the United States is a grievance equally intolerable and disgraceful."

However, probably no ship raised the ire of the British more than the 356-ton American schooner *Chasseur*, the "Pride of Baltimore." Armed with sixteen long-range twelve-pounders, she carried a crew of 150 sailors, and her captain was another fighting Irishman, Thomas Boyle. On her first cruise, the ship reportedly captured eighteen merchant ships, a staggering number of prizes.

That cheeky impudence which seemed so characteristic of the U. S. merchant marine found its voice in Captain Boyle. He issued his own "Proclamation," heaping scorn on Britain's blockade of American ports, and declaring a blockade of his own:

I do, therefore, by virtue of the power and authority in me vested (possessing sufficient force) declare all the ports, harbours, bays, creeks, rivers, inlets, outlets, islands and sea coast of the United Kingdom of Great Britain and Ireland in a state of strict and rigorous blockade. And I do further declare, that I consider the force under my command adequate to maintain strictly, rigorously and effectually the said blockade. And I do hereby require the respective officers, whether captains, commanders or commanding officers under my command, employed or to be employed on the coast of England, Ireland and Scotland to pay strict attention to the execution of this my Proclamation.... And that no person may plead ignorant of this my Proclamation, I have ordered the same to be made public in England.

And make it public, he did. Rubbing salt water into the wounds of British pride, Boyle somehow arranged to have his Proclamation posted publicly on the door of that great English insurance institution, Lloyd's of London.

The British Navy went gunning for Boyle. But in a series of encounters, he always seemed able to evade disaster at the last moment. According to his ship's log, Boyle managed to escape unharmed from four warships on one occasion, and then encountered two others. After being fired upon, Boyle returned fire and "displayed the Yanky [sic] flag, hauled upon a wind, and outsailed them both with ease." The following day, he escaped capture by three more warships, and then "was chased by four men-of-war but outsailed them with ease." The British, despite their power and might, were never able to force Captain Boyle to strike his "Yanky flag."

To Boyle's credit, he also displayed on occasion a nice sense of compassion. After a heavy exchange of broadsides, his ship closed with the British schooner *St. Lawrence*. His orders to his men to board induced the English ship to strike its colors. A number of seamen from both ships died or suffered serious injuries. Boyle carried all the wounded ashore for treatment out of "motives of humanity."

The British captain presented Boyle with a letter which said, in part: "In the event of Captain Boyle's becoming prisoner of war to any British cruiser I consider it a tribute justly due to his humane and generous treatment of myself, the surviving officers, and crew of His Majesty's late schooner *St. Lawrence*, to state that his obliging attention and watchful solicitude to preserve our effects and render us comfortable during the short time we were in his possession were such as justly entitle him to the indulgence and respect of every British subject."

Privateering served the United States well in its conflicts with Britain. And the practice of issuing Letters of Marque continued into the mid-1800s, with European maritime powers finally abolishing the practice in 1856. The United States declined to approve the agreement, however, and remnants of privateering persisted during the early stages of the Civil War, when sea tactics changed. Northern ships blockaded southern ports and effectively prevented the Confederacy—which was more likely to benefit from privateering—from hauling prizes into ports. Without that incentive, ships captured were simply destroyed.

It took a little dickering to put an end to the practice. In April 1861, President Jefferson Davis announced that the Confederacy would issue Letters of Marque and Reprisal. Lincoln responded that the Union would regard privateers as pirates. The deadlock stood until the crewmembers of the captured Confederate ship *Savannah*, all privateers, were tried at New York for piracy. The seamen were saved from the gallows by a Confederate declaration that an equal number of Union officers would meet the same fate. Sanity prevailed, and privateering ceased.

As an alternative to privateering, the South bought a number of fast British-built raiders, powered by steam as an auxiliary to sail, to seek out and destroy the much slower northern merchant ships. The most famous—or notorious, depending on one's point of view—was the *Alabama*, commanded by a former U.S. Navy officer, Raphael Semmes. British tars, lured by a Confederate promise to pay them prize money at war's end, crewed the ship.

Alabama lived up to expectations, preying on northern shipping over a period of almost two years. She captured sixty-four northern merchant ships, fifty-four of them torched at sea. A familiar pattern evolved: those set afire were first divested of rigging and stores and their officers and crew removed as prisoners; a few ships were allowed to proceed on their way after promising to pay a certain sum to the Confederacy after the war's end.

The full measure of the captain of the *Alabama* shines through the description furnished us by Union Admiral David Porter, who admired and disliked Semmes with equal intensity:

Was there ever such a lucky man as the Captain of the *Alabama*? If he wanted a cargo of provisions it fell into his hands. If he required to visit a dockyard to fit out his ship, a vessel came along filled with cordage, canvas, and anchors. If he wanted lumber, a lumber vessel from Maine came right into his path; and if he needed to reinforce his crew, renegades from captured vessels would put their names to the Shipping Articles, after listening to the thrilling tales of the Norsemen, of burning ships and abundant prize-money.

On one notable occasion, *Alabama* fired on the bark *Alert*, forcing it to heave to. The southerners confiscated the ship's stores and cargo, allowing her captain and crew to sail to nearby land in their own boats. *Alert*'s fame stemmed, of course, from former crewmember Richard H. Dana, Jr., who later wrote of his exploits in *Two Years Before the Mast*.

Semmes did the Confederacy proud. Eventually, however, he met his match at the hands of the Union warship *Kearsage*. And it happened in an unlikely spot, off Cherbourg, France, while the *Alabama* was docked there for repairs. The *Kearsage*, learning of the southern ship's arrival, took up station outside the harbor.

The ships were mismatched in weaponry. The *Kearsage,* a man-of-war in the best sense of the phrase, carried much heavier guns, a sizeable advantage. The *Alabama*, on the other hand, was of lighter construction, having been designed primarily for speed. The end was not long in doubt, and heavy fire from *Kearsage* sank *Alabama* in little more than an hour.

Other southern ships continued the fight, but none equaled *Alabama*'s record in destroying northern shipping. However, southern strategy did have one unforeseen effect: the damage inflicted by raiders such as the *Alabama* drove insurance rates, and consequently the cost of shipping, sky-high. Foreign ships picked up the slack by carrying American cargo—financier R. B. Forbes, in a letter to the Secretary of the Navy in July 1863, noted that 146 of the 180 ships in New York were at one point flying foreign flags—self-interest had driven northern ship owners to sell out to foreign interests. Such sales increased from 17,408 tons in 1860 to 300,865 tons four years later.

Following the end of the Civil War, the U.S. merchant fleet declined as American goods continued to be carried on foreign ships. In 1905, for example, the United States had 1,333 ships engaged in foreign trade, as opposed to Great Britain's 11,365. Worse, in terms of technology, 73 percent of the U. S. fleet was powered by sail while less than 20 percent of the British fleet suffered that handicap. And yet, the decline occurred despite U.S. foreign exports increasing five-fold since the end of the Civil War.

That downward spiral continued into the early 1900s, when several events began to arouse interest in a strong U.S. maritime presence on the oceans of the world. The United States ascent to power argued for a strong Navy to protect the nation's interest, and a naval buildup followed. Then, with the advent of World War I in Europe and America's possible involvement in it, the need for a strong merchant marine was recognized. No other means existed to carry the millions of tons of bombs, tanks, and legions of American troops that would be needed on foreign shores.

These evolving challenges marked the end of an era. With a strong Navy to defend the country, an O'Brien or a Boyle would no longer sail their civilian ships and crews into battle. Instead, merchant ships in times of war would mirror their transportation role in peacetime, carrying troops and military goods rather than civilian goods from port to port. But that single function would prove critical to a modern military force, a point World War I drove home.

Anticipating the need, Congress, shortly before entering the War, considered ways to expand the merchant marine. Its handiwork, the Shipping Act of 1916, marked a major milestone. For the first time, a legislative act authorized the U.S. government to build and operate its own merchant fleet. However, there was one concession to private ship owners leery of government intrusion: the United States had to dispose of its fleet within five years after the end of the war.

Based on the Act, the U.S. set about creating a new design for a merchant ship, and began constructing shipyards to build it. The most celebrated yard was on Hog Island, near Philadelphia. A simple distinctive design—a ship featuring the blunt look of straight steel plates in the ship's bottom, sides, bow, and stern—was created to take advantage of the unskilled labor then available. "Hog Islanders" continued to sail long after the end of the War. This shipbuilding program made the U. S. one of the leading seafaring nations of the world.

But these merchant ships could no longer depend on speed to outrun enemy warships, a fact brought home when German subs, in an undeclared war, began sinking American ships. The first was the schooner *William P. Frye,* bound for Queenstown, Australia, with a load of wheat in January 1915. A German raider came upon the vessel, ordered the crew off, and sunk the ship with gunfire.

Not long afterwards, the newly built American tanker SS *Gulflight,* bound for a French port with a load of gasoline and oil, also fell victim to a German sub. Sailing off the English coast on her maiden voyage, a torpedo found its mark, slamming into the starboard bow of the ship and taking her down.

But more than any other incident, a single torpedo fired by a German sub in 1915 galvanized American public opinion against Germany. It sank the British passenger liner *Lusitania,* the ship going down in eighteen minutes, taking with it 1,198 passengers and crew, including 128 Americans. The sinking garnered worldwide headlines, and prompted President Wilson to strongly protest the taking of so many American lives.

Possessing no guns, merchant ships were not much more than targets in a shooting gallery. To remedy this lack, and with the quickening tempo of approaching war, President Wilson issued an executive order placing naval armed guards on board all merchant ships sailing in dangerous waters. In an interesting turn of events, the Navy was now furnishing firepower aboard a civilian-owned and -crewed ship.

For its part, the Navy acted quickly, recruiting and training sailors for the job, as well as fitting ships with the largest weapons the ship's structures could tolerate. Arming merchant ships became an important defensive, and sometimes offensive, tool throughout the First and Second World Wars.

Following the formal declaration of war on Germany on April 6, 1917, the naval armed guard quickly justified its presence. A few months later, fittingly on the Fourth of July 1917, the American steamer *Navajo* encountered a submarine in the English Channel. In a running gun battle with the German sub—unheard of before the advent of the armed guard—a shell from the American ship hit the sub near her conning tower. As the report of the battle stated, "The men who were on deck at the guns and had not jumped overboard ran aft, the submarine canted forward at an angle of almost 40 degrees, and the propeller could be plainly seen lashing the air." The sub went down.

A few months later, the U.S. cargo ship *J. L. Luckenbach*, bound for a French port, engaged in an unusually extensive gun battle with a German sub. One shell exploded in the armed guard's quarters, starting a fire and disabling the ship's firefighting system. Another burst in the engine room, seriously wounding two engineering officers. One of its guns was destroyed by a direct hit. The *Luckenbach* broadcast an SOS. The signal was picked up by the USS *Nicholson*, a destroyer sixty miles away, which immediately proceeded to the scene.

In the normal course of events, the German sub would have chalked up another win. However, the *Luckenbach*'s armed guard proved to be the equalizer, enabling the ship to hold its own until help could arrive.

The ships continued maneuvering for advantage, neither able to gain an edge over the other. The continuing exchange of gunfire eventually took its toll on the *Luckenbach,* and she began to take on water, causing her to list to one side. However, she held her own until the destroyer arrived and added its considerable weight to the battle. A shell from one of the American ships exploded on the sub's foredeck, driving the sub under. The battle was memorable for the length of time the ships exchanged gunfire—four hours, and hardly without respite.

Another striking example of the naval armed guard in action, but with a startling twist to it, involved the American freighter SS *Norlina*. The ship had discharged her cargo at a British port in June 1917. While returning to the U.S., a half-ton German torpedo struck the hull of the ship with a tremendous roar. Every man aboard feared that an enormous explosion had torn the ship apart. The captain gave the order to abandon ship and all boats were safely launched. However, several men were somehow left aboard. The commander of the German U-boat, seeing the crew abandon ship, assumed it was sinking, and left the scene to pursue several other merchant ships in the area.

In a highly unlikely turn of events, the men still aboard the *Norlina* discovered that the ship was not taking on water and not in danger of sinking. In fact, it had sustained no damage whatsoever since the torpedo had not exploded, but had apparently bounced off the hull and sank. The sound of the "explosion" heard by the crew appeared to have come from the torpedo slamming into what was, in effect, a huge metal "drum," the empty hull of the ship. The lifeboats were called back; a chagrined master and crew reboarded the ship; and in a turn of events reminiscent of the merchant marine's penchant for impudence, the *Norlina* became the pursuer of the sub—the fox now after the hounds. Coming into range, the armed guard aboard the American ship opened fire.

Meanwhile, an equally chagrined German U-boat commander brought the sub about and headed for the *Norlina*. The American ship's radio operator recalled what happened next:

> When about six hundred yards off our starboard quarter, a shell from our forward gun hit her and she submerged. Again she appeared, and our after gun hit her and blew away her periscope. Another shot from our forward gun fell right on top of her. There was a shower of black specks rising high in the air, followed by a great commotion of bubbles of water and a light blue smoke arising from the stern of the submarine. Our crew, which were lined up against the starboard rail watching the battle, gave a hearty American cheer when the submarine disappeared. The *Norlina* fired nineteen shots in all. One of the gunners afterward said we ought to have given them two more and made it twenty-one shots, the presidential salute.

In other battles, however, the pursuer, gaining on the pursued, unexpectedly meets its match. The U.S. tanker *Silver Shell,* loaded with gasoline, sighted a German sub while in the Mediterranean in May 1917. The tanker turned about and attempted to outrun the sub. Then ensued a battle that lasted more than an hour and a half.

Cranked up to full speed of fourteen knots, the *Silver Shell* was slowly but surely losing ground to the sub, much to the disadvantage of the German sub, as it turned out. A shell from the tanker hit a cache of ammo on the deck of the pursuing sub. "There was a flash of flame," the captain of the *Silver Shell* reported, "and within a minute she had disappeared."

Eventually, American might proved decisive in World War I. By its end, the United States possessed a merchant fleet capable of dominating world transport, most of it steam powered, fueled by oil of which the country had a plentiful supply. Foreign shipping generally depended on coal, which Britain monopolized through its international web of coal bunkering stations. The U.S. had neatly sidestepped that monopoly.

War experience drove home the critical need for a strong U. S. merchant fleet. Congress responded with the Merchant Marine Act of 1920, which established a national policy of developing a merchant marine large enough to carry most of the country's commerce. Best known to merchant seafarers as the Jones Act, the law restricted the transportation of goods coastwise and intercoastal to American-flag ships. Beyond that, it spelled out a policy of developing a merchant marine to "serve as a naval or military auxiliary in time of war or national emergency." While carving out a military role for the service, it nevertheless provided for private ownership by U. S. citizens. With this nod to private interests, most of the government-owned ships built during and after the war went on the auction block at rock-bottom prices.

Cheap ships and plenty of cargo served the U.S. maritime industry well in the years immediately following World War I. However, other countries, building newer ships and able to cut costs, soon posed tough competition. The reality was that, for various reasons, U.S. shipping was a high-cost operation and thus at a competitive disadvantage. And yet the country needed a strong merchant marine to serve its international interests. The Merchant Marine Act of 1936, still the defining maritime policy today, attempted to deal with this challenge.

Merchant ships, under the Act's main provisions, would be designed to be readily convertible to wartime use. Ownership was restricted to the private sector and, as far as practicable, to U.S. citizens. Recognizing the necessary role for the merchant marine in the nation's defense, the Act authorized government money, construction and operating subsidies, for certain merchant ships.

American shipyards experienced a building boom as a result of the 1936 Act. By the end of 1939, 127 cargo ships were under construction, while Britain had let contracts for the building of sixty ships of its own in U.S. yards. The British design, thanks to its simplicity, became the model for the highly successful U.S. wartime Liberty ships. At its height, a Liberty could be built in a remarkable fourteen days, and over 2,700 were built before the end of World War II.

But the Liberty had one major problem: it was slow. A faster ship, the Victory, capable of speeds up to seventeen knots, followed. The first Victory was launched in February 1944. Eight months later, eighty-two of the ships were in commission. Both models were the mainstays for the enormous transport of war goods needed in almost every part of the world during World War II.

Notwithstanding this surge of shipbuilding, the U. S. was largely unprepared for action in the early stages of the war. The Germans took advantage of this, their U-boats experiencing much success off the North American coast. During the first nine months of 1942, German subs sank 520,000 tons of Allied and neutral shipping, more than half of which occurred on that coastal battleground.

A major part of that loss was attributable to a deplorable lack of elementary precautions. Despite being at war, for example, coastal resort cities continued to light up the sky much in the way they had done in peacetime, nicely outlining ships for the Germans to torpedo. In addition, ships' running lights continued to burn brightly, and lighted beacons still illuminated the nation's waterways.

Thanks to research by historian Michael Gannon, the consequence of that failure can be viewed through the eyes of an amazed Captain Reinhard Hardegen and his watch officer aboard the German sub U-123. The American tanker SS *Gulfamerica*, loaded with fuel oil taken on at Port Arthur in April 1942, was on her maiden voyage, bound for New York. Ship and sub crossed paths. The sub launched a torpedo at the American ship. "Both men," Gannon reported, referring to the German sub's two officers,

> stared at the large fast-moving shadow now sharply outlined against the brilliant Jacksonville Beach lights . . . the western sky suddenly erupted in a blinding red-and-yellow explosion . . . [Hardegen] watched the tanker torch break apart in the middle and its photoflash illumine the beach as brightly as though it were noon. In the incandescence he saw people on shore pour out of their hotels, homes, and places of entertainment. It was 10:20 P.M. local time, which was a little late for American supper, but the bars, dance halls, drive-ins, and amusements were still going strong [because] it was the end of the week and the beaches were crowded with sailors from the training base, Jacksonville NAS, twenty miles inland from Mayport on the St. Johns; soldiers in basic training from Camp Blanding in the interior; and high-spirited youths and civilians of all walks and ages to whom Friday night in Florida was party time.

Not for all, however. A winter vacationer named McCollum, in a remarkable display of compassionate bravery, set out in a rowboat to help rescue the unfortunate men of the *Gulfamerica*. Favorable winds drove him out to the flaming tanker and, lacking navigational tools, past it. A rescue ship discovered him the next day, some twenty miles out from the shore.

The *Gulfamerica* subsequently went down, taking nineteen of her crew with her, a testament to the need for lights-out along the nation's coasts. Florida, for one, turned off its coastal lights. Britain, on the other hand, had blackouts as early as 1939.

An officer aboard the American freighter SS *Lemuel Burrows* offered a different view, but the same story. Twenty of its crewmembers died when a German sub torpedoed the ship off the Atlantic coast in March 1942. Others successfully abandoned ship, and soon found themselves with a ringside view of Atlantic City. As one of the men, the ship's second engineer, reported, "We might as well have run with our lights on. The lights were like Coney Island. It was lit up like daylight all along the beach. We're going to lose boats every day if they don't do something about it."

The "something" was an order for a "dimout"—total blackouts were not considered necessary. Even with dimouts, however, vessel silhouettes could still be seen as far as ten miles at sea. One Army study found that, "like targets in a shooting gallery, our ships are moving in off a backdrop of hazy light."

Aside from the lighting problem, the failure to sail ships in convoys under a protective escort also contributed to the "kills" chalked up by German subs. The Navy eventually recognized this, and merchant ships began sailing in convoys, escorted by destroyers. Later, "baby flat top" aircraft carriers and land-based airplanes would prove effective in cutting the number of ships lost to submarines. The results were dramatic: losses in the second half of 1943 dropped by three quarters. The Allies finally began to gain the edge in the "Battle of the Atlantic."

The merchant marine remained active in all theaters of the war. A particularly challenging one was getting wartime supplies to the Russian port of Murmansk, located some 900 miles from the North Pole. Drifting icebergs, frigid cold, and violent storms marked the route. The military threat included not only German subs, but warships, dive bombers, and torpedo planes operating out of nearby Nazi-occupied territory. Murmansk itself suffered almost constant air bombardment.

Typical of ships and men subject to the onslaught of violence on this route was a thirty-four-ship convoy sailing from Russia back to England in February 1945. In the midst of it sailed the Liberty ship *Henry Bacon,* carrying thirty-five Norwegian refugees and a remarkably brave crew.

Two violent storms with winds blowing up to sixty miles an hour battered the convoy, scattering the ships. Naval escorts tried to round up the fleet, but the *Henry Bacon* lagged behind, disabled by a damaged steering engine.

Once repaired, Captain Alfred Carini got his ship underway at maximum speed, but could not reach the protective cover of the convoy—the Liberty ship could only make 11 knots. An armada of twenty-three German airplanes, enough power to sink a battleship or aircraft carrier, homed in on the lone merchant ship. Every gun aboard the *Bacon* began firing away in a futile attempt to stay the inevitable. Carini managed to zigzag away from one torpedo, but the odds proved too great. Two torpedoes hit the ship in rapid succession. The captain ordered the crew to abandon ship.

Two lifeboats were safely launched. However, twenty-two men went down with the ship, including Captain Carini, bravely standing on the ship's bridge, and Chief Engineer Donald Haviland, who committed a singular act of bravery. Managing to reach the safety of the lifeboat, the chief spotted a less fortunate youngster still aboard. "Put me alongside," he shouted to the third mate. "Let that kid have my place. It won't matter so much if I don't get back." The two men exchanged destinies.

Merchant ships, carrying the very goods needed to support military operations, were the natural prey of subs—none more so than tank ships. Oil was the life's blood of the military juggernaut. Cutting its flow stopped the mechanized military forces in its tracks.

For the brave men sailing these tankers, life was one step away from a spread of torpedoes speeding out of the darkness and slamming into their ship. A freighter might have a few moments to set things right. A tanker's cargo of oil and gas, torched by a torpedo, was likely to become a raging inferno in short order. In all likelihood, the ship would sink quickly, leaving the crew without time to get the lifeboats over. And burning oil would invariably spill into the ocean around the ship, closing off the only avenue of escape. Seamen, desperately jumping into the water, either died in the flames surrounding the tanker, or had to plunge through a heavy curtain of thick, blinding oil to get away. This scenario happened to a swarm of tankers throughout the war. The *R. P. Resor* was only one of them, but notable for the speed of its destruction and the obstacles posed by its cargo of oil to men desperately trying to escape. This single ship carried 4,955,125 barrels of petroleum products over the course of fifty-six voyages during the period 1939–42. On her last voyage, the *R. P. Resor* departed Houston, Texas, with a cargo of fuel oil bound for Fall River, Massachusetts. Shortly before midnight on February 26, 1942, sailing off the New Jersey shore, a torpedo exploded on the ship's port side. A raging inferno almost instantly swallowed up the *R. P. Resor* from her bridge amidship to her stern.

Able Seaman John J. Forsdal, a lookout near the bow of the ship, found a line hanging over the side and lowered himself into water that was ice cold. He began to swim away from the ship. About fifty yards away, he heard a second violent explosion, which set the oil in the water ablaze. Forsdal continued struggling, trying to put distance between himself and the burning oil.

At some point, Forsdal heard two voices calling out. One of them was the ship's radio officer, Clarence Armstrong, with a raft. Blanketed with heavy oil, Forsdal fought gamely and finally reached Armstrong who was clinging to one side of a raft about a half mile out from the burning ship. The seaman hung on to the opposite side, exhausted from struggling in the freezing cold and heavy oil. A Coast Guard picket boat later arrived on scene and hauled the luckless seamen aboard. Other boats picked up Daniel Hey, an armed guard coxswain from the ship, and the lifeless body of the radio officer.

According to Chief Boatswain's Mate John W. Daisy of the rescue team, "Forsdal was so coated with thick congealed oil that we had to cut his clothes and his life jacket off with knives. [He was] so weighted with oil we couldn't get him aboard. Even his mouth was filled with a blob of oil." Forsdal and Hey were the sole survivors of the *R. P. Resor*. The men's fate, and the conditions that surrounded the sinking of the tanker, were not unusual events.

In 1942, the SS *Benjamin Brewster* became both rescuer and rescued in the space of two months. In May of that year, coming upon three life rafts adrift, the ship rescued nineteen survivors from the torpedoed Gulf Oil Corporation tanker *Gulfoil*. Again, illustrating the effects of oil on survivors, the captain of the *Brewster* reported that the men rescued were "so thickly covered with oil that it took an entire barrel of kerosene to get it off."

Two months later, having delivered the men ashore, the *Benjamin Brewster* departed Baytown, Texas, with a load of aviation gas and various grades of oil, bound for Tampa. Near midnight, while off the coast of Louisiana, two torpedoes hit the ship on her port side. She immediately burst into flames and sank within the space of three minutes. Fifteen of the forty persons aboard survived in spite of the ship being surrounded by a ring of flaming gas and oil.

Second Engineer Claus Bertels, refusing to give up, grabbed a life jacket after the first hit. He recalled dropping the jacket after the second torpedo hit and then finding himself trying to swim in a river of oil. His left arm, injured and bleeding, was useless. Shipmates had boarded a burned-out lifeboat still afloat close by, but were unable to maneuver the craft to him. Guided by sounds from the boat, and struggling to breathe through a curtain of oil, he eventually reached the boat and joined other oil-covered survivors aboard. Prevailing winds pushed the boat ashore where they were rescued.

Oil provided the fuel for the blazing torch the *Benjamin Brewster* had become as she lay sunk in relatively shallow waters off the coast of Louisiana. Wicking up the oil from the ship's tanks, the fire continued to blaze for nine days, leaving a molten mass of twisted metal as a tombstone to mark the spot.

It helps, sometimes, to have "man's best friend" along. The SS *E. G. Seubert,* a tanker bound for the Mediterranean in February 1944, was torpedoed. The ship, carrying seventy men and a canine companion, went down in twelve minutes. Ship's Clerk Harold Myers remembered the explosion throwing him to the deck. His dog, a Persian deerhound, began whimpering. Myers located the dog, buckled on his collar and leash, and carried him to the bridge. Both quickly ended up in the water, swimming for their lives.

The dog swam ahead. Myers, injured and blinded by the thick oil coating the water, followed his buddy, holding on to its leash. The dog unerringly led him to a life raft where both were hauled aboard. Later Myers gratefully shipped his "seeing-eye dog" to his home in St. Louis, saying, "He had saved my life, I did not want him to go to sea again during the war."

Occasionally, a tanker does in its tormentor. That happened to the SS *Frederick C. Kellogg* as she desperately tried to escape from a submarine. The ship, enroute from the Canal Zone to Aruba in December 1942, encountered a submarine near the Gulf of Venezuela. Captain Anthony J. Coumelis immediately sounded the general alarm and maxed out the ship's speed, hightailing it out of the area with the sub in hot pursuit.

The ship's naval armed guard opened fire at the sub's periscope, barely visible in the churning wake of the *Kellogg* as she sped on her way. As Naval Reserve Ensign Elmer C. Brewton, commander of the gun crew, reported, "Our sixteenth round knocked the periscope off. [A] shot hit in the wake of our ship, making a direct hit on the submarine; a black puff of smoke and explosion of projectile was seen as the shell hit the water line of the periscope." The report concluded that the sub appeared to have been sunk and that "our ship resumed normal course." No doubt, with a bit of a swagger and justifiable pride.

Most of the ships sunk during World War II involved torpedoes, either from planes or, more likely, from submarines. However, one of the memorable legends of the war involved the Liberty ship *Stephen Hopkins* and two German surface raiders, the *Tannenfels* and the heavily-armed *Stier*, which had already sunk four merchant ships.

An unusual running gun fight between a merchant ship and naval vessels, reminiscent of nineteenth-century sea battles, began. Closing to within a thousand yards, the German ships added small-weapons fire to its regular armament. Aboard the *Hopkins*, seamen encouraged one another and volunteered where needed to help their comrades. Navy gunners shot down at their posts were replaced by regular crewmembers stepping up to the challenge. Individual stories of heroism became commonplace: the bosun died while trying to rig an emergency antenna on the bridge; a shell killed the radio officer as he tried to key an SOS; the captain was blown off the bridge while directing the battle; nineteen-year old Edwin O'Hara, an engine cadet from the Merchant Marine Academy, led wounded gunners to the rafts, and then returned to their gun station to fire the remaining shells. The valiant cadet was gunned down by enemy fire while trying to help launch a raft.

A shell finally hit the engine room and the ship's boilers blew up. The crew managed to get over one lifeboat moments before the ship went down. Nineteen men of the *Stephen Hopkins* survived, five of them seriously wounded. The *Stier*, herself engulfed in flames and smoke, followed the *Hopkins* into the deep.

The American ship, heavily outgunned by two German vessels, acquitted itself in heroic fashion. A bronze plaque honors the ship at the Kings Point Merchant Marine Academy. But a remarkable honor also came from her German adversary. One of her seamen later wrote: "On the German side we had four dead and twenty injured. Despite a search of two hours we did not find any survivors of the American ship. With our flag at half-mast we made a full circle around the spot where the Liberty ship had sunk thus rendering the last honors to our brave adversary."

With so many ships sinking, one wonders what happened to the survivors who fell into the hands of the enemy. The answer depended largely on who the enemy happened to be.

In June 1942, Able Seaman Raymond Smithson and Ordinary Seaman Cornelius F. O'Connor found themselves struggling together in a thick scum of oil after their ship, the tanker *M. F. Elliott*, had been torpedoed (as described in Chapter 6). They fashioned a "raft" out of pieces of ship's gear floating nearby. Three planes appeared overhead, and one dropped a float. In the dark, the men were unable to find the float. Just as they were ready to give up, a huge black shape surfaced—the German sub that had torpedoed their ship.

Two seamen on the bow of the sub heard their cries and they were taken aboard. The submarine commander agreed to take them in the direction of the rafts. The Germans gave the two seamen water, hot tea, and graham crackers. O'Connor recalled:

> One of the officers asked me, "What do the people in America think about the war?" I told him after a little hesitation that they thought they would win. He laughed and asked, "What do you think about it?" I said, "Well" about a dozen times and then said, "In time we should win." He laughed again and said, "Germany is stronger than you think."
>
> We were then blindfolded and taken to the torpedo room, where they washed us in petrol to remove some of the oil and fed us graham crackers and water. We were taken back to the control room and the blindfolds removed. The commander said, "We are going to give you our lifeboat and water and bread. Row six miles south and you should find your comrades. If you do not, keep heading south and you will reach land. This is war, and it is all that I can do."

Both men were later rescued.

Other German U-boat commanders displayed a similarly generous spirit. The SS *Esso Houston* took on a full cargo of oil at Aruba, and set sail for Montevideo in May 1942. A torpedo struck the ship amidship, breaking its "back" and ripping the hull open, spraying fire throughout. Chief Engineer Charles A. Hicks recalled being immediately covered with fuel oil and being thrown out of the cargo space by the explosion. He managed to find his way to No. 3 lifeboat which upended while being launched, dropping him nearly thirty feet into the water.

Swimming away from the doomed ship, the chief eventually was taken aboard a lifeboat. Shortly afterwards, he heard a submarine blowing its tanks. "The submarine surfaced quite near us," he recalled,

> and we could see the men in silhouette manning the guns. A voice with a German accent shouted to us, "Is the captain on board?" Captain Wonson answered "Yes." After several routine questions had been asked and answered the voice inquired as to our

welfare—Have you a steering compass? Do you need any food, water, or medicine?—when Captain Wonson had replied the voice said "It's the war, captain. Pleasant voyage." Then the U-boat disappeared.

We were using a flashlight to direct any survivors to the boat when the submarine returned and the German voice again called out "Captain, sixty meters astern of your vessel, one of your lifeboats is sinking. It has three men in it." The skipper thanked him and we rowed toward the ship. There were seven men in No. 3 lifeboat and it was swamped. These men would have been lost if it had not been for the submarine commander.

Occasionally, a harsher reality intruded. Danish survivors of the torpedoed Panamanian-flag *Esso Copenhagen*, clinging to an overturned lifeboat, looked for help from the German submarine that surfaced alongside. The sub declined. "Don't forget," the response came, as the sub hurried on its way, "we are at war!"

Even medical treatment was sometimes available. The MS *Arriaga*, crewed by American seamen, was hit by a single torpedo off the coast of Colombia in June 1942. The sub surfaced some 300 feet astern. The Navy armed guard fired at the sub, missing by a close margin. The *Arriaga* then took a sudden list, the angle rendering the gun useless, and the sub crash-dived before a second shot could be fired.

With the ship settling, the crew abandoned ship in a lifeboat and one raft. Shortly afterwards, the German sub resurfaced, displaying a striking ace of clubs painted on her conning tower, and signaled the crew to pull alongside.

Captain Gunnar Gjertsen reported what happened next.

The commander asked us, in fairly good English but with a strong German accent, "What is the name of your ship and where was she bound?" I replied that she was the *Arriaga*, coming from Baltimore and bound for Aruba. He then inquired if we had any injured men. One of the U.S. Navy gunners, suffering from a strained back and also from oil in his eyes, was helped aboard the submarine and treated in the conning tower by her surgeon. A few minutes later he was helped back into our boat and the commander bade us farewell and wished us good luck. Before that he had given us five packs of German cigarettes and ten boxes of French matches. He told me the course and distance to the nearest shore.

Not so fortunate were the survivors of the Liberty ship *Henry Knox*. Under way in the Persian Gulf in June 1942, the ship was hit by a torpedo, setting it ablaze and causing her to take a 20-degree list to port. The crew quickly abandoned ship. According to a report by Cadet Midshipman Maurice Price, two Japanese subs surfaced nearby and waited until the *Henry Knox* went down.

"Then they prowled the surface, seeking survivors," he said. "Number One lifeboat was stopped. The Japanese took the sails, mast, charts, flashlight, and rations, broke the oars, and departed. One of the subs came within seventy-five feet of our boat but the men hid under blankets and the submarine passed by. We were in the lifeboat eleven days before we reached safety."

Far worse was the fate of the survivors of the Liberty ship *Jean Nicolet,* torpedoed by a Japanese submarine while in the Arabian Sea in July 1944. All hands safely abandoned ship. The sub surfaced and began shelling the deserted ship. A voice ordered the four lifeboats and two rafts to approach the sub one by one under the point of a machine gun.

As the first group climbed aboard, Japanese sailors snatched life preservers off their backs, and stole their watches, wallets, shirts, and shoes. The men were then forced to kneel on the forward deck where their hands were tied with wire behind their backs. Men were clubbed with pipes and cut with knives and bayonets. Some of the men, succumbing to the beatings, were thrown overboard. Others were forced through a gauntlet of clubs and knives. When six men of the ship's naval armed guard tried to get away, the Japanese opened fire on them.

This torture continued until a patrol plane approached. The sub quickly submerged, leaving the survivors on her deck to be washed overboard. Of the ninety-nine men aboard the *Jean Nicolet*, twenty-three survived to tell the tale.

Occasionally, survivors had not only the worry of being gunned down by the crew of a hostile sub, but also had to deal with the fear of attack from another source: sharks.

Herman Kastberg was the chief mate of the SS *Esso Gettysburg*, hit by two torpedoes while en route from the Gulf to Philadelphia in June 1943. The tanker caught fire, and when attempts to lower one of the lifeboats failed, the mate and others dove over the side.

The mate described his experience in the water:

> While swimming away from the ship, six of us got together. Suddenly a shark was among us. As I had previously got rid of my shoes, I felt him brush past my bare feet. Only three of us had life jackets, and we were supporting the other men. The shark circled off toward the ship but came back again and charged. [Thomas] Chapman grabbed a knife, but we cautioned him against using it except as a last resort. We all kicked and splashed and the shark again swerved away, but a few minutes later he made a second charge. We repeated the kicking and thrashing in the water and he went off.

The men survived the attacks and were later rescued.

Beyond the acts of kindness, and cruelty, and fear of sharks were the occasional snafus as well as the unusual and inexplicable happenings that occur in the chaos of war.

While in convoy, the tanker *J. A. Mowinckel* was one of three ships torpedoed in rapid succession off the coast of Cape Hatteras in July 1942. The bulk carrier *Chilore*, under way from Baltimore to Trinidad, was another.

The commodore of the convoy detailed the Navy ship *Spry* to escort the *Mowinckel*, and the *Chilore*, to a "safe" area. While en route, the commodore, who took up station aboard the *Mowinckel,* observed a Navy blimp dropping smoke bombs overhead. He took the display as a warning that German subs were in the area. Sure enough, a mysterious explosion rocked the tanker on her port side a short time later. The *Spry* immediately opened fire on "some target" and dropped depth charges. A second mysterious underwater explosion followed and a slug of oil burped to the surface.

The *Chilore* meanwhile suffered damage from a third unidentified explosion. With wounded men on board, and fearful of further "attacks," the captains of both ships ordered their crews to abandon ship. The seamen managed to reach land safely. A tug sent out to assist was rocked by a fourth underwater explosion. Meanwhile the tanker, which had been successfully beached at Hatteras Inlet, sustained damage from still a fifth mysterious explosion. Later investigation showed that the explosions, which damaged the *J. A. Mowinckel*, the *Chilore*, and the tug sent to assist, were from underwater mines—U.S. mines. The Navy had escorted the ships into the middle of a U.S. minefield.

Occasional foul-ups were not unknown to the German fleet. Although it seemed their guns and torpedoes rarely missed their targets, a few red-faced episodes eventually came to light. One involved the British-chartered motor vessel *Kattegat,* en route from Capetown to Montevideo in May 1942.

According to the U. S. Navy Department, the ship came under the guns of an unseen German surface raider firing away at night. Shells hit the ship's bridge, stack, radio room, and engine room. Abandoning ship, the *Kattegat*'s crew was taken aboard the German ship and confined below deck.

The German skipper kindly invited the captain of the *Kattegat* to join him on the bridge to witness the destruction of his ship. Broadside to the vessel, with the luxury of unlimited time to zero in on a fat target dead in the water, the German crew took careful methodical aim and, no doubt aware of their captive audience, proudly fired torpedo No. 1. Onward the torpedo sped, the British captain watching spellbound as it headed directly for the middle of his ship where it would undoubtedly crash in an earth-shattering blast, sending his beloved ship to the bottom. At the last moment, however, as if having second thoughts, the torpedo nose-dived *beneath* the ship's hull, a clear miss.

Presumably slightly upset, the German commander maneuvered his ship closer for a second deadly shot. Again the careful aim, the deliberate countdown, the push of a button, and the swish of a torpedo as it sped out towards a target begging to be hit. Again, a near miss, the torpedo passing free across the bow of the ship.

The British skipper was banished below deck. Their confidence no doubt flagging, and taking no chances, the German crew hauled over TNT by boat. A boarding party planted two bombs in the engine room and hung another over the side. This time, they couldn't miss, and they didn't. The crew of the *Kattegat* maintained their sense of civility and lived to tell the tale.

Even though torpedoed, some ships managed to survive. The SS *Brilliant*, owned by Standard Oil Company of New York and chartered to the U.S. Maritime Commission, was one such ship. What made the ship unique was that she owed her survival to the navigating skills of a junior third mate sailing on his first ship as a deck officer.

The *Brilliant*, under way in November 1942 with 112,000 barrels of fuel oil bound for Belfast, Ireland, was torpedoed without warning roughly 400 miles off St. Johns, Newfoundland.

Junior Third Officer James C. Cameron was on watch on the bridge at the time of the explosion. He immediately awoke the captain who casually instructed him to put some cigarettes in his lifeboat. Cameron did better than that; he picked up the sextant, code book, and a few other essentials and placed them near the boat. Returning to the bridge, he passed the third mate who seemed incoherent, a partly-clad second mate, and the gunnery officer, who suggested that the general alarm should be turned off although flames at this point were licking at the topmast.

Cameron next discovered the captain's boat gone. Inexplicably, the sextant, code book, and flashlight remained where he had placed them earlier. He then called the engine room from the bridge, and spoke to one of the third engineers, who reported that all was well in the engine room but who wanted to know "what in the hell is wrong up there?"

With the ship on fire, Cameron and the radio officer turned on the fire control system. The engineer also switched on the steam smothering line from the engine room, as well as water on deck. With those systems working, Cameron and the radio officer subdued the fire by exhausting all the fire extinguishers and flushing the deck with water.

Initially, the *Brilliant* was listing heavily to starboard and appeared to be settling in the water. However, the ship righted itself and otherwise appeared to be seaworthy. The chief engineer reported that the engines were operable. Cameron mustered the crew and discovered nine men missing, including the entire complement of deck officers: captain, chief mate, second mate, and third mate. Realizing he was now "captain" by default, the junior third mate got the ship underway and headed for St. John's.

Shortly thereafter, according to a report of the event, "the tanker had not proceeded any distance before a motorboat crossed her bow, circled the ship, and a voice was intercepted by members of crew asking why they had not abandoned ship in accordance with the captain's instructions. The tanker was then proceeding full speed ahead, and although she slowed down, there was no effort made by those in the motor boat to board." No explanation was ever forthcoming concerning this mysterious motorboat.

According to the report, after the *Brilliant* had been torpedoed, the captain and others on the bridge deck, believing the ship to be doomed, left in a lifeboat, presumably taking the pack of cigarettes with them. The boat capsized shortly afterwards, and they were rescued by HMS *Bury,* an escort ship. Discovering that the *Brilliant* was afloat, the captain was prevented from rejoining the ship by the *Bury*'s surgeon who considered him and the other deck officers physically unfit.

The *Brilliant* docked at St. John two days later. Considered seaworthy enough to return to the States, the ship left port on December 17, returning the following day after encountering problems while underway. In January, she again departed St. John under tow bound for Halifax. Ironically, the *Brilliant* broke up while underway, taking down with her the two men primarily responsible for seeing her safely to port in the first place: the junior third officer and the radio officer.

The Navy lieutenant preparing the summary concluded that "the Junior Third Officer, who assumed responsibility for the ship's safety and successfully by his leadership and good seamanship, brought his ship to a safe harbor with cargo of 58,000 bbls. of fuel oil still intact, is to be commended, especially since it was his first voyage as an officer."

Countless other ships in a myriad of other battlefields played out their destinies in World War II. This summary, with its highlights of dramatic moments in the history of the merchant marine, can hardly begin to do justice to those ships and the brave crews who manned them. But statistics do tell part of the story. At war's end, 6,845 of the 250,000 merchant seamen who sailed during the conflict gave their lives on behalf of their country. According to Bruce Felknor, editor of *The U.S. Merchant Marine at War*, the 2.74 percent who died compares favorably with the average death rate of 1.05 percent sustained by all the armed forces. Only the U.S. Marines had a higher death rate than the merchant marine. Yet, these civilian seafarers, who faced the same dangers as the military, were denied any government recognition for their service, and received none of the benefits given military veterans.

It was not until 1988 that the Pentagon, under order of a federal judge, granted the status of veterans to members of the merchant marine who sailed during the war. The decision, more cosmetic than substantive, formally honors the contribution of the merchant marine to the war effort. It also entitles its members to have their caskets draped with an American flag furnished at government expense, as well as enabling them to join various veterans' organizations. Some merchant mariners have done so; others have established their own, among them the American Merchant Marine Veterans' Association, and the U.S. Merchant Marine Veterans of World War II.

The end of World War II marked the beginning of the Cold War.

For the merchant marine, that standoff meant it would continue to play a prominent role as an auxiliary to the military in the event of another war. A fleet of roughly 4,000 merchant ships were then available. Half were Liberty ships having little value in the commercial marketplace; the rest consisted of Victory ships, C-2s, C-3s, tankers, and troop carriers. Congress made such ships available to U.S. and allied shipping interests, and sales of about 2,100 ships were split roughly between the two. Ships not sold or scrapped were retained for possible future use in the new National Defense Reserve Fleet, a system of ship's anchorages on the nation's coasts and waterways.

A familiar scenario developed after the war. American shipping and shipbuilding declined, largely because of cost factors that made both non-competitive. Some federal help came in the requirement that all military cargoes and 50 percent of other government cargoes be carried on U.S. flag ships. With the invasion of South Korea by North Korea in June 1950, the United States paid immediate attention to the merchant marine.

Following U.N. approval, President Truman immediately ordered American troops into battle. Merchant and Navy ships were given the job of getting the troops to the battlefield. In September 1950, 230 naval and merchant ships carried U. S. soldiers in a successful attack behind enemy lines at Inchon. The troops then headed north, reaching as far as the Chinese border. China then entered the war and drove American armed forces back.

Naval and merchant ships were then charged with removing troops and military supplies to a safe area. Sailing some two hundred voyages, these ships were credited with rescuing roughly 105,000 U.S. and South Korean troops, as well as more than 90,000 civilian refugees from the North Korean port of Hungnam. A single merchant ship, the SS *Meredith Victory,* rescued 14,000 of those refugees in what has been described as the greatest rescue by a single ship in maritime history.

The *Meredith Victory,* government-owned but operated by a private steamship company, Moore-McCormack Lines, was crewed by American merchant seaman. It was one of hundreds operating under the control of the Navy's Military Sea Transportation Service to carry supplies to American troops.

Captain Leonard P. LaRue, master of the *Meredith Victory*, ordered his crew to take on as many refugees as the ship could hold. Cargo nets were draped over the side, and a mass of humanity—thousands of men, women, and children—scrambled aboard. Every available space on the ship—cargo holds, passageways, top decks from stem to stern, inside quarters—were crammed full with people.

Little food or water was available for such a horde. Nor was there a doctor or even an interpreter. There was only a captain and crew determined to save as many lives as possible. Leaving port, the ship had to run the gauntlet of a thirty-mile minefield on its journey south, as well as jury-rig a nursery to tend to the births of five babies born during the ship's three-day run.

The *Meredith Victory* arrived at her destination, fifty miles southwest of Pusan, on Christmas Eve 1950. Captain LaRue, moved by the rescue and the holiday, wrote in the ship's log: "The nearness of Christmas carries my thoughts to the Holy Family—how they, too, were cold and without shelter. Like the crucified Christ, these good people suffer through the actions of guilty men." Captain LaRue left his calling later to take up a new one: religious vows under the name of Brother Marinus, Order of Saint Benedict, at Saint Paul's Abbey, Newton, New Jersey.

Once again, the merchant marine proved its value to the nation in wartime. During the three years of the Korean War, 38 percent of the materiel needed in Korea was transported by U.S. commercial vessels; the remainder was carried by the Military Sea Transportation Service in its own ships or on the 180 ships activated from the National Defense Reserve Fleet.

In the years that followed, the cold war and other conflicts kept the merchant marine operating—most notably Vietnam in 1961. Public awareness for the need of a U.S. merchant marine again rose as one consequence of this war, particularly in light of a substantial expansion of the Soviet naval and merchant fleets.

Still, many people thought that getting the military goods to Vietnam could be done by aircraft, Robert McNamara, Secretary of Defense, among them. However, as the war expanded, it soon became obvious that merchant ships would again be needed to do the job. Consequently, 170 ships were activated from the National Defense Reserve Fleet. By 1967, at the height of the war, more than 500 ships, which represented 40 percent of U.S. commercial capacity, were involved. The total included scores of privately owned merchant ships chartered by the Military Sea Transportation Service to carry bombs and other supplies to the war zone.

The SS *Badger State* was one such ship.

CHAPTER 8

Flying Dragon

Captain Wilson fumbled with the buttons that held him captive in a rumpled khaki shirt and trousers. Exasperated, he gave up and dropped fully clothed on his bunk. A long spell in the wheelhouse, worrying the ship along its troublesome path, overlapping watches by the crew, had driven him below to rest.

But sleep would not come. Too many images cluttered his mind— the ship struggling on its way, bombs coming loose, and the haunting faces of his men drawn tight by work and tension. Added to that was the sheer physical discomfort imposed by the ship's jerky roll. It pulled at his body, forcing him to brace his arms and legs as he laid in his bunk. Turning and twisting brought no relief. The favorable weather forecast was somewhat hopeful, but even so, doubts were beginning to nag at him.

To distract himself, Wilson forced his mind to look for a memory, anything, to mentally take him away from his surroundings. And then he remembered a pushy little fellow and his dour-looking assistant. They were the "official greeters" who met the bus at Vickery Gate, the entrance to Kings Point.

It was the summer of 1950 and Wilson, having been nudged out of the family nest, had traveled alone across country by train, past a host of cities with familiar names and others he had never heard of. The train stopped briefly at Chicago, and then it was on to New York State, memorable to a teenager because eighteen-year-olds could have a beer there. To prove it, once the train had entered New York's border, he went back to the club car and downed one, just to show he could do it. It was a liquid milepost on the road to adulthood.

He blended in at Kings Point, one more high-school grad among scores of others able to get past the written and physical exams. As helpless plebes, he and his fellow classmates were anchored to the bottom of the school pile, fair game to the upperclassmen who would arrive in due time to make life hell for them. School life followed the military model: uniform blue shirts and trousers; standing at attention in spit-polished shoes; punishment for real and imagined breaking of the rules; and marching in formation everywhere. Plebes always marched to the right, took the corners square, and tried desperately to avoid upper classmen who might take offense at anything. But that was part of the game; his turn would come. Meanwhile, he spent most of his days trying to keep his head above water, and studying.

Thoughts of Kings Point brought to mind his heroes in those younger days: his dad, who had given him a legacy of values that had stood him well over the years; President "Ike," at whose inauguration Wilson and his class had the honor of marching; John Tucker, the regimental commander who went on to command the pride of the merchant fleet, the SS *United States*; scoutmaster Hugh Conway, and high-school advisor Ted Tajima. These were a few of the men he had somehow tried to emulate, whose images came to mind, only to drop out as a particularly hard roll of the *Badger State* threw him over on his side.

He tried to recapture other memories of Kings Point, but the moment gave way to the reality of the *Badger State* battling its way across the north Pacific. And with that awareness slowly came the nagging doubts in earnest. *Where were those decreasing winds that had looked so enticing? Where were the seven- to eleven-foot seas projected by Fleet Weather Central?* He tried to waylay the thoughts, seizing on a brief respite in the rolling, his hopes rising. But then would come the rebuttal, his jerking body giving the lie to what his mind was unwilling to believe. Giving up, he grabbed the low railing along one side, rolled off his bunk, and climbed one deck to the wheelhouse.

Christmas Day, early morning, the beginning of the mid-to-four watch. Third Mate Burnette, looking worn behind a week's growth of whiskers, had the watch. "Tough sleeping, Cap'n?" he said. It was more of a statement than a question.

"Yeah, it'll take forever for all of us to catch up once we hit port," Wilson said, as he rubbed his eyes hard, as though trying to scrub away the tiredness of the past few days.

Able Seaman Ed Hottendorf, looking scruffy in fatigues, entered the wheelhouse to relieve the helmsman on watch. He clutched a ham sandwich wrapped in a grease-smeared paper towel that he had squirreled away from the galley. He handed it to Wilson.

Wilson, taken unawares, could only nod in appreciation. He turned away, swallowing hard, a lump in his throat. A warm feeling welled up deep inside. The seaman's gesture was an indication of sorts that the crew had noticed his long hours on the bridge and his work in trying to bring some order out of the turmoil that threatened them all. But Hottendorf was not the first to express indirect concern over the way the Old Man was driving himself. Deck Utility man Lawrence McHugh remembered, "The Captain never had any sleep for at least four days that I know of. I gave him an apple I had in my pocket when I went up to the wheel. As far as I know, that's all he had to eat in those four days."

Wilson inhaled deeply as his eyes viewed the bow of the ship, hazy in the morning darkness, rising and falling in the rough waters that continued to tumble over it. This was not the relatively placid scene he yearned to see at this particular moment.

Captain and watch officer talked about the weather. "That Navy forecaster had better turn in his badge, Cap'n, because I sure can't see any improvement out there," Burnette said, shaking his head. "Looks pretty much like the same stuff we've been dealing with for the past week, and then some."

Wilson could only groan in response. Burnette had confirmed what he did not want to believe. But he could no longer disregard the evidence of his own eyes. The dim light made it difficult to see clearly, but the skies that earlier seemed to be clearing—a sign that fit nicely with Fleet Central's favorable weather report—were again clouding over. Waves seemed to be mounting higher, swells running deeper. And the slant of the deck under his feet that previously had become tolerable began again to tilt sharply in response to an increasingly steeper roll.

Wilson squinted as he bent down to check the barometer. It was dropping rapidly in anticipation of a storm, confirming what his eyes were telling him. He moved to one side and fished a weather report out of a basket on the chart table, rereading it again for the umpteenth time. "I can't understand how they could be so goddamn wrong," he said to no one in particular, a note of dejection in the tone of his voice. Hardly more than a few hours had gone by since the ship received favorable weather reports the previous evening.

Aside from his own disappointment at the turn of events, Wilson was more concerned about the reactions of his men. Captain and crew had taken the favorable forecast as gospel, a sign that the worst might be behind them. Given the forecast, they could have reasonably expected to be docking at a safe harbor within a few days. The cargo could then be unloaded and re-stowed the right way once and for all.

Wilson rechecked the barometer, staring at it with disbelieving eyes. It was in a free fall to one of the lowest levels he had ever seen. And he had been through almost every imaginable weather situation in the course of his years at sea. The steep decline in pressure was unmistakable. The Navy's forecast was dead wrong.

For the first time, Wilson noted a change in the direction of the wind. It was blowing from a single direction, from south to southeast. Years of hard-knocks experience told him that the combination of changing wind direction and falling barometric pressure usually predicted foul weather ahead, regardless of what the experts were divining from their charts and graphs and readings.

There were also other signs of trouble. It's a rare moment when a sea captain fails to notice unusual sounds that suggest something may have gone wrong. What he invariably hears when he tunes in to it are the familiar background sounds of the ship working the seaway, a symphony of noises from the booms and tackle and the countless parts of the vessel moving roughly together in the water. An intimate part of every sailor's existence, it fades into the background after the first few days at sea only to emerge again when the ship is under stress.

Wilson began to pick up a major sign of that stress: gale force winds starting to whistle through the rigging. These winds, gradually increasing in intensity, tore at the vessel, shaking it from stem to stern. Gathering more force, they carried a blanket of wind spray to the ship's upper reaches, obscuring the vision of the men there. Wilson logged the force of the wind as No. 8 on the Beaufort Scale, fresh gale winds blowing thirty-nine to forty-six miles per hour. That's how British officer Sir Francis Beaufort would have described it in 1805, as he sought to develop a simple numerical scale to describe wind velocities acting on the sails of a "well-conditioned man-of-war."

The *Badger State* unquestionably had serious problems. But it was not the only ship dealing with a raging storm on her lonesome trek across the north Pacific. Nor was she alone in the struggle to contain wartime cargo within her holds in the midst of it. Unbeknownst to Wilson, south of the *Badger* near Midway, the SS *American Robin* sailed. In an ironic twist of fate, while Wilson's ship was westbound carrying bombs to Vietnam, the *Robin* was eastbound carrying broken-down tanks, jeeps, a caterpillar bulldozer, and other damaged military items—"retrograde equipment" in military talk—from Vietnam back to the States for repair.

The twenty-six-year-old *American Robin* had its own problems in trying to secure its bulky cargo. The vehicles were awkward-sized and hard to handle; some were extremely heavy, tipping the scales at over thirty-six tons each; and securing points in the cargo holds were few and far between. The ship's crew had little choice but to handcuff the vehicles together, one to another, and then wedge heavy-duty twelve-by-twelve lumber between them to serve as supports.

The same optimistic weather reports received by the *Badger State* also reached the *American Robin.* Likewise, the ship encountered thirty-five-knot winds rather than the predicted fifteen-knot winds, with a corresponding increase in the height of the waves. The combination caused the ship to roll fifteen to twenty degrees. Winds increased dramatically to fifty knots and the seas to an estimated thirty-five feet later in the day. The ship's roll then jumped to over thirty degrees. It was enough of a tilt to break loose all the cargo in No. 3 lower tween deck. Heavy tanks and trucks began marching across the steel deck, crashing with a tremendous roar against the metal sides of the cargo hold. The impact of metal against metal sent tremors throughout the ship. There was one slight saving grace in this turmoil: no explosives were in the ship's holds.

John McDonnell, the chief mate aboard the *American Robin,* hesitant to risk the lives of his men, worked his way alone down into the hold to survey the damage. In the dim light cast by a single overhead cargo light and a flashlight that he held with shaking hands, he confronted chaos. The sturdy foot-square lumber used for support had been reduced to kindling. Tanks and trucks were running amok, sliding back and forth, eerily suggestive of out-of-control highway traffic. A bulldozer, crushed like an accordion, was barely recognizable.

Trying on his own to stem the flow, the mate danced nimbly between the sliding vehicles, shoving pieces of wood into the treads of the tanks, hoping to jam them up. Recognizing the futility of his efforts, he marshaled the crew and proceeded to chain the cargo to padeyes located overhead, much like a hammock. This was a reversal of the usual practice of securing the cargo to the deck.

It worked, after a fashion—enough to allow the ship to reach San Pedro. Shipyard repair workers there replaced parts of the framing and plating in No. 3 hold, bowed out some six inches from the pounding the ship's hull took.

News of the *Badger State*'s plight later reached the *American Robin.* And with it an awareness that, being shipmates in distress, neither was capable of helping the other if called upon. The mate recalled that a ship's lights had earlier been sighted on the horizon. The *Badger State?* Or just a quirk of wind and waves bouncing back the lights of the *American Robin* at its lookout? No one would ever know for sure.

Aboard the *Badger State,* events escalated rapidly. In quick order, strong winds drove heavy seas over the bow and across the main deck, cascading over ventilators, windlasses, and pontoon-covered hatches. The ship shuddered under the onslaught. The deck under Wilson's feet slanted higher as swells, grown huge, teeter-tottered the ship from side to side.

"Hard right!" he barked to the helmsman who repeated the order in confirmation, and immediately turned the ship's wheel in an arc to the right as fast and as far as he could go, the unseen ship's rudder mimicking his actions. Wilson watched in the dim light as the bow of the ship began to turn hesitantly to starboard. Taking in what he perceived to be the direction of the swells, he ordered "rudder amidship," followed by "hard left!" It was a defensive series of maneuvers choreographed by Wilson to deal with the offensive mounted by the sea.

As the winds became stronger, the waves deeper, the battle seemed joined between the elements and the Old Man. In the darkness of the wheelhouse, Wilson crouched with intensity as he strained to pierce the darkness and gloom of the early morning hours, his eyes red and swollen from the effort. The commands he gave came from deep within him, gruff-sounding, short, to the point. He focused on keeping the ship headed into the direction he chose, always looking for the center of the confused swells meeting the ship. It was a process of feeling his way along, trying to sort out the phantom swells from the real thing, a skill honed over the course of hundreds of voyages.

"Keep an eye on the inclinometer, Mr. Burnette," he said. The instrument—a simple curving water tube marked off in degrees—recorded the extent of the rolling of the ship.

"Aye, sir."

With his two hands firmly grasping the rail in front of him, eyes focused on the waves ahead, Wilson continued to call out his orders to the helmsman. Despite his efforts, the roll of the ship continued to intensify.

"She's at 40 degrees," Burnette said, pausing as the ship rolled to her opposite side. Then, "She's reaching 45, Cap'n."

Wilson gritted his teeth, saying nothing.

"The cargo pallets can't hold up to this kind of—." Burnette's words broke off as a huge wave unexpectedly caught the ship off her starboard side. The ship began to roll to port. "Hard right!" Wilson ordered, his voice sharp.

"She's past 40 degrees, Cap'n. It's up to 47, 48 . . . it's at 50!" Burnette exclaimed, the words tumbling out quickly.

Wilson felt his heart skip a beat, a tightness in his chest. The *Badger State* lay over on its port side, rails dipping under water. Seconds seemed like hours, as the ship hovered there as though it might continue to roll over into eternity. He braced himself with both hands holding tight, his feet grabbing at the steel deck to keep from being bowled over. "Hard left!" he snapped at the helmsman. The ship suddenly jolted back to the center where momentum took over and drove her in the opposite direction.

Wilson inhaled through clenched teeth, trying to conceal his anxiety. But that proved to be the high point as the fury of the storm gradually began to subside. Winds began to ease off; darkness retreated as morning approached; and overcast skies opened to show patches of light. Captain and crew welcomed the new day.

Still, Wilson kept his guard up. It was not the ship itself that concerned him the most, but the cargo. After all, the *Badger State* had sailed through the worst of storms over the course of her twenty-five years at sea and, like the ship's animal namesake—the wily, tenacious, and scrappy badger—had survived all of them. The ship would see them through.

Wilson sent the lookout to get the mate. While the skies continued to clear, worse weather might still lie ahead and they needed to prepare for it. And, without doubt, the roll of the ship to the steepest angle yet must have created more problems in the hold.

That observation proved prophetic. The mate reported to Wilson that he had inspected the holds and found cargo loose in almost every one of them. The 50-degree roll seemed to have brought on most of the problems. Bosun and crew were already at work trying to deal with it.

But lumber was becoming scarce, and they would have to think about using a substitute of some kind to shore up the cargo.

That was one major concern. Another was the 2,000-pound bombs in No. 5 tween deck hold. The mate reported that he had inspected the hold and the pallets seemed to be holding up. That was good news to Wilson since the sheer weight of the bombs would make working with them almost impossible.

The final concern weighing heavily on Wilson was the mate himself. He was getting along in years and had been in the middle of the battle below decks since the ship had weighed anchor. Wilson suggested he have one of the younger mates take over some inspections, but Cobbs assured him he was still up to the work.

After the mate left, Wilson leaned against the bulkhead, staring out the porthole wild-eyed, as though trying to divine the future, his mind wearied from its preoccupation with ship and cargo. The hazy outline of a familiar windblown form came floating into view, grabbing his attention. It was one of their companions, a great seabird gliding effortlessly up and down, staying ahead of his ship, seemingly oblivious of wind and water, hundreds of miles away from its land base. A free spirit, he thought, feeling grudging admiration for a creature that not only survived but seemed to thrive in a hostile setting.

In a way, Wilson reflected, letting his mind wander in a moment of fancy, every ship had that same kind of free spirit, with its constant movement—its yawing, twisting, rolling—hundreds of miles from shore, unrestrained and liberated from its ties to the land. But there the similarities ended. Birds were as free as the wind. Ships needed a guiding hand.

Turning away, Wilson weighed the problems at hand: loose cargo in most of the holds; shoring materials running low; perhaps another storm in the cards—possibly a more violent one. There was a real possibility they would require outside help. In any event, it would be prudent to ask for it, perhaps even an escort. He thought about that for a few moments, as he considered his options. The ship needed help—there was no alternative.

With those thoughts in mind, he handed a message to his radio officer: REQUIRE ESCORT ASAP. WENT THRU STORM LAST NIGHT, ROLLED 50 DEGREES. CARGO LOOSE ALL HATCHES. PRESENTLY ROLLING TO 45 DEGREES. UNABLE TO HEAVE TO BECAUSE OF CONFUSED SWELL.

Several hours later, Wilson sent a second message updating the ship's position. He again repeated the need for a ship escort and requested extra shoring materials as soon as possible.

Below deck, good-natured griping became the order of the day. And many a piece of lumber was accompanied by the imprecations of men denied the comforts of home and family. Hard work and tough living aboard the *Badger State* undoubtedly gave the men reasons for considering spending the following Christmas at home.

Bosun Dick Hughes continued to boss the crew despite his injured back, doing what he could to maintain high spirits. He moved from hold to hold to keep the work flowing, encouraging the crew. "Great job!" he might say, no matter how shoddy the work of men from the steward's department, who thought a hammer was used to tenderize steak. "You put the guys over in Number Four to shame!" he would say, clapping guys on the shoulder. Chests would pop out a bit, and the men would usually go back to the job with a little more pep, a little more of a smile. "Hey, we're pretty dang good!" they might brag. "Think I'll sign on with the deck department next time around." That was not too far-fetched since almost anyone could sign on in one of the entry ratings: ordinary seaman on deck, or wiper in the engine room. Jumping those levels required experience and knowledge—a minimum time at sea plus passing a Coast Guard exam.

Bosun Hughes had met those requirements easily and had been sailing for some time in that rating. His wife, Nancy, a tall, willowy woman with dark brown hair that swirled across her forehead framing an appealing heart-shaped face, tended to their home. She described her husband as a devoted son to his ailing mother, and a father who doted on his young daughter, Jennifer. A photo she treasured—a curly-headed father tenderly gazing down at Jennifer, barely a few months old—brought that image to life.

The arrival of Jennie, their only child, was memorable for both of them. But for Hughes, adopted when he was barely a year old, the feelings probably ran a little deeper. Somehow that obscure beginning seemed to shadow him and make life a little more difficult in later years when he seemed to try to come to terms with it.

When they got married, his adoptive mother needed care and they welcomed her into their first home. Nancy recalled her husband's sorrow when his mom died, and his last words to his mother: "Mom, talk to me; talk to me," he had implored her, as though she might have secrets he desperately needed to hear.

He also had a closeness with Jennie, and it had been that way since the day she came into the world. Whenever he was home, she would latch onto him like she was afraid he would never come back. Being away for weeks and months on end, it was easy to see why. So he babied her, carried her around, put her in the car when he had an errand to run. She would chirp at him, mouthing sounds only a parent could understand. And he would chatter right back at her.

Nancy remembers that Jennie even became a fixture on some duty weekends at the union hall where he held down the job of patrolman. "Hey," he might say to Jennie, "let's go down to the hall . . . time to go to work!" She knew what "hall" meant and she would become unglued, running around the room while Nancy tried to get her to stand still long enough to put some decent clothes on her. Then off in the car they would go, father and daughter.

Christmas evening, the bosun and the mate met with Wilson in the wheelhouse to give him some good news: the crew had been able to repair the damage resulting from the earlier storm. Again, their main concern was the heavy rolling of the ship, but that was a matter beyond their control.

The bad news, the men reported, was that they were just about out of shoring. The bosun had his men scour the ship from the paint locker to the engine room. They could come up only with scraps here and there and had been forced to use anything at hand. For captain and crew, this marked a major moment in the voyage.

Wilson talked over the situation privately with the mate. The crisis below decks was getting out of control. They needed help quickly. Wilson grabbed a pencil and scribbled out a message to his headquarters, reiterating a need for an escort as soon as possible: ATTEMPTING TO RESECURE CARGO WITH ALL AVAILABLE MATERIALS. STILL REQUIRE ESCORT ASAP AND SHORING MATERIALS IF AVAILABLE.

Several hours later, the *Badger State* received a response: IN ORDER TO PROVIDE SAFE PORT FOR RESECURING CARGO AND AWAITING WEATHER ABATEMENT, DIVERT FROM PRESENT POSITION TOWARD MIDWAY.

Sure, Wilson thought, *great idea. Complex problem; simple solution. Just go to Midway!* That was precisely what he had been trying hard to do for the past several days. Forward progress had nearly come to a halt, particularly since repairs to the leak in the hull had forced him to reduce speed. The problem confronting them lay in trying to get south without aggravating the ship's tendency to roll violently. And yet their current westerly heading wasn't working either. It looked like a no-win situation.

Within a few hours, Wilson received another message, advising that help was on the way. The SS *Flying Dragon,* a United States-owned merchant ship, had been directed to meet and render any assistance the *Badger State* needed. Both ships were ordered to sail to Midway.

Captain Stephen H. Toohey of the *Flying Dragon* received the message from the naval commander of the Hawaiian Sea Frontier, and immediately changed heading to intercept the *Badger State,* several hundred miles distant. Heavy winds and high seas slowed the ship on her new course.

Wilson closed his eyes and inhaled deeply. Help was on the way!

CHAPTER 9

A Mighty Wind

God is against thee old man; forbear! 'tis an
ill voyage! ill begun, ill continued; let me
square the yards, while we may . . . and make
fair wind of it homeward. . . .

—Herman Melville, *Moby-Dick*

S o argued Starbucks, the mate, to Captain Ahab, master of the fictional whaler *Pequod* at a moment when their ship seemed bound for disaster. His words find a real-life echo in the voyage of the *Badger State*: battered by unpredicted storms, compromised by hull and gear failures, and sailing on to a destination firm, but a future shrouded in uncertainty.

However, the parallel has one striking difference. Ahab angrily sought to settle scores in a personal vendetta, looking to harpoon the great white whale that had bitten off his leg. Wilson's assignment was on behalf of his country at war, and the nation's order to him was clear: "Continue on assigned mission."

But there was much more to it than a question of official orders. Part of the indoctrination that maritime school cadets receive is that every merchant marine officer has a "duty to cargo." The obligation begins at loading; it ends when the cargo is offloaded at her destination. Captain

Felix Riesenberg, in his *Standard Seamanship for the Merchant Service*, neatly defines the duty: "This old sea term stands for the integrity of merchant seamen. It sums up their faithful care and handling of the goods entrusted to them." Clearly, bringing the ship about 180 degrees and slinking home with its military cargo undelivered could never be an option for an American merchant ship.

Christmas morning 1969 followed a night of violent storms and a mountain of work for the crew. Few of the men had ever endured such violent winds and seas, made all the more damning since the circumstances flew in the face of the forecasts. In spite of them, their ship continued to edge gradually south as wind and seas allowed.

In the face of a catalogue of uncertainties, every man coming off watch invariably got the same grilling: *What's the latest? The Old Man say anything? Messages? The* Flying Dragon *still on track?* Bits and pieces of overheard conversations, dispatches sent and received, what an officer might have said—all formed a mosaic of sorts which kept the crew remarkably abreast of everything relating to ship and cargo.

For the men, this holiday suffered miserably by comparison with the happy celebration of the holiday at home. For those ashore, Christmas meant fellowship, good cheer, and, most important of all, a gathering of immediate and extended family to exchange gifts and love. At sea, it's the usual work, euphemistically referred to as "holiday routine"—keeping the ship on course, wrestling cargo in the holds, tending to the engines, and trying to cook and serve chow. With work a foregone conclusion, recalling warm memories of the past and marking one less day before the ship reached its destination was the extent of the "celebration".

Still, a few traces of the holiday were in evidence. Someone had brought aboard a stunted Douglas fir and tried to hide its imperfections under a shower of silver balls and a gaudy string of lights. The tree stood uneasily on a table off to one side of the mess hall, telegraphing every twitch and roll of the ship as it swayed, threatening to nose-dive down to the deck. Twine crisscrossed the branches in a hopeful attempt to anchor tree to table.

True to their calling, the steward's department cobbled together a semblance of a holiday meal—roast turkey, giblet gravy, potatoes, and the trimmings. But with half of the department unavailable—everyone except the steward, one cook, and a messman worked the holds—some dexterity and hard work were needed to pull it off.

Of course, a seaman could not be forced to eat that sumptuous meal. Instead, unlikely as it might seem, he could elect to demand his whack. In sailor talk, a seaman's whack is a minimum scale of food that the captain must provide him daily. It's part of the Shipping Articles signed by captain and crew. The menu includes biscuits (one half-pound daily), salt pork (one pound every other day), fresh bread (one and a half pounds daily), and the like, including an ample portion of lard, pickles, molasses, and vinegar. Three ounces of dried fruit is also called for every other day. Presumably, holiday routine simply calls for more of the same.

A far cry from hamburgers and fries, this legislative diet stemmed from early sailing days. Seafarers then engaged for long voyages often contracted scurvy, a condition characterized by loosened teeth, spongy gums, and a general weakness. Doctor James Lind, aboard the British ship *Salisbury* out of England bound for the Plymouth colony in 1747, helped end it. In true scientific fashion, he divided the men into six groups, each one receiving a different food. The group given two oranges and a lemon daily fared best, suggesting that a lack of ascorbic acid commonly found in fruit caused the disease. Lime juice, which contains more acid than lemon juice, became part of the menu on British Navy ships—thereafter lending its name to the sailors who became universally known as limeys.

Once a seaman—presumably one rope end short of a two-end splice—demands his whack, the skipper has no choice but to haul out his scale and dole out the portions. Either that or pay a fifty-dollar fine. Some skippers advocate a reciprocal penalty: require the complaining seaman to eat the stuff.

In spite of the cooks' best efforts aboard the *Badger,* the crew could not enjoy the luxury of sitting down to enjoy the meal. Steve Bordash recalled what it was like. "Unbelievable!" he exclaimed. "Out of twenty chairs in the officer's mess deck, there were only eight usable on Christmas day. Nobody could sit there. If you tried to sit down, it would throw you clear across the deck as the ship snapped back and forth. I think it was the day before that we were having so many problems in the engine room. The violence of the rolls was beginning to bring things loose that had never been loose on that ship before. I think some of the stuff had been bolted down for twenty years."

Despite those miserable conditions, the mess deck remained the only area large enough to accommodate more than a handful of men. And so they met there, these seafarers who undoubtedly felt an urge to huddle with each other—they were all literally and physically in the same boat. In this congregation, long faces hid under a two-week stand of whiskers. Work-stained dungarees, shirts, and a dangling Lucky or Camel completed the image—the men were, by and large, recognizable only to one another. If any were to find comfort, it would be in his own thoughts, probably of home and family. Hanging on to a plate and knife and fork was futile, and hunger drove many to settle for a cut of turkey slipped between two slabs of bread, washed down with black coffee.

The cargo continued to demand everybody's attention. The bosun brought the word. *Need help!* he would holler. A handful of men would then reluctantly tear themselves away from the area, grumbling and cursing. Others would just as reluctantly join them.

No. 3 upper tween deck hold was one of many cargo holds that needed attention. For a change of pace, it held small-arms ammo stowed in boxes, and there was enough broken lumber in the hold to work with. The containers went adrift, and Henderson and a few other men went in to try to tie the boxes down. It took some high stepping to keep from being run down. "It started on the starboard side aft," Henderson explained. "As the cases ran back and forth, they broke the banding on the other pallets, and we had a mass of small boxes running back and forth. When the ship wasn't rolling too much, we would build shoring in the corner. We put two-by-twelves against the cargo and then put four-

The SS *Badger State*, then known as the SS *Starlight*, at launching, 1944. (Charles Wilson Collection)

The SS *Badger State* sinking in the north Pacific Ocean, 1969. (Official U.S. Air Force photograph)

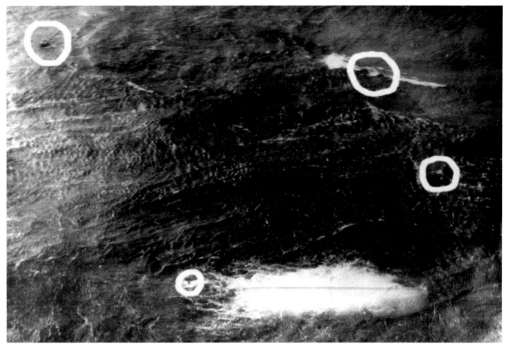

Capsized lifeboat and survivors *(circled)* from the SS *Badger State*, December 26, 1969. (Official U.S. Air Force photograph)

Burial at sea, SS *Steel Rover*, off Guam, 1968, Captain Charles Wilson officiating, reading from *The Book of Common Prayer*. Name of decedent unknown. (Charles Wilson Collection)

Captain Charles T. Wilson: *(left)*
Midshipman, 1954; *(above)* sailing,
1981; *(bottom)* with wife, Mary, 1973.
(Wilson Collection)

Bosun Dick Hughes:
(above) with daughter,
Jennifer, 1966;
(left) with wife,
Nancy, 1964. (Nancy
Keys Collection)

At the White House, 1970, President Nixon presents the American Merchant Marine Seamanship Trophy, honoring Bosun Richard D. Hughes, to his wife, Nancy, and daughter, Jennifer. To the President's right is Joseph Curran, president of the National Maritime Union; to his left, Maritime Administrator Andrew E. Gibson, and Robert B. Stone, president of States Marine Lines, Inc., owner of the *Badger State*. (Courtesy *NMU Pilot*, in which photo, believed to be by a White House photographer, was published.)

SOME WHO SURVIVED. Captain Niros, master of the *Khian Star*, Greek seaman K. Ionas, and Captain Charles Wilson. (Courtesy National Maritime Union, AFL-CIO)

Left: George Henderson *(standing)*, Florencio Serafino, Samuel Kaneao, James McLure, and Charles McCullar. (Courtesy National Maritime Union, AFL-CIO)

Below: Agent G. Sanford, Engineers Richard Pattershall, Steven Bordash, and Neal Kirkwood. (Courtesy the Marine Engineers Beneficial Association)

Richard Hughes,
Bosun

Joseph Candos, AB

Nelson Fabre, AB

Floyd Rilling, AB

Francisco Nunez,
Oiler

Nick Barbieri, Oiler

Leonard Scypion,
Fireman-Watertender

Mohamed
Al-Muwallad, Wiper

SOME WHO WERE LOST.
These are some of the men
who gave their lives on
behalf of their country.
(Photos of Baker and Woods
courtesy the Marine Engineers
Beneficial Association; all
others courtesy the National
Maritime Union, AFL-CIO)

Chief Gilbert Baker

Kinnie Woods

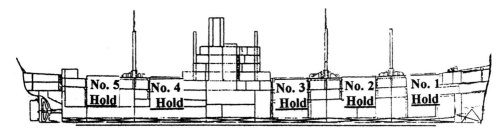

Diagram of a C-2 ship similar to the SS *Badger State*. (U.S. Maritime Commission; digitally enhanced by Koepnick Enterprises.)

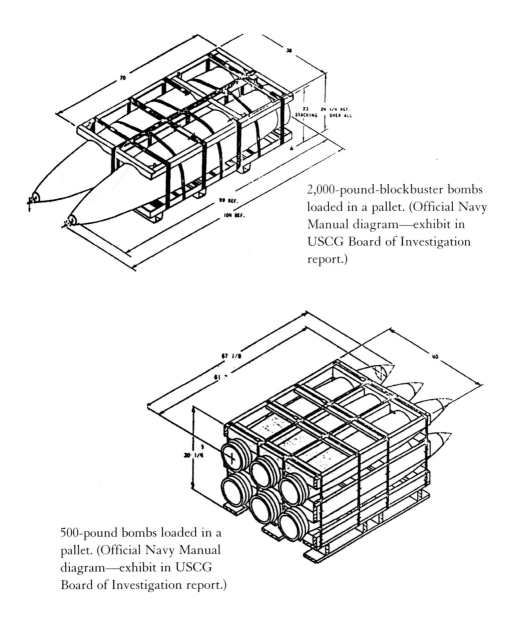

2,000-pound-blockbuster bombs loaded in a pallet. (Official Navy Manual diagram—exhibit in USCG Board of Investigation report.)

500-pound bombs loaded in a pallet. (Official Navy Manual diagram—exhibit in USCG Board of Investigation report.)

by-four braces in as close as we could get them. But then the cargo would shift away from us and we would wait for the cargo to shift and then drop more material in. But when it drifted back, it was just too much weight. It would shatter the four-by-fours." It was a battle hard to win.

Some blockbuster bombs in No. 5 also began to make a disturbing move during the day. The big ones got the respect they deserved fast. Three or four pallets of the bombs had shifted—Bangor had loaded some pallets with the bombs nose to nose without any shielding between them. The bombs tended to nuzzle close and climb up on each other. The stress of this amorous coupling caused the metal bands holding the pallets together to snap. Weighing tons, the crew couldn't budge any of it. Bombs and pallets were left where they were, with the crew improvising as best they could. Given the layout, the job went easily enough, and the crew felt that No. 5 hold, once shored up, was probably in better condition than most of the others.

Near the end of the day, the mate and the bosun checked in with the captain. They briefed him on the work in progress in the various holds, and about the dangers faced by the men. The men were getting by using broken lumber, scraps of wood in the holds, and anything else made of wood around the ship. Still, they noted optimistically, the men seemed to be handling the work well, most of them believing they were keeping on top of the situation.

That was the last report Wilson got from his key men late on Christmas day. But, despite their generally upbeat report, he could not dispel a sense of unease as he reflected on the ship's precarious condition. The men were beat—one could see the signs of it in their half-shut eyes, pasty complexions, and slacked jaws. The breakdowns were continuing, and their concerted efforts were just barely keeping the day of reckoning at bay.

Third Mate Burnette joined Wilson in the wheelhouse for the midnight-to-four watch on the 26th. It was the second time in as many nights that the two men shared the same watch. They exchanged upbeat talk, agreeing that the worst might well be behind them. The *Flying Dragon* was on its way, and to have help within shouting distance would ease everyone's concerns. But the *Dragon* was still several hundred miles away. Distance, plus bad weather, meant that it might be several days before it could reach them. The men had reasonable grounds for optimism. They had coped with nearly everything that could go wrong, and had risen to the challenge.

Wilson comforted himself with the notion that no storm could beat the one they had sailed through. It had rolled the *Badger* over to a dangerous angle—proof of the size of the waves battering the ship—but they had survived it. As every sailor knows, not all ships *do* survive.

Huge ocean waves, along with Davey Jones and sea serpents, are the stuff of maritime legend. While the latter remain questionable, rogue or freak waves, typically described as looking like "walls of water," have taken on new credibility in the scientific community. How they develop is not well understood. One theory is that they arise out of the head-on collision of powerful storm waves and equally strong currents. The impact squeezes together storm swells, superimposing their frequencies. Giant waves can develop from this combination of forces, attaining unbelievable heights of a hundred feet or more.

Other theories attempt to explain phenomenons such as the one sometimes referred to as "three-sisters"—three huge waves following in rapid succession. That theory holds that the chaotic nature of the ocean itself will at some point produce a high wave, and that it will most often arise in groups of three.

Ship designs have been generally based on the assumption that a chance meeting with a rogue wave was an event highly unlikely to occur. However, research and increasing reports of such encounters caught the attention of Naval architects. One such study by marine consultant and former professor of naval architecture Douglas Faulkner showed that out of sixty supercarriers that were lost over a recent twenty-five-year period, rogue waves took down a staggering twenty-two of them.

Reports and studies are one thing, but seeing is believing, and Captain Ronald Warwick, skipper of the *Queen Elizabeth II*, en route to New York in 1995, saw one coming. It looked like a mountain in the night, he reported. When it struck, it broke over the bow of the equally huge *QEII* and sent a shudder rippling through the giant ship. Two waves hammered the ship in rapid succession. As the *QEII* fell into the "hole" created by the first wave, the second swamped the foredeck, tearing off the forward mast. The crest of the huge wave approximated Warwick's line of sight on the bridge, about ninety-five feet above the surface of the water. A Canadian weather buoy moored in the vicinity measured it higher, at nearly a hundred feet. To Captain Warwick, all that white water "looked as if we were going into the white cliffs of Dover!"

A predecessor to the *QEII*, the Cruise liner *Queen Mary*, experienced a similar freak wave in 1942 while sailing the north Atlantic. She was battered by a seventy-five-foot wave that nearly capsized the ship and would have taken her down with the 15,000 troops on board. More recently, another British ship, the *Oriana*, had six of its ten decks swamped when a seventy-foot wave washed over it.

Any wave larger than normal might appear to be a rogue wave, depending on the experience and background of the sailor or passenger. Exact measurements are hard to come by. However, one of the largest waves ever recorded was by Navy Lieutenant Commander R. P. Whitemarsh, whose findings were published in the U.S. Naval Institute Proceedings in August 1934.

Whitemarsh sailed aboard the USS *Ramapo*, a Navy tanker under way in the Pacific Ocean. A storm arose and gale-force winds of forty-seven to fifty-four miles per hour—the same as those met by the *Badger State*—hammered the ship. The winds later increased to near hurricane-force of sixty-nine to seventy-six miles per hour. A massive wave slammed into the ship. Whitemarsh and his crew, hanging on to everything in sight on the ship's bridge, were able to measure the height of it by lining up its crest with the horizon and a point on the ship's mast (a horizontal line) while the stern of the ship sagged to the bottom of a trough. The wave measured a staggering 112 feet, as high as a ten- or eleven-story building.

Often, there are no survivors to brag about how big the wave was.

The ship just disappears. That happened to one of the largest super-tankers ever built, the German Navy ship *Munchen*. En route to the United States in 1978, the ship simply sailed into oblivion. No message; no sightings; no wreckage. She was gone. One of the widest-ranging searches in history, covering every conceivable point along the ship's route, resulted in the recovery of only one of the ship's lifeboats, battered almost beyond recognition. The entire crew of twenty-six had vanished along with the huge ship. An official inquiry into the cause of the disappearance concluded that the sinking was a highly unusual event that had no further implications.

Measurements of rogue waves might be more accurate if made against stationary objects such as lighthouses. Waves have reportedly sprung over the seventy-five-foot-high lighthouse on Minots Ledge, Massachusetts; others have reached high enough to carry rocks through the glass of the Tillamook Rock Lighthouse in Oregon, which stands 133 feet above the water. (Fortunately, no lives were lost there.)

Less fortunate were the Coast Guardsmen at Scotch Cap Lighthouse on Unimak Island in the Aleutians—a site so isolated that the original keepers got a flat one year off for every four years they tended the light. In 1946, a one-hundred-foot tidal wave swept lighthouse, crew, and every recognizable sign of human habitation into the sea.

Wilson could only hope that a giant wave was not in the cards for the *Badger State*. But another storm could be—he began to feel winds picking up around the ship, possibly a prologue to the chorus. The tempo, slight at first, enabled Wilson and Burnette to disregard the sign as nothing of consequence. But then the deck began to angle up a few degrees and the winds to increase a notch or two, until, by slow stages, they escalated to near gale-force, while waves—a confused mix which had bedeviled the ship almost continuously since leaving Bangor—kept pace. Seas began to smash over the bow, rushing down the forward section of the main deck and spilling over the side.

The barometer had already begun its familiar plummet, a sure sign of bad weather ahead. It didn't seem possible to Wilson that a second unpredicted storm could hit them, but the signs were ominous. Wilson resumed his litany of orders to the helmsman. "Hard right"—then "hard left." The seaman at the helm bent to the task with each command. Soon the occasional order "steady as she goes" was followed by an order to turn to one direction or the other. It was a high-stakes game of chess, the sea attacking on one quarter after another, the captain defending, moving, striving to protect his queen, his ship.

"Winds are picking up, Captain," Burnette reported. "Better than forty knots . . . and shifting." Gale-force winds.

Wilson nodded. The Navy told him to divert, but that was out of the question. Trying to bring the *Badger State* to a direct southerly heading with the winds and waves as they were would be suicidal. Wilson was content to continue westerly, dropping down into a southern track whenever the seas lightened up. The ship, still at reduced speed, was making little headway west. Its track showed it being literally pushed slowly south.

Wilson copied down the ship's position and speed, and drafted the following message to Navy Headquarters: NEW POSIT LAT 36-50N LONG 172-24W. SPEED 6 KNOTS. PRESENTLY RUNNING BEFORE WESTERLY GALE. SHIP IS VERY STIFF. HAVE ALREADY ROLLED TO 50 DEGREES. FEAR ANY DIVERSION AT THIS TIME TOWARDS MIDWAY WILL CAUSE SERIOUS CONSEQUENCES TO CARGO ALREADY RESECURED IN HOLDS.

The winds continued to intensify, the seas breaking in huge waves with deep broad swells coming at the ship from multiple directions. Rain pelted the ship off and on. The ocean became increasingly agitated, waves breaking over the ship at regular intervals.

At four bells, marking two hours into the watch on the morning of December 26, Wilson remained at his post conning the ship. On watch almost continuously for the past four nights, the lack of sleep played games with his eyelids and reflexes. An immense feeling of weariness left him weak and unable to concentrate. Staring into the blackness, his mind wandering, he drew a blank. He felt his head drop, and caught himself with a start. His vision blurred. He shook his head vigorously from side-to-side. A watchstander, understanding the motion, handed him a glass partly filled with water. Wilson let a sip trickle down his throat, and then flipped the rest at his face, gasping as the cold spray wet his skin. It caught Burnette's attention.

"Why don't you turn in, Cap'n," Burnette suggested. "I'll take over."

"No, no thanks, Mr. Burnette. I'm okay," said Wilson, rubbing his eyes with the palm of his hand.

"With all due respect, Captain. Maybe I need to pipe down, but I'm afraid you're trying to—" Burnette suddenly stopped talking, gasped, and shouted, "Good God, Captain! Off the port bow . . . a monster wave. Watch out!"

Wilson, jolted awake by the shout, his heart pounding, glanced quickly to his left. A huge wall of water, appearing out of nowhere, loomed monstrously large over the *Badger State*.

"God help us!" The prayer ripped out of Wilson. "Hang on!" he shouted as loud as he could, grabbing the rail in front of him, instinctively hunching his shoulders tightly together as though to protect himself. A shudder rippled through the ship, passing through his body as a massive wall of seawater engulfed the ship, lifting the bow high and thrusting it over on a side. He hung on with all his strength as the ship rolled 45 to 50 degrees to starboard. The fate of the *Badger State*, now thrashing about wildly, was out of his hands.

The ship, hovering sickeningly on the cusp of a roll, snapped rapidly back to its center as the wave carried the 441-foot ship and her crew, who were hanging on to bulkhead, railing, whatever was close to hand's reach, on a heart-dropping, roller-coaster ride over the top of the massive wave. Momentum carried the vessel down sideways, curling her over into a roll on her port side.

The *Badger State* lay there helpless, on the verge of rolling completely over. "She's at 52 degrees, Cap'n!" Burnette shouted, his words punctuated by the screeching sounds of the chart table breaking loose from its moorings and sliding crazily across the deck of the wheelhouse. Charts, pencils, sextants, ashtrays, and other gear followed, clattering across the deck. Fifty-two-degree rolls were not on the minds of the shipbuilders when they built the *Badger State*.

The bedlam topside was matched by chaos below deck. Refrigerators and other fixtures, welded to the metal of the ship when she was built two decades earlier, also came loose and spilled their contents everywhere. The fixtures were joined by a torrent of pots and pans, tools, and a hodgepodge of bric-a-brac that defined the necessities and comfort of life aboard ship.

"It was some time after midnight," Bordash recalled. "I was thrown completely out of my bed, and there was a loud noise outside my room and it seemed to get progressively worse. I remember very well that I had an awful time putting my clothes on because the rolling would throw you back and forth. I finally got to the officer's mess deck, and the second and the third engineers were there. None of us were able to stay in bed."

Fireman-Watertender James Beatty was one of the men active in trying to secure the holds in the late hours of December 25 and extending into the following morning. "I worked up until midnight with the chief mate," he said.

Then I grabbed a cup of coffee at midnight and the bosun said "I know you are tired, but can you give me a hand in Number Three?" Eddie Hottendorf and George were working down there, shoring along the side of the ship, and Hughes was cutting lengths of four-by-fours. I stayed down there until approximately two-thirty A.M. and I told Mr. Hughes that I was getting very tired and ought to get a little bit of rest because I had to go back on watch in the engine room at four o'clock, and he said, "Yes, go ahead."

I went up to my room and this was about two-thirty A.M., I guess, and I laid down on my bunk. The ship took a big roll and my feet went against my locker. My locker was at right angles to my bunk and I was literally standing on the side of my locker when we took such a roll. I couldn't get any sleep. So I got up and I went back in the mess hall and I heard Dick Hughes talking about the emergency we had.

Lawrence McHugh was at the helm when the ship took its 52-degree roll. "That is something I don't want to go through again," he recalled. "I have sailed the Aleutians and all over Alaska, and I have never sailed on a ship that rolled like that—three 45-degree rolls in a row, plus a 52-degree roll!"

There was pandemonium in the wheelhouse, suddenly punctuated by an excruciatingly loud banging noise as though the ship had been hit by a battering ram, vibrating through the structure. A pause, and then, as the ship rolled, the same banging sound again reverberated through the wheelhouse.

Reacting to the event, Wilson shouted at the watch officer, "See what the hell's going on out there!"

Burnette moved quickly out to the wing of the bridge, holding on to the ship's rail. He returned shortly, his eyes wide, water streaming down his face. "Lifeboat's broken loose, Cap'n," he declared, his voice rising.

"Which side?"

"Port side. She's hanging by a thread on just one davit, just dangling there, stern down, banging against the ship."

"Christ!" Wilson exploded, shaking his head in disbelief as the disabled boat again crashed against the steel of the ship. "What the hell next? That leaves us with only one lifeboat. We need—"

He was interrupted by the mate, poking his way in, wiping water from his face, shaking. "Captain," he said excitedly, panting from exertion, struggling to catch his breath, "port lifeboat—"

"I know about the boat," Wilson interrupted him.

"There's also bombs loose in Number Five and—"

"What?" Wilson shouted, his heart beating rapidly.

"Number Five, Cap'n!"

"Upper or lower?" Wilson said, struggling to regain control.

"Upper tween deck, Cap'n. You can hear the bombs rolling back and forth. Sounds like a freight train down there. I was on my way down to get the bosun and take a look . . . thought I'd better get word to you on the double." The words tumbled out of his mouth, one after the other in an unbroken stream.

No. 5 upper tween decks hold contained the 2,000-pound bombs.

CHAPTER 10

Pandemonium

No. 5 upper tween deck cargo hold squats just below the *Badger State*'s main deck level near the stern of the ship. The mate, as he later reported to Wilson, accompanied by the bosun, looking like spacemen in their bulky foul-weather jackets and trousers, climbed down into the hold. Stopping, the men clung to their perch like barnacles to the ship's hull, shivering, staring downward with fear and a morbid fascination.

Scarcely more than an anchor's length beneath them, 2,000-pound blockbuster bombs swirled around like sharks gone berserk in a kill frenzy. As the deck slanted back and forth, the one-ton monsters stampeded across the deck, collided with each other, or smashed into the metal skin of the ship, punching holes in the hull. Showers of fiery sparks shot out as metal slammed into metal, setting off an incessant roar that reverberated throughout the chamber—sound waves bouncing off the metal of the ship's hull, deck, and overhead.

The pallets were destroyed, broken down into unrecognizable fragments and pulverized by the mass of rampaging metal. The bracing—the thick 4-by-4 and 2-by-12-inch lumber that seemed solid enough in the serenity of the harbor left behind—had been reduced to splinters. Spaghetti-like strands of wire, the broken remnants of the metal banding that held the bombs to the pallets, whipped around wildly, also throwing off sparks.

The mate and the bosun scrambled out on deck, shaken, and then climbed to the wheelhouse. Other seamen, attracted by the noise, checked out the scene on their own.

Fireman-Watertender James Beatty had trouble sleeping in the early morning hours of December 26. "I got up and went into the mess hall," he said, "and I heard the bosun talking about the emergency we had in Number Five. He said the bombs were loose; the hold was in a mess, and they were rolling all over. This was about three-thirty A.M. I didn't have time to help since I had to go on watch at four. Mr. Reiche, the engineer on watch, and I were both frightened. We could hear the bombs going boom, boom every time the ship took a roll. The bombs would smash into the side of the ship, and the noise in the engine room was tremendous. It was like being trapped inside a big drum with somebody hammering the outside of it!"

As if the problems in No. 5 were not serious enough, other holds were also presenting concerns. "We had something loose on the forward end on the starboard side of Number Four," Steve Bordash recalled. "I thought it was going to go through the side of the ship. I don't know what cargo was there, but it sounded like it was rolling over an area of about six feet and then slamming against the side." However, there were no 2,000 pound bombs in No. 4, and the big bombs got top priority.

In the wheelhouse, the two men barged in to find an anxious Wilson waiting for them. Wilson wanted to know immediately how bad it was, mentally bracing for the worst as he took in the ashen face of the mate. Cobbs described the chaos the two men had witnessed.

Wilson's first reaction was to try to figure some way to dump other items into the hold—tables, bunks, whatever. "We'll use the bunks for bracing," he said. "We've got plenty around. We can—"

"No, no, no, you don't understand!" the mate interrupted him, his voice rising. "The two-thousand-pounders in Number Five are out of the pallets, all of them. They're crashing into each other. It's hell down there!"

Losing control of the 2,000 pounders was catastrophic. The ship's roll to 52 degrees—an angle akin to that of the roof of a house in snow country—had snapped the bombs loose. At that position, the side-to-side cumulative weight of the pallets of one-ton bombs, one literally on top of another, must have broken the pallets apart.

There didn't seem much that anyone could do. Putting a man in the hold would be suicidal. And even if that could be done, it would accomplish nothing. There were no pallets standing; nothing to work with. Bangor's advice never considered the possibility of bombs breaking loose from their restraints and running amok in a ship's holds. It simply had never happened before.

But *something* had to be done. The flow of bombs had to be stopped or, at the least, slowed somehow. The only hope seemed to be to try to smother the bombs—to dump materials on top and in between the moving bombs to slow them down. Pondering the options, Wilson tried to recall Bangor's cautionary words. Ironically, the only warning that came to mind was the admonition to avoid sparks in the holds. Smothering the bombs was the only option.

He ordered the two men to round up everything movable aboard the ship—mattresses, steward's linens and stores, engine room packing—and dump all of it into No. 5 on top of the moving bombs. Start with the mooring lines, he told them. They had hundreds of feet of flexible line and that might prove effective in stopping the flow. Every single available man had to turn to, Wilson stressed.

That was the Old Man's order. Then came the real problem: how to get the stuff into the hold. It would be impossible to squirrel all of it through the narrow access hole used by the crew to get down into the hold. The only other option was to take one or more of the steel covers, the pontoons, off the opening to the hold.

A cargo ship is designed to allow easy access to all the holds in port for loading and discharging cargo. At sea, all those openings need to be slammed shut and battened down. That's the purpose of the bulky, heavy, steel pontoons covering the holds. They are hauled off in port to allow easy access to the ship's innards. Once loading or discharging is done, the pontoons are dropped back over the holds, sealing them off from the elements until the ship can reach the next port. As added insurance, a waterproof tarp blankets the pontoons to keep the ocean out.

The ship's own booms—long metal cylinders, similar to derricks ashore, with cables for lifting attached to them—are used in port not only to shift cargo, but also to remove the pontoons. The booms can lift roughly five tons or more of cargo at a clip. The *Badger State* carried more than a dozen such booms strategically located next to the five holds. When not in use, the booms were lowered to rest in cradles located directly above the pontoons.

"I can give it a try," the bosun said.

"How?" Wilson asked, sounding dubious about the idea of lifting the huge metal covers in a surging sea.

"Don't worry, Captain, I'll figure out a way."

Wilson nodded. The past few days had convinced him there wasn't anything his bosun couldn't do. "Then let's get to it!" he said abruptly.

Wilson leaned wearily against the bulkhead after the two men left, squinting and staring, his face dark and pinched tight from lack of sleep. The unending series of life-and-death decisions had taken its toll. Slouched forward against the bulkhead of the wheelhouse, struggling to resist the urge to lie down, he continued to maneuver the huge ship, heading her bow into the confused swells. Given the necessarily erratic maneuvering and the low speed, dead-reckoning plots showed the ship's progress west as almost zero.

There were other problems for Wilson to think about. Use of the port lifeboat had been lost. Still attached to the ship at one end, it dangled at an awkward angle over the side of the *Badger State,* banging against her side with every roll of the vessel. It sounded a mournful requiem to the shriek of the wind and the metal-to-metal clashing of the bombs in the holds. He considered the possibility of cutting the boat loose, but concluded there was not enough manpower to spare for the work.

Wilson still harbored the hope, more tenuous with each passing moment, that the ship might yet reach a safe harbor. A brief spell of mild weather would do the trick. On the other hand, ship and crew could go up in one humungous, earth-shaking blast. The danger was real. Sparks could ignite powder spilled in the hole, which would be enough to set off everything. For good reason, no ship in a convoy wanted to buddy up with an ammo-loaded ship sailing next to it.

Such was the dramatic case for several unlucky ships sailing close to the SS *Mary Luckenbach*, while in a convoy bound for the Russian port of Murmansk in the fall of 1942. Grouping merchant freighters and tankers together in a convoy, accompanied by a protective covey of Navy warships, proved effective in cutting the terrible loss of such ships to German subs during the early stages of World War II.

Heavily loaded with explosives, the *Luckenbach* was hit, not by a torpedo from a sub, but by a German Junkers 88 torpedo bomber. Other ships in the convoy had riddled the plane with gunfire. Perhaps knowing he was doomed, the pilot took dead aim at the *Luckenbach*, and crashed his plane, torpedo and all, onto the deck of the unfortunate ship. The resulting explosion literally vaporized the vessel and every man aboard her.

Several eyewitnesses from other ships in the convoy attested to the ferocity of the disaster that enveloped the *Mary Luckenbach*. "There was," by one account, "one great boiling mass of grayish-black smoke and flame, which must have reached a thousand feet in height." The smoke was so thick that other ships in the convoy lost track of each other.

So devastating was the explosion that the crew of the SS *Nathaniel Greene*, sailing immediately ahead of the *Mary Luckenbach*, thought *their* ship had been hit. As reported by Lieutenant (jg) R. M. Billings, Commanding Officer of the *Nathaniel Greene*'s naval armed guard, his ship felt a tremendous explosion. Shrapnel from the explosion cut down some crew members and the blast caused an incredible amount of damage: doors and bulkheads were blown out, cargo boxes and glass ports destroyed, ventilators caved in, hospital demolished, and bullets and shrapnel all over the place.

The certainty of an explosion aboard was so strong that the captain of the *Nathaniel Greene* immediately ordered the crew to their boat stations. Life rafts were pitched overboard, and the ship's engines stopped.

The ship dropped back from the convoy. At that point, one of the engineers reported to the bridge that he could find no damage in the engine room. To prove his point, he quickly got the engines running again.

A more thorough check-up followed. The ship was declared seaworthy and without any obvious critical damage. The *Greene* resumed her place in the convoy. It was only then that captain and crew learned the truth: what they had assumed was a torpedo hit on their ship was in fact the massive explosion aboard the *Mary Luckenbach,* sailing a bare two hundred yards off her starboard quarter.

The SS *William Moultrie*, in line directly behind, sailed over the very spot in the water where the *Luckenbach* had been only moments before. Not a single piece of that unlucky ship could be found in the area, so complete was its destruction.

The SS *William Pierce Frye*—not to be confused with the schooner *William P. Frye*, sunk during World War I—loaded to the gunnels with high explosives, was another such victim. In 1943, the ship departed an American port in company with dozens of other ships in a convoy bound for England. The convoy encountered fog and foul weather, both menaces to safe navigation by ships within sight of each other. But far worse than the elements were the subs, looking for easy game and nipping at the heels of every convoy. Lame-duck stragglers fit the bill nicely. The *Frye,* encountering engine problems, began to lag behind the other ships. However, the convoy continued on track, the fate of the whole enterprise taking precedence over the possible loss of a single ship.

The captain of the beleaguered *Frye* had no choice but to stop the ship's engines while the crew attempted repairs. A German sub came upon it wallowing helplessly in the water, took aim, and fired two torpedoes. Both missed. Still, the narrow escape concentrated the efforts of the crew wonderfully in hastily finishing repairs. The ship got underway and at once proceeded under forced draft in an attempt to reach the safety of the convoy, now miles ahead.

The sub, in a cat-and-mouse game, paralleled the ship's course some distance away, seeking the advantage of a broadside attack. Bad weather and evasive maneuvering by the skipper enabled the *Frye* to win a reprieve, but it was short-lived. Two torpedoes eventually found their mark, setting off the explosives. The massive explosion drove the ship down quickly, leaving only a handful of lucky survivors blown clear in its wake to tell what happened.

The SS *Timothy Pickering* suffered a similar fate while taking part in the invasion of Sicily in July 1943. One plane managed to dump two bombs into the ammunition loaded in the ship's holds. The *Pickering* disappeared in a funeral pyre of fire and smoke, carrying burning debris along with it. Some of that blazing material dropped on the nearby tanker *O. Henry,* setting off an explosion on that ship as well.

Still, those explosions do not begin to compare to the fate of the SS *Paul Hamilton*, a Liberty ship sailing in a convoy in the Mediterranean Sea in 1944, with bombs in her cargo holds, as well as 498 Army Air Corps passengers. A German plane, hit by British gunners and afire, managed to get off a torpedo before crashing, and made a direct hit. The ship disappeared into dust, taking every person on board with it. In terms of human lives, it was the most devastating loss ever sustained by a single Liberty ship during World War II.

What set the *Badger State* apart from those doomed vessels was a unique circumstance: the danger confronting the ship was internal. No armada of Navy cruisers and destroyers in a convoy could lessen that danger; no sister ship sailing close by could lend a helping hand. The crew had to deal with it, doing the best with what they had available.

Other ships have undoubtedly experienced a breakdown in cargo over the years—in the *Odyssey* Ulysses expresses concerns for his cargo, gourds of mellow wine, as his ship fights to weather the storms thrown his way by angry gods—but rarely, if ever, is the loose cargo explosive. Rule books are silent on the subject of bombs running loose in a ship's holds.

With the ship in this cliffhanger situation, Wilson had no choice about what needed to be done next. It would be the ultimate step every skipper dreaded: keying out an SOS.

Wilson turned his attention to the chart table. The second mate had penciled in a dead-reckoning position. Wilson hurriedly scribbled notes, crossed the wheelhouse to the radio room and handed the message to his radio officer.

"Send this now!" he ordered, his voice cracking. There was a pounding in his chest. It was almost as though having made up his mind, the feelings inside of him were almost too much to bear.

The officer's eyes opened wide as he glanced at the note. "I'll get it out right now, Captain," he responded. The officer quickly keyed the following distress message to the maritime world: SOS SOS SOS. KWGE KWGE. POSIT LAT 36.48N, LONG 172.40W. (KWGE was the radio call sign of the *Badger State*.)

The letters SOS, almost as ancient as wireless telegraphy, fit well with the popular idea that SOS means "Save our Ship" or "Save our Souls." But its exact meaning is unknown. Letters may simply represent a rhythm easily keyed by an operator, ones not likely to be confused with other letters.

Before the discovery of wireless telegraphy by Marconi, ships casting off their mooring lines also cut their link with the larger human community. If the ship did not reach its destination within a reasonable time, it was simply assumed lost. Wireless changed that scenario dramatically by establishing a link between sea and shore, extending to a sinking vessel the possibility of being rescued.

In one of the earliest such cases, Lightship No. 58, braving a hurricane on station at Nantucket Shoals in 1905, sprang a leak in her hull. Water came in faster than the crew could bail. The ship had wireless aboard. However, no recognized signal for distress existed at the time. The ship could only bleat out in Morse code the single word "H-E-L-P" repeatedly, the earliest known use of wireless in the United States to call for help. The lightship received no reply to its plaintive plea; fortunately, the naval station at Newport intercepted the call and passed it on. A lightship tender, the *Azalea*, proceeded to the scene and took the lightship in tow. Although the ship sank before reaching port, her thirteen crew members were saved, thanks to wireless telegraphy.

The United States finally adopted SOS as its distress symbol following the dramatic rescue of roughly 1,500 passengers and crew from the White Star liner *Republic* off Nantucket Island in 1909. The ship departed New York harbor, bound for the Mediterranean, with 440 tourists on board. Meeting heavy fog south of Nantucket, her captain cut speed slightly, relying on the eyes and ears of the ship's lookouts to spot other ships—radar was not available until decades later. A ship's whistle sounded dead ahead. The captain at once ordered the engines reversed, but it was too late. Steaming out of the dark and fog, the Italian ship *Florida* rammed the *Republic* amidships, leaving a calling card, its anchor in one of the ship's staterooms before pulling back and disappearing into the mist.

The *Republic* quickly took on water and developed a heavy list. The engine room flooded and the ship lost all power. In the normal course of events, the ship would have gone down with all persons on board. However, in a serendipitous turn of events, the *Republic* had brought aboard a brand-new Marconi radio before sailing. The radio was hooked to emergency batteries, and the ship's operator broadcast the distress signal CQD—the first two letters came from their use by the British ashore as a general call preceding time signals and other notices; the letter "D" stood for distress (the British passenger ship *Titanic* broadcast both CQD and SOS as its distress signals). Wireless saved the *Republic*'s passengers and crew.

The SOS broadcast by the *Badger State* reached the U.S. Coast Guard at Honolulu, which at once sent its own planes to look for the ship, and promptly notified Hawaii-based Air Force and Navy people who had communications and rescue capabilities of their own. Since the ship was carrying bombs for the Air Force under Navy charter, both branches of the service had a direct interest in the fate of the *Badger State*. Hickam Air Force Base planes joined the search, their mission to pinpoint the ship's location, to pass that information on to any rescue units on scene; and to drop rafts and supplies to men found in the water.

Using its more powerful transmitters, the Coast Guard also keyed the following message to all ships at sea: URGENT MARINE INFOR-

MATION BROADCAST. VESSEL BADGER STATE/KWGE HAS
BROADCAST DISTRESS SIGNAL ON 500 KHZ IN POSIT 36–48N,
172–40W. REPORT ANY SIGHTINGS TO COMMANDER FOUR-
TEENTH COAST GUARD DISTRICT HONOLULU HAWAII.

Dial 911 in any city, and fire fighters, police, ambulances, and para-
medics race to the scene, lights flashing, and sirens screaming to clear
the road. No need to guess about location; no obstacles clutter the highway; no worries about weather conditions. Help arrives quickly, and
another disaster is usually averted. Keying SOS at sea is an exercise in
patience and, usually, frustration. The receiver, another ship or agency, is
unknown; it may be hundreds of miles away; and the distressed vessel's
position on a vast ocean must be pinpointed—not an easy matter, and
much less so in earlier years when navigation was more conjecture than
science.

Planes rush out to find the ship, but they are restricted to confirming
the ship's location and dropping rafts and supplies. The real workhorses,
the rescue ships, must sail long distances over an obscure, ever-shifting
"highway" at ten to fifteen miles an hour, land speed. Arriving on scene,
perhaps days later, the tough part begins: taking the seamen off the
stricken ship or, worse, hauling them out of the water if the ship has
been abandoned. The entire operation is a ponderous, slow-motion
response to an event in which time is of the essence.

This inevitable delay places the ship in even greater peril. Storm conditions are usually at the heart of the problem in the first place. Consequently, winds are likely to blow stronger, waves mount higher, and the
combination relentlessly batter the ship even more. All too often, by the
time the rescue ship reaches the scene, the crew and stricken vessel are
already doomed. The *Badger State* was fast approaching that point.

At sea, firefighters, ambulances, and police are all embodied by a
single agency, the United States Coast Guard. Its sailors go by a handful
of names, including coasties, shallow-water sailors, hooligans, rum-
runners, the Guard, and, now, the Home Security guys. It's a proud
outfit, composed of too few men dealing with too many of the nation's

problems. Their official motto, *Semper Paratus* (Always Ready) speaks volumes; their unofficial motto, *You have to go out, but you don't have to come back*, speaks louder.

Captain John F. Mundy, a graduate of the Pennsylvania State Nautical School and a veteran Coast Guard officer, attributes the saying to the Outer Bankers, those hardy souls who manned the first lifeboat stations on the outer banks of North Carolina: Cape Hatteras, Cape Lookout, and Cape Fear. To the men who rowed out in double-ended surfboats in the fury of Atlantic storms to rescue fellow seamen in danger, the motto expressed the reality of the life they led. Their children absorbed it along with their oatmeal and milk, and later carried on the family tradition by serving in the Coast Guard. More likely, according to this outspoken Old Salt, when one is faced with extreme danger, disaster lurking in every direction, and you know "you have to go out," the motto gets shortened to the universal "Aw, shit!" Then you go out, he says, deal with it, and hope like hell you get back where you started from.

The Guard dates from 1790 when Congress decided it had had enough of smugglers—a fine enough occupation during colonial times when Americans wanted to tweak the British nose, but now the United States was itself being tweaked. Out of that concern came the Revenue Marine, the predecessor to the Coast Guard, whose close partnership with the Navy eventually developed when Congress later designated the Coast Guard "a military service and a branch of the armed forces of the United States at all times."

Flexing a little of this muscle, the Guard fought in every war in which the U.S. has been involved, declared and undeclared, typically as a part of the Navy. But it is best known for its peacetime exploits: overseeing the U.S. Merchant Marine; seeing to the security of ports; tending to buoys that line every waterway; dealing with oil spills; keeping track of icebergs; and, among the best-known of its jobs, rescuing people and ships, perhaps even an airplane or two, at sea. The name *Bermuda Sky Queen* still resonates with old salts more used to dealing with ships than planes.

The *Bermuda Sky Queen* was a passenger plane that, unfortunately, ran out of gas in the middle of the Atlantic Ocean in 1947. In the normal course of events, passengers and plane would have bought a one-way ticket to the next world. However, the Coast Guard Cutter *Bibb* happened to be cruising around on "ocean station patrol," transmitting weather reports in those presatellite days. Plane and cutter set up radio contact, and the pilot, bucking stiff winds and thirty-five-foot waves, miraculously crash-landed the aircraft onto the water. Then began the ticklish job of ferrying the sixty-two passengers and seven crew members from plane to ship. Lifeboats, rafts, nets, and Coastguardsmen over the side did the trick. The cutter did its job.

Naturally, every rescue of a plane or ship had to be reported up the line to Coast Guard headquarters. A typical message, whether involving a plane or a fishing vessel broken down off the Grand Banks, would include certain vital stats. Such a message might read like this: THIS DATE, REMOVED PASSENGERS AND CREW FROM DOWNED AIR- CRAFT BERMUDA SKY QUEEN 800 MILES SOUTH OF ARGENTIA NFLD. PLANE SUNK. VALUE OF PROPERTY $1,000,000. 62 PASSEN- GERS AND 7 CREW MEMBERS ABOARD. ALL 69 SOB RESCUED.

A number of tax-paying ham operators tuning into Coast Guard frequencies years ago took exception to the Guard apparently referring to persons rescued as "sons of bitches." The Service bowed to the adage that says if you have to waste a lot of time explaining something, it's best to just go ahead and make the change. Consequently, in all future messages, the time-honored term SOB was changed to POB—or from "souls on board" to "persons on board."

But it is the Coast Guard's rescue capability that generally gets the headlines. Those confronted by any problem at sea—whether cargo ships and oil tankers bested by monstrous weather; fishing vessels or scallop draggers on the Grand Banks who have exhausted their fuel and their luck; or solo recreational boaters testing their fifteen-foot outboards beyond the breakwaters—all look to these sailors for a helping hand.

To deal with these jobs, the Guard has its own fleet of ships— everything from self-bailing, self-righting boats that can spin around 360 degrees in a roaring surf, to speedboats and large, oceangoing rescue cutters. It even has its own air force—choppers and long-range planes that operate out of dozens of air bases scattered around the country.

The Coast Guard acts directly in most cases, giving it a personal touch. If a ship is in danger far at sea, as was the case of the *Badger State*, it can also act indirectly through a program called AMVER, short for Automated Mutual-assistance VEssel Rescue. AMVER is a computer-driven, dead-reckoning plot on vessels who radio in periodic position reports. It's strictly a voluntary program, and takes extra time, but skippers recognize that one day it might be *their* turn to send out an SOS. The *Badger State*'s turn came on December 26.

Dick Hughes had just come from a meeting with the mate and the captain, and he immediately huddled with a few key men on his crew. They had a major problem, he told them. They were out of shoring, and the Old Man wanted loose stuff around the ship dumped into No. 5 to try to smother the flow of bombs. A way had to be devised to lift one of the pontoons covering No. 5 in order to gain access to the hold. A plan to do so gradually emerged: the crew would use the booms, stretched horizontally across the top of the pontoons, as anchor points for a block and tackle, a line would be rigged to run to one corner of the pontoon, and applying power to the line should be enough to lift a corner of the pontoon.

The plan was carried out. As Henderson explained:

We took the tarp off the forward end of Number Five and put straps around the booms. We then attached lines to the straps. We had a snatchblock on one side and a snatchblock on the other side. That didn't work and so we ran it through a shackle, secured it to the pontoon, and lifted the pontoon. As the ship rolled, we could see the bombs running from one side of the hold to the other; you could see where the bombs had punched holes in the side of the ship on the starboard side.

We started putting material in there. Started with the mooring lines; fed the lines from aft across the deck and down into the hold. We put in all the line we had back aft. We could see the bombs as they ran across the deck were creating a lot of sparks. And so we tried to make sure that the stuff we put in wouldn't be combustible.

We had a lot of material in the holds, just below the first pontoon, but we could see that the bombs were running in all parts of the hold. We had to get into those areas. So we took another line, moved a sling up, and then lifted the after pontoon up.

We put in mattresses, spare life jackets, personal effects, steward's stores, chairs, anything that was loose on the ship. We had enough in to slow the majority of the bombs down. We started bringing more line that we had aft and dropping it down through the masthouse. We couldn't seem to get enough material in.

Other men testified to that fact as well. Ordinary Seaman James McLure remembered meeting the bosun early on the morning of December 26.

I asked him if I should go on watch and he said, "Negative. We've got to get every available man down in the hold that we can possibly find." So we got everybody we could down there. George [Henderson] and I and Little Joe [Candos] worked on the hatch to open it.

It became daylight about 0700. The sea was a little bit calmer then. George and the bosun discussed what they should do to keep the bombs from sliding back and forth, and he says, "Red, I want you to bring the pallets and anything you can find and just drop it into the hold to stop it." We went down and took up all the line from the fantail and brought it up. The sea was just—well, you could just barely work, you know. One man thought he saw a Navy vessel twenty-five to thirty miles out at sea, but nobody else saw it. We kept working on Number Five hold. I was up on the hatch bringing these boards, throwing them in. The more gear we brought, the worse the sea got and the sea was just going back and forth. We had one heck of a time trying to save our own skins, let alone keep the bombs from shifting.

After we got all the line from the fantail to Number Five hold, then we went down in the galley, and started bringing up the sheets

and pillow cases and what have you, whatever was available, everything we could find—meat, chickens, sausage.

Wilson was on the open wing of the bridge. "You're doing well!
Keep it up, men! Keep going! We'll get through this!" he shouted down
to the men. Most looked up, and nodded or waved a hand.

After the crew finished its work, and as later reported to Wilson,
Hughes collared the mate for a joint check of the hold. The lines and
mattresses and other items thrown into the hold seemed to have helped
somewhat, but it was obvious that the moving bombs were beating down
the materials thrown in. However, a new danger grabbed their attention:
some of the decking that separated the upper tween deck hold from the
one below it had split open. Bombs were sliding through that opening into
the lower No. 5 hold. That bottom hold contained smaller bombs in pallets—2,000-pound bombs were dropping down onto 750-pound bombs.

Mate and bosun returned to the wheelhouse to brief Wilson on conditions in the hold. The danger of bombs falling on bombs in the lower
hold was obvious—it was metal-to-metal contact on a major scale—but
nothing could be done about it. The immediate focus would have to
remain on the 2,000-pounders. But, with the shoring gone, and with the
crew having scavenged up most of the loose stuff available, there was
nothing left to work with except the huge one-ton pontoons themselves.
Dumping in one or two of those might conceivably keep the bombs in
check, perhaps slow or stop their shifting. It might buy time, a factor
that grew more crucial with the passing of every day.

Dumping the pontoons into No. 5 was a desperate gambit by men
made desperate, a move no one aboard had ever experienced or heard of
before. Sheer size and weight posed real problems and considerable
danger. Lifting a pontoon by a corner was one thing. Lifting the whole
five-by-twenty-foot slab of steel, and then trying to kitty-corner it
through the hole it normally covered was quite another. Imagine tilting
the cover of a cardboard shoe box into the box itself, using string and a
hook. But this was far more complicated. For one, the location of the
booms directly over the hold crowded whatever workspace remained for

the crew to work in. For another, the rolling of the ship made handling a pontoon a threat to life and limb. If the crew lost control of it—a real possibility—the one-ton cover might caterwauler across the deck like a giant scythe, cutting down everyone in its path, or maybe carry somebody over the side. A seaman overboard would be dead—no one could possibly be rescued in the waters that raged around the ship.

Even if they could somehow pull it off and get the pontoons into No. 5 hold, Wilson wondered, *What then?* The pontoons themselves might in some fashion join the bombs careening across the hold, adding another huge battering ram to the melée below.

Captain and crew were in uncharted waters, but, Wilson reflected, it was a risk they had to take. They had run out of any conceivable form of shoring—everything had been swallowed up in the hold. The bombs were still loose; there was no rescue ship on hand; and they were still a long stretch from the nearest safe port.

Wilson told the mate and the bosun to go ahead with the work, but to use as few men as possible. He then pulled the mate aside and the two men discussed their mutual concerns about the ship's predicament and about the crew sliding the pontoon into the hold. Both recognized they were running out of options. Wilson told him that he had sent out the SOS, and that he hoped that help would soon be on the way.

After the mate left, Wilson watched from the open wing of the bridge. The bosun was bossing a handful of seamen gathered around the pontoons covering No. 5 hold. In the thick of it was Henderson, who remembered the problems they had:

> We had a hard time getting the pontoon to drop in. We couldn't drop the first pontoon because there is a lip on the coaming, so we moved our gear to the second pontoon. Because of the booms laying in their cradles over the hatch, it did not allow enough room to pull the pontoons to one side or the other. So we tried to upset the pontoon by jerking it. As the ship rolled, we jerked the pontoon and one end, the port side, fell in on the material that we had in the hold. This secured a number of bombs that were on the port side.

The pontoon was down in the hold at an angle with one end up; about two or three feet of it was sticking up out over the coaming. We waited for the roll of the ship to carry it down into the hold.

It worked and the pontoon gradually slid out of sight into No. 5 hold.

So calm and dispassionate a report leaves out the tumult one can only imagine. Rain and sleet poured down at intervals on the heads of the men; the deck beneath their feet threatened to throw them down and maybe overboard; the ship continued its jerky twelve-second rolling; and oceans of water still inundated the ship. On this slippery, slanting, roller coaster platform, a small band of seamen, untrained in longshore work, jury-rigged and lifted a ton of awkwardly shaped steel off its base, and then slid the whole of it through the smaller opening it covered. All too likely, that ton of steel, free of its base, could have wiped the deck clean of everything in its path, but the *Badger State*'s crew did it.

The hope was that the pontoon would help to stymie the motion of the bombs. But reports from the mate grew increasingly pessimistic. The bombs were still roaming loose, he told the Captain, flattening everything.

Below deck, the crew shared the mate's pessimism. While morale seemed to be holding up well, there were disturbing signs of increased concern. "There was the feeling that we were in trouble," Bordash said. "When I was talking to the bosun, he had told me one of the other crew members had been in Number Five to reinspect it—excuse me—at Number Five, the term used was "gone". I guess he was referring to the load being beyond control. We knew that there was a layer of large bombs in that hold. I kind of felt sorry for the bosun at the time because I thought the man was totally exhausted. I knew that he had been on his feet almost day and night from possibly the second day out of port, trying to secure the cargo."

The concerns about the problems in No. 5 hold seemed justified. In spite of everything thrown in, the bombs there pretty much had a free run, with nothing in the way to stop them. Most of the other C-2 ships had a barrier in the middle of the hold, a centerline bulkhead, or wall, in the tween decks that divided the hold into two halves. The bulkhead was missing on the *Badger State*, probably removed when the ship was converted to a troop carrier during World War II.

But Wilson didn't need any reports from his key men to understand the seriousness of the problem. He could hear it, loud and clear, the banging of metal against metal. The steeper the roll, the more horrific the noise. He could even feel it, the deck shuddering beneath his feet as bombs crashed into each other in No. 5 hold.

CHAPTER 11

One Last Hope

The *Badger State*'s radio officer prefaced the ship's SOS with four long dashes, a signal that triggered an automatic alarm on ships sailing within roughly a two-hundred-mile radius. The signal rang bells on the motor vessel *Khian Star,* a foreign-flag merchant ship out of Piraeus, Greece, underway within the area.

Without the alarm, the SOS would have disappeared into nowhere since the MV *Khian Star*'s radio officer was off duty. That also happened to the *Titanic*. After that ship crashed into an iceberg, her radio officer keyed the distress symbol CQD as well as SOS. The ship *Carpathia* received the message and turned about in response, but she was hours away. The *Titanic* needed help immediately. Close by, however, and in position to rescue *Titanic*'s desperate crew and passengers, sailed the liner *Californian,* en route from London to Boston. Brief radio contact had taken place earlier between the two ships. The *Californian* attempted to inform the other of ice in the area, but was curtly told, "Shut up! I am busy." Rebuffed, and it being the end of a long day, the radio officer clicked off the ship's radio and turned in for the night, effectively shutting down the ship's ability to receive messages of any kind.

Marconi began experimenting with a means of dealing with this problem. A simple concept eventually emerged: a sequence of Morse code signals, four or more dashes of four seconds duration each, would trigger a bell in the radio shack, the bridge, and the radio officer's sleeping quarters of the receiving ships. The system worked and is now mandatory for all maritime nations.

Radio Officer Dimitrios Kosmas, awakened by the bell ringing aboard the *Khian Star*, took down the distress message. He at once passed the word to Evangelos Niros, the master of the ship. Captain Niros, a handsome man, thin, slightly built, and with an intense air about him, ran a check on the *Badger*'s position, calculating it to be roughly forty miles east of the *Khian Star*. He reversed the ship's course and headed toward the position given by the stricken vessel.

Wilson could not have contacted a better-equipped ship and, as it turned out, a more helpful and compassionate crew. The 466-foot-long *Khian Star* had barely slid off the shipyard ways, having been built in a Tokyo shipyard earlier in 1969. She boasted the latest technology, including an automated engine room featuring diesel engines directly controlled by the master from the wheelhouse. No need for oilers and firemen and wipers below—the ship got by with three engineers and two apprentices. For that reason, and despite her size, she carried a total crew of only twenty seamen, half that of the *Badger State*.

The *Khian Star* had cast off her mooring lines on December 12 at Portland, Oregon. There, giant funnels at a grain elevator—huge cylindrical concrete silos fronting the harbor—blew some 14,000 tons of grain into the ship's holds, destined for delivery in Yokohama, Japan. The grain was loaded loose in bulk—master and crew of the *Khian Star* had no call to worry about crumbling pallets.

Wind and sea played no favorites in the north Pacific, hammering the *Khian Star* as badly as it had the *Badger State*. "I have been making trips to Japan since 1957," noted Captain Niros, a seafarer for over seventeen years, "and I have never before seen such continuous bad weather, with the seas so high and the winds so strong. The highest waves were forty feet, and there were many of these. On the 25th, the wind force was 8, 9, and 10; on the 26th, it was 9 to 10."

Winds of that magnitude are considered gale-force, ranging from forty-seven to sixty-three miles per hour. The effect was predictable. Waves slammed over the bow of the *Khian Star*, reaching all the way up to the bridge, situated some forty feet above the water at the stern. Wind and waves combined to slow the ship down to about one-half its normal speed of 13.5 knots.

Captain Niros's actions in immediately heading his ship to the scene stemmed from a humanitarian urge to help fellow seamen in need. In some cases, such an impulse might also involve the law of salvage which, in its earliest form, provided that one who preserved another's property was entitled to compensation from the owner. A "volunteer adventurer," one court called it, one having no connection to the ship in need.

Rescuing a sinking ship is the first thought that comes to mind in terms of salvage. But also reclaiming marine property from pirates qualifies. One unique salvage case involved two ships, both needing help.

The captain of the American brigantine *F. I. Merryman*, sailing to Boston in 1886, died of an unknown sickness. Unfortunately, he was the only navigator aboard. The ship, a distress flag fluttering from her mast, without the eyes and calculations of her master to guide her, sailed aimlessly until, by accident, she stumbled upon the German bark *Friederick Scalla,* a sister ship also flying a distress flag. The *Scalla* had sprung a leak and was in immediate danger of going to the bottom. A happy encounter between singles looking for a partner, as it turned out. Skipper and crew of the German ship abandoned her to the deep and boarded the American ship. The German master then helped the American ship find its way to a safe port. In the matter of who saved whom, the court gave the award to the German skipper. He had saved the *Merryman*, the court reasoned, by guiding the ship to a safe harbor.

Even a paying passenger on a liner might get a salvage award, provided he did more than merely man the pumps, handle lines, or lower the lifeboat. Some extraordinary contribution was needed. Mr. Candee rendered such unusual assistance while he was a passenger aboard a river steamer in the late 1800s. As fire swept through the ship, the crew threw overboard flaming bales of cotton. With the fire out, the ship's master ordered his crew to retrieve the cotton. Half of them threatened to desert rather than do so. Mr. Candee, an enterprising person, offered each man three dollars to do the work. They accepted the offer and, under his direction, recovered a part of the ship's cargo. The passenger walked away with the salvage prize.

Aboard the *Khian Star*, Captain Niros was undoubtedly preoccupied with more pressing concerns. Now on her new course, he radioed the *Badger State*: WE ARE PROCEEDING TO YOU. WE'LL BE THERE THREE HOURS LATER.

Shortly after that, the ship sent a second message: WHAT KIND OF DAMAGES DO YOU HAVE?

From the *Badger State*: WE ARE BREAKING UP. CANNOT GIVE YOU MORE INFO DUE HEAVY ROLLING.

The *Khian Star* again: OK. DO NOT SCARE. WE ARE COMING TO YOU.

Preparing for rescue, Captain Niros ordered his crew to gather lines, pilot ladders, net slings, and life jackets to be dropped over the side. Launching the ship's lifeboat was not an option, given the rough state of the weather.

A later exchange of messages followed:

Khian Star:	WHAT IS YOUR CARGO?
Badger State:	HAVE BOMBS ON BOARD AS CARGO. THEY ARE LOOSE. WHAT ARE YOU DOING TO HELP US?
Khian Star:	WEATHER PERMITTING, HAVE YOUR LIFEBOATS READY.
Badger State:	[No answer.]

Knowing that the *Badger State* carried bombs in her holds had to have worried Captain Niros—they presented an element of risk, the extent of which could not be gauged. He had his own responsibility to his crew and to the owners of the ship. Despite the potential danger, however, he proceeded at maximum speed to the *Badger State*. At the same time, concerned about his crew's possible adverse reaction, he ordered his officers to keep news of the bombs confidential.

At 7:30 A.M., the *Badger State* showed up as a blip on the radar screen of the *Khian Star*. Captain Niros, anticipating arrival within half an hour, ordered his crew to prepare to stand by their rescue stations.

The *Badger State* was a disaster waiting to happen. Bombs roamed around in her belly, threatening unimaginable consequences. The ship could only limp along at reduced speed. Diversion orders, a jumble of words on paper, had no prospect of being carried out. The ship could only stumble along in fits and starts, with Wilson continually trying to nudge it south toward Midway and Pearl. Given such a pessimistic outlook, the *Khian Star*'s message, crackling across the divide of an angry sea, would seem to be timely and comforting.

It was, and yet Wilson found himself confused by a swirl of conflicting emotions. On the one hand, he was relieved to know that a rescue ship was nearby. On the other, it disturbed him that he and his crew were in the position of needing any help at all. Those feelings may have stemmed from the fact that, to an outside observer, the ship appeared to be seaworthy. It still floated on an even keel; the crew stood by to carry out orders; and the engines remained ready to do the master's bidding.

Still, while harboring misgivings about abandoning the ship, Wilson realized ship and crew had to prepare for that possibility. A semblance of a plan began to take shape in his mind. He conferred with the mate, reviewing his plans for action when the *Khian Star* arrived. If forced to leave, the crew would go in the only boat left, the starboard lifeboat.

Enough volunteers would need to remain aboard to get the lifeboat safely over the side. Once that was done, the volunteers would use the ship's life rafts to try to make it to the rescue ship. Department heads needed to be checked to see how many men would be willing to stay aboard with him to launch the lifeboat. The mate volunteered himself, but Wilson told him he would be needed as senior officer in the lifeboat.

The *Badger State*'s two lifeboats were attached, bow and stern, to cradle-like metal davits by separate wires that led through a series of pulleys to a winch. With this type of davit, no power is needed to lower the boat; gravity moves it down. Once a boat dropped into the water, a releasing gear frees the boat from the falls fore and aft simultaneously.

Such boats have certain special characteristics: both ends are shaped like a bow to increase maneuverability and seaworthiness; built-in air tanks or buoyant materials keep them afloat should they sink or capsize; and grab rails, riveted to the outside of the boat, provide a seaman the means of clinging to an overturned boat while awaiting rescue.

While some boats have oars or even diesel engines, the *Badger State* had hand-propelling gear. Crewmembers provided the horsepower, pushing and pulling lever handles, sticks they called them, to send power to the boat's propeller. It was precisely the type of complicated gear, Wilson remembered, that never seemed to work properly when it was most needed.

A number of essential items were stowed in the lifeboat: bailing bucket; bilge pump; hooks; compass; hatchets; lantern (with a nine-hour supply of oil); portable mast and sail; matches; storm oil to spread on the water to help prevent breaking seas; and a sizeable package of other items that conceivably might come in handy for a crew in a small boat floating on the open ocean.

With all this gear, it would seem that a sailor or passenger might have little concern about safety. If the ship must be abandoned, one jumps into the lifeboat that is then dropped into the water, and off one goes to the rescue ship waiting conveniently nearby. That neat scenario probably works well when a ship is moored at a dock, or floating in a dead calm sea. Unfortunately, ships are abandoned in the worst possible sea conditions—huge waves; rain and sleet; high winds; rolling and pitching. Given such circumstances, the launching of the boat is often an exercise in confusion: shouting, crying crew and passengers, all desperately hanging on; the boat banging back and forth against the mother ship; touching water, only to find the releasing gear malfunctioning, with the boat being yanked out of the water and unexpectedly slammed back into it; or worse of all, being upended and thrown into the water.

Small wonder, then, that a recent study made over a ten-year period by the Marine Accident Investigation Branch of the United Nations International Maritime Organization suggested that "anyone using a lifeboat, be it in a drill or a genuine evacuation, runs a risk of being injured or even killed." The most significant problems were blamed on the handling of power winches and release hooks. The study went so far as to question the need for a ship to carry any lifeboats at all, arguing that they are "a legacy of conditions applicable in the early twentieth century and before." The crew of the *Badger State*, oblivious to the report, was grateful to have some means of leaving the ship behind them.

One way to deal with the real-world problems cited by the study was through practice. Regular boat drills are mandatory for most ships like the *Badger State*. Such drills are typically low-key affairs without too many hands paying much attention. However, for James Beatty, one crew member who had experienced the real thing, boat drills were a serious matter. "I'll never laugh at another boat drill," he said. "They are very necessary!"

Still, when the time came for the *Badger State*, a lifeboat was the only option. And once past the initial pitfalls, the tenacity and will of the human spirit to survive in one sometimes borders on the miraculous. Poon Lim, a Chinese steward on the British ship *Benlomond*, torpedoed in the Atlantic in 1942, survived for 133 days until being rescued. Malnourished and unable to walk, he recovered, and was said to be anxious to return to sea.

Another notable example of perseverance by the crew was the Lykes Line SS *Prusa*, torpedoed a hundred miles off the coast of Hawaii during World War II. She went down quickly, springing loose her deck cargo of mahogany logs that shot rapidly to the surface. Four boats were launched. Two of them succumbed to battering by logs and seas; the remaining boats set sail for land. The Coast Guard rescued the men in one boat twelve days later; the other lifeboat, holed and leaking badly, remained lost at sea. The crew plugged the leaks with their clothing, yarn, cotton, anything available, and bailed water constantly. Without controls, the boat drifted near the equator where the men were exposed to intense heat by day and a shivering chill by night. Several died of exposure. The emergency rations and water that had been stowed aboard kept most of the men alive. Thirty-one days later, the boat made it to the Gilbert Islands after a voyage estimated at 2,700 miles.

Strangest of all perhaps was the story of Jesse Roper Morohovicic. Reversing the tradition of naming ships after individuals, his mother named him after a ship, the destroyer USS *Jesse Roper* that rescued them both. The child survived birth in a lifeboat that was launched from the torpedoed SS *City of New York* during World War II—the ship was evacuating his pregnant mother and other consular employees, including a physician, from Nairobi. The doctor delivered Jesse in the lifeboat.

With its many potential problems, the lifeboat offered the only reasonable means of escape from the beleaguered *Badger State*. Wilson gave one final order to the mate: he wanted every man aboard to strap on a life jacket. He also shared with Cobbs the hope that after most of the men were seen safely off, he and the other volunteers remaining aboard might still be able to save the ship. If that didn't work, then perhaps the crew in the lifeboat might somehow be able to return to take them off the vessel.

It was that incredible desire to somehow still salvage his ship that drove Wilson on. *His* ship—that was the key word. Only another seafarer, faced with the loss of his ship could truly understand that emotional feeling.

The Standard Oil tanker SS *Esso Bolivar*, for one, found itself in far greater danger of sinking. One of her officers, knowing he was on a ship beyond hope of saving, seemed to echo the emotional feelings that consumed Wilson.

The *Bolivar* departed Newport News in February 1942 bound for Aruba to pick up a cargo of oil. While off Guantanamo Bay, Cuba, she came under gunfire from a submarine apparently intent on saving its torpedoes for bigger game. The ship broadcast an SOS. Then ensued a one-sided demolition derby, the American ship being unable to bring the sub under the guns of its armed guard.

Shells began to explode on the *Bolivar* as the sub zeroed in on its target. Shrapnel put the radio out of commission; the galley exploded in flames, shooting a fireball fifty feet into the air; flames quickly spread throughout the ship, bulkheads caving in from the intense heat; cylinders of acetylene stored on deck contributed to the conflagration; 300 gallons of paint in storage near the engine room exploded in flames; a shell toppled the smoke stack; shrapnel destroyed the fire room; gunfire killed the captain and, later, shot down the mate; and shells destroyed the steering gear, causing the rudderless and leaderless ship to roam wildly in a tight circle. A crewmember finally sounded the abandon-ship signal.

Engulfed in chaos and pandemonium, Chief Engineer Thomas J. McTaggart calmly said, "I decided to stay a few minutes. If we could leave the engines and boilers in good shape, we could save the tanker if there was any possibility of coming back. We still had lights in the engine room and it seemed a shame to run off and let everything go to pieces." The good chief did finally leave in a lifeboat riddled by shrapnel but kept afloat by the boat's air tanks. A shell killed the mate in charge of the boat. Chief McTaggart, suffering shrapnel wounds, took over.

The *Esso Bolivar,* still afloat but fortunately not carrying her usual cargo of oil, withstood the storm of torpedoes and gunfire aimed at her by the enemy sub. A wounded chief engineer and thirteen survivors, with Navy help, later reboarded a battered and still blazing ship. Thanks to McTaggart's earlier precautions, they were able to bring the burning ship, under her own power, into port. Eventually, "McTaggert's miracle," as the deck crew aptly took to describing the ship, was put back together and returned to the high seas to sail again. President Franklin D. Roosevelt bestowed on Chief McTaggart the Merchant Marine Distinguished Service Medal, the citation praising, "His extraordinary courage and disregard of danger to life or limb in the protection of his vessel constitute a fidelity to trust which will be an enduring inspiration to seamen of the United States merchant marine everywhere."

Another skipper, Captain John Cameron of the sailing ship *Beluga* expressed his feelings at witnessing the destruction of his ship. The *Beluga* departed San Francisco in May 1917, bound for Sydney, Australia, with a cargo of 15,000 cases of benzine in her holds. Also aboard was the captain's wife and six-year-old daughter; little danger was expected as the ship's route would be thousands of miles away from the World War I zone of hostilities.

However, the *Beluga* crossed the path of another vessel, one flying the German imperial navy ensign at her jackstaff, that signaled to the *Beluga* to heave to. The German ship uncovered its guns and fired a shot across the *Beluga*'s bow. The captain was understandably shocked to have been stopped by a German raider in the south Pacific, 15,000 miles from any war zone.

A small boat filled with German seaman soon came alongside. An officer stepped aboard the *Beluga*, saluted, and questioned the skipper in excellent English. The Germans then searched the ship and confiscated everything of value. Captain Cameron, his family, and all his crew were taken back to the German ship. The raider chose to destroy the *Beluga* by gunfire.

Cameron watched as a shell hit amidship of the *Beluga*, igniting the benzine cargo which flung burning petrol for miles. He observed:

For some time the beauty of the sight caused me to forget that it was our little home that was burning. There were a great many satisfied "aahs" from the German crew as the ship disappeared; a general feeling of satisfaction among them. For myself, I am afraid there was a tear in my eye, and all that I can wish these destroyers of good, honest ships is that sometime when they are standing around with empty bellies waiting for a chance to earn a living as a sailor, they may think of how they smiled when they sunk these ships. I can understand a landsman sinking a ship and thinking it a joke, but a sailor, to my mind, should feel sad at seeing the end of an honest vessel, whether she belong to friend or enemy.

Driven by similar emotions, Wilson was not about to give up. One last option remained to save the *Badger State*. If that failed, they would have to abandon ship. All of them. Together.

CHAPTER 12

Khian Star

S hip off the port bow!" bellowed the lookout on the wing of the *Badger State*'s bridge, his words swallowed up in the howling shriek of the winds battering the ship. The seaman turned, water curling down the whiskers of his unprotected face, and banged on the porthole. Wilson glanced up. The lookout repeated the words, mouthing them silently as he pointed frantically toward a point off the ship's bow.

Wilson waved in acknowledgment, straining to see through a dense curtain of swirling rain and rampaging water ahead. Gradually, the unearthly outline of a dark hull and the stick-like structure of masts rising and falling began to take shape. It seemed hardly more than a phantom, in view one moment, out of sight the next.

Wilson inhaled deeply, letting the air out slowly with a rasping sigh of relief. "There can only be one other ship in this godforsaken place," he said to Bob Ziehm, the second mate by his side on the bridge. A message crackled through the radio, choked with static. It was from Captain Niros, *Khian Star*, to *Badger State*: ARE YOUR LIFEBOATS READY?

Given the breakdown in the ship's cargo holds, the answer would seem simple enough. But there were other matters to mull over. The Navy's order, unchanged, directed Wilson to continue on assignment. A second one, given only hours earlier, directed the ship to divert to Midway. Coupled with those orders was a reluctance by captain and crew—evidenced by a report from the mate that the entire crew had elected to remain aboard with Wilson—to leave the security of their home at sea for the savagery of the unknown elements that surrounded them.

It was the unknown that gave them pause. In the remote ocean setting, winds blow fiercely, roiling the seas into mountainous waves. Storms follow like clockwork, with nature giving no quarter. But somehow a seafarer's puny ship, even as it tosses, pitches, and rolls, sees them safely through the worst of it. A ship, a patchwork thing of metal and wires and a sailor's gear, breeds confidence, and a rough affection, in a high-stakes game.

For the captain, there is also the emotional and practical link that arises from the assumption of enormous responsibility. The multimillion-dollar investment represented by the value of ship and cargo rests on his shoulders. Karl Barslaag, writing in *Famous Sea Rescues,* refers to the "voluminous rules and regulations of the government, seemingly forgotten until after a disaster, when they are dusted off by the prosecutors and rubbed under the noses of the surviving victims. Ships are operated to make money," he added, "and to complete their voyages speedily and woe unto the luckless captain who forgets these cardinal commitments."

Much more important to Wilson, however, was that the law of the sea entrusted to his care the safety of every seaman aboard, symbolized by the tradition that the captain be the last to leave a distressed ship. Examples of such bravery abound. Ironically, however, Wilson need not look far to find a classic example of it close to home: the captain of the *Panoceanic Faith,* sister ship of the *Badger State.*

The sisters were built simultaneously on adjoining ways at a North Carolina shipyard toward the end of World War II. One of the ships, assigned Keel No. 102, was christened the SS *Midnight* at launching. The other, Keel No. 103, was christened the SS *Starlight.*

Both ships subsequently changed ownership and names: the *Midnight* became the SS *Panoceanic Faith*, the *Starlight* the *Badger State.* They seemed to have little in common except for their dates of construction and their classification as C-2s. But there was another, less apparent similarity.

The *Panoceanic Faith* had sailed from San Francisco barely more than two winters earlier, bound for Bombay by way of Yokohama. Ten thousand tons of bulk ammonium sulphate, a salt-like material used primarily as a fertilizer, filled her holds. No need to worry about palletized cargo—the sulphate was loaded loose in bulk directly into the holds.

Several days after sailing, the captain radioed that the ship was encountering "boisterous weather" and that he had cut the ship's speed. In later messages, he reported the ship being slammed by continuous gale winds and mountainous seas; the crew being forced to jury-rig numerous repairs to boilers, condensers and auxiliaries; and noted that the ship was running short of fuel and water. Consequently, because of continuous gale winds and leaking boiler tubes, he cut the ship's speed to four knots (about four and a half land miles per hour).

The ship was then sailing on the north Pacific, on a route similar to that later followed by the *Badger State*. The master, perhaps surmising that safer waters might lie south of their course, tried several times to bring the ship about to a southerly heading. Wind and sea proved too much, forcing the ship back on her northerly track where she remained for the duration of the voyage.

Several days later, the ship began taking on extremely heavy seas over the bow. Worse, part of the tarpaulin covering No. 1 hatch, the closest to the bow, tore adrift, allowing water to find its way into the ship. Two days later, the *Panoceanic Faith* began to list to starboard, a sure sign that the ocean had breached the ship's watertight integrity.

The inexorable march of calamitous events quickly forced the master to order all hands to put on life jackets and stand by for an emergency. A sheaf of radio messages told the story of a ship headed for tragedy: Taking water in No. 1 and No. 2 holds; Requesting ships in the area to standby to render assistance; Developing a heavy starboard list; Violence of seas and swells intensifying; Unable to increase speed due to boiler problems. Finally, in desperation, the master broadcast an SOS.

In the early morning hours of October 9, 1967, the *Panoceanic Faith* again began to list heavily to starboard, ship and ocean becoming locked in a death embrace. The crew tried to launch one of the lifeboats. A mechanical failure upended the boat, throwing some two dozen frightened seamen to their deaths in the frigid waters of the north Pacific. The ship's list increased to 35 degrees. Barely a few seconds later, the *Panoceanic Faith* went down with most of her crew, five surviving to tell her story. Her master was last seen bravely standing on the port wing of the bridge, piloting his ship into oblivion.

The heroics in a few cases defy description. The fully loaded tanker *Esso Nashville* was under way in March 1942, bound for New Haven, Connecticut, when she was torpedoed. Captain Edward V. Peters reported that "a terrific crash occurred on the starboard side abaft the midship house, raising the vessel up bodily and throwing her to starboard and then keeling her to port so violently that I feared she was going to turn over. The entire ship was flooded with oil which spouted as high as the foremast; dense smoke and sparks emanated from the explosion of the torpedo."

Captain Peters at once ordered the crew to abandon the ship. As the boats were being lowered, he dutifully struggled to return to the bridge to get the codebook and other secret documents aboard—Naval orders required that he pitch these critical documents over the side. But smoke and fire stopped him in his tracks. He then scrambled back to the lifeboat. Reaching it, he lost his balance and skidded across the oil-slick deck into the sea, breaking his leg and crushing his chest. The crew managed to get the boat over. Captain Peters, fighting for his life in the oil-covered water, but fearful that the crew might be killed if the boat slammed into the ship, bravely ordered the boat away.

A testament to the will to survive, the captain then floated himself over to the midship section of the tanker where the ship's deck was awash, crawled back to the engineers' quarters, and roughly bandaged a badly swollen leg. To let the world know the ship had not been completely abandoned, he strung a white sheet alongside a ship's rail and hoisted the ship's ensign on the flagstaff aft of the tanker. If the ship finally went down, he was prepared to go with it.

Fate decreed otherwise as he was subsequently rescued by an American vessel, and part of the ship salvaged. The torpedo had broken the "back" of the tanker with the bow eventually separating and drifting away. Navy tugs towed the floating after section, the engine room still intact, to a shipyard. A new forward section was grafted on and, ten months later, a rejuvenated *Esso Nashville* returned to the battle zone.

But it was the fate of the *Panoceanic Faith* that seemed most disturbing to Wilson. The similarities were eerie. Sisters born at the same time and place; sailing the north Pacific in winter; encountering storms and violent seas; the master unable to bring the ship to a southerly heading; boiler and equipment problems; and a series of inexorable events leading to emergency conditions. The *Badger State,* sailing in the same general area, seemed headed toward the same fate that had claimed the *Panoceanic Faith*.

Wilson reached a decision based on a simple premise: act on the courage of your convictions. He had never forgotten Captain George Fredrick Lindholm, who did exactly that, leaving an indelible mark on an earnest, impressionable, young Cadet Wilson.

It happened on the Grace Lines SS *Santa Juana*, Captain Lindholm commanding. Wilson was then in his "sea year" at Kings Point, getting on-the-job training as a deck cadet. It was a taste of what his future would become.

The cruise south hit most of the "dog holes" on the coast, including Buenaventura, Guayaquil, Chimbote, Callao, Mollendo, and a brief stopover at Antofogasta, Chile.

Then came Chanaral, an incident that marked the first occasion on which Deck Cadet Wilson was called upon to offer written testimony:

30 May 1952

Statement: Striking unknown submerged object on arrival Chanaral, Chile, 27 May 1952

We were proceeding, as usual, under the pilot's direction to the buoys and anchorage at Chanaral, Chile, 27 May 1952. The captain, pilot and second mate were on the starboard wing of the bridge. The helmsman and the deck cadet were in the wheelhouse.

The wheel was hard left and the engines full ahead. The master, Capt. Lindholm, ordered the cadet to turn the ship's searchlight on the beach off the starboard bow. This was done. The wheel was ordered amidships by the pilot. The Captain countermanded this by ordering the wheel put hard right. The order hard right was obeyed. We then apparently touched a submerged object a few seconds later. On touching, the pilot ordered the engines put full astern. The Captain countermanded this order by putting the engines on stop. The ship then cleared the object.

Charles T. Wilson, U.S.M.S., U.S.N.R.

Ships' pilots typically are former oceangoing masters and mates who have acquired specialized knowledge of a local port. They hire out that knowledge and talent to oceangoing ships looking for entry into, or departure from, a port.

Countermanding the orders of a pilot, one employed specifically because of his background and knowledge of local conditions, is not an everyday event. It wants a stiff backbone by the master, and a strong conviction to go with it. He can do so—he is charged with the overall responsibility for the safety of ship and crew—but if his actions are ill-advised, his license and reputation may be at risk.

Captain Lindholm's decisions were prompted by his close observations of the harbor and his prior experiences there. If he had not countermanded the pilot's orders, the *Santa Juana* would have sustained heavy prop damage that would have guaranteed expensive repairs in a shipyard. As it was, the ship sustained minor damage to its bilge keel.

The lesson, and the courage Lindholm displayed, stayed with Wilson for the rest of his sailing days. And it now helped him make up his mind. Conferring with the mate, Wilson laid out his plan: they would make one final attempt to carry out the last diversion order, to put the ship on course to Midway. If that didn't work, only then would the crew abandon ship.

It was an overcast day, intermittent rain mixing with sleet. Sky and sea blended into a single seamless blanket, a mottled, dark-gray shroud pressing down hard on the ship. Waves leaped high, and strong winds whipped spray off the crests in tattered streaks of foam. Swells, in confused ranks, marched endlessly across the ocean.

Wilson heaved open the door of the wheelhouse and stepped outside onto the open wing of the bridge. He grabbed the railing with one hand, shielding his eyes from the rain with the other. He checked the open deck, fore and aft. Not a man could be seen on the cold, wet expanse— the mate had seen to it that all hands were safely inside. Hatches were closed and dogged down tight, and the starboard lifeboat hung over the water, ready to be lowered.

Satisfied, Wilson returned to the wheelhouse. "Stand by," he told Ziehm. "I'll handle this." He grabbed the sound-powered phone connected to the engine room, turning a hand crank with his free hand. After a pause, the rasping voice of Third Engineer Kinnie Woods could be heard. "Yes, sir."

"I want full speed ahead, every RPM you can squeeze out," Wilson ordered.

"Aye, aye, sir. Full speed ahead!"

Wilson waited until the telltale sounds of the engines being revved up reached his ears. He felt a slight tingling in his fingers as the ship, driven by the powerful thrust of her engines, began to vibrate. *It's now or never*, he told himself, as he turned to the helmsman. "Hard left," he ordered, his voice crackling with tension.

"Hard left, sir," the seaman replied, grabbing the spokes of the wheel and spinning it in the direction of the turn.

The *Badger State* slowly began to heed her rudder, bucking against a wall of water that rose to resist her motion. The seas spilled over the side of the bow. The vessel lurched sideways, then began to pitch violently fore and aft. Heavy swells caught the ship on her port beam, resisting the turn. The sheer brute power of the ship's engines could force the *Badger State* around to a new southerly course and overcome the enormous resistance posed by wind and water. But Wilson, his eyes taking in the seas surrounding him, sensed a far more serious problem: the ship would be subjected to greatly intensified rolling while turning, as well as when it reached its new southerly heading. Increased rolling would generate more pressure—the very force they were desperately trying to avoid—on what was left of the broken-down bomb containers.

"Ease off," Wilson ordered, "ease off, damn it. Ease off!" The sharp tone of his voice, ringing through the tension-filled wheelhouse, betrayed the bitterness that seemed to consume him. The helmsman quickly returned the wheel to amidship. The *Badger State* began to settle uneasily in the seaway, rolling steeply from side to side.

"We're taking a beating in Number Five, Cap'n," Ziehm said suddenly in a high-pitched voice.

His senses at fever pitch, Wilson could feel the movement of the bombs, and hear the bedlam in No. 5 tween deck hold, the hammer blows of metal banging against metal. Grim reality set in. There was no way he could get the ship to a southerly heading—and no way he could continue on the present northerly course. It was all over. They had to abandon ship.

"Need to get the damned lifeboat over," he muttered to himself, going over the drill in his mind. "Need to cut speed and get the boat into the water."

He rang up the engine room. "Bring her down to half speed," he barked. "Now!" The words were barely out of his mouth when the jarring sound of an explosion reverberated throughout the ship. Wilson's heart jumped as shock waves rippled through the metal deck under his feet. The explosion came from aft, and Wilson knew instantly what had happened.

Below deck, George Henderson recalled the event:

I went up to see the bosun. I met him in the passageway, and he said, "get everyone off the deck; we are going to try and make a run for Midway." So I went back on the starboard side and there were a number of fellows still there. I told them to go in the midship house. Then I went back aft, and there was the day man, McHugh, and AB Joe Candos. We all went back up the deck. For some reason, we stopped and closed the resistor house door. We went up the port side and stepped through the hatch. We were dogging the door when there was an explosion and looking out through the glass, you could see fire and smoke. Alarm sounded then.

Earlier, James Beatty also met the bosun, who told him, "I want everybody off the deck. We have nothing left; there is nothing more to put down on these bombs. All we can do is pray to God and I want everybody off the deck and back inside the house!" Beatty went inside at that time, and

I got my wallet, my seaman's papers, my discharges, my union receipts, my passport, and my wife's wedding ring. I put them in my pockets along with a new package of Salem cigarettes. We were having tremendous difficulty trying to remain on our feet. The ship was rolling, plunging, pitching, tossing. Then the explosion occurred. I ran inside and looked down in the engine room. I saw the fireman and oiler come running out with life jackets on. I put one on. Then I saw Bordash and Woods coming through the alleyway from the engine room and they had life jackets on. I knew there was nobody left there. I ran back up the ladder and up to the boat deck. I ran back on the boat deck and I could see the smoke boiling out of Number Five hold.

The explosion could be seen from a distance of four to five miles. Captain Niros, aboard the *Khian Star*, saw plainly a flash of light on the *Badger State*, followed by black smoke pouring out from the after end of the vessel.

Following the explosion, Wilson ran out to the port wing of the bridge, and strained to see aft of the ship. Several of the huge pontoons which had covered No. 5 hold were upended like a giant hand of playing cards, blown off by the force of the explosion. Black smoke from the explosion billowed out, highlighted by tongues of flames flashing in the dark interior of the hold.

Wilson clambered down to the main deck, moving quickly. The rain swept over him, pelting his face and uncovered head. Scurrying aft, he instinctively reached out to grab handrails and lifelines to keep from being pitched over the side of the steeply rolling ship. He caught glimpses of his men as they began to pour out on deck.

Reaching the vicinity of No. 5, he ducked under the curtain of black smoke shooting out of the hold. An odd stench of burning metal and cooked beef filled his nostrils. Bits and pieces of kapok-filled life jackets, along with charred meat and other debris the crew had used to smother the loose bombs, were now fueling the blaze.

Wilson rushed back to the wheelhouse, and at once ordered Ziehm to sound the alarm. The watch officer moved quickly to grab the wooden handle of a line dangling from overhead. He pulled on it hard, and a mournful requiem sounded through the wind and rain. Ziehm pulled on the line seven more times, holding it down seconds longer on the last whistle. The sequence of seven short blasts, followed by a long blast, signaled the crew to abandon the *Badger State*.

The moment had come. Swaddled in bulky life jackets, seamen spilled out on deck. Nondescript dungarees bore the stains and rips of hard work in tight spaces. Most of the men sported a week's growth of whiskers camouflaging sunken cheeks. Their bloodshot eyes automatically looked upward to the flying bridge and their captain for guidance.

Wilson stared back at them. He felt an overwhelming sadness for these men who had gone through incredible hardships and yet had risen to meet the challenge. "Don't give up!" he shouted to them. "A rescue ship is nearby. We'll get through this somehow if we pull together!"

The thirty-foot-long metal boat dangled over the sea, swinging precariously. Davits, with wire lines ending in metal hooks, linked the boat fore and aft to the ship. A hand brake controlled the lines. After the men were aboard, the brake would be released, allowing gravity to take over and drop the lifeboat into the sea. Waterborne, it would remain tied to the *Badger State* by a painter—a manila line. In the normal course of events, the painter would help the lifeboat get clear of the doomed mother ship.

The lifeboat seemed pitifully inadequate to carry thirty-five seamen to safety, but it was all they had. Two rubber life rafts, compact enough to be thrown over the side, backed up the boats. A manila line attached to each raft served a dual purpose: holding the raft to the ship, and automatically triggering a mechanism that would inflate the raft when it hit the water. If the ship sank unexpectedly with no one being able to pitch the rafts overboard, a hydrostatic device would automatically pull the trigger on an air cartridge to inflate the raft and allow it to float free. The raft was designed to be accessible to seamen in the water who, for whatever reason, had not been able to board the lifeboats.

Several men, including the bosun, Neal Kirkwood, and George Henderson, removed the life rafts from their moorings and pitched them over the side. The rafts inflated on schedule, but lost their line connection to the ship. The men could only watch helplessly as the rafts skipped away on wind gusts into the wide expanse of the ocean.

Wilson shook his head in dismay at this turn of events, but he had other urgent matters to attend to. He called the engine room, and ordered all engine throttles stopped and the fires pulled from the boilers. "I want the emergency generator put on line for steering, and all hands evacuated immediately," he barked into the phone. "Everyone get out of the engine room as soon as possible!"

"I was standing [in the engine room] when there was a violent explosion," Bordash recalled. "Shortly after that, the alarm rang. Mr. Woods, the third assistant, was near the throttle. He said the captain wanted to stop the engine. So he shut the throttles. The fireman on orders pulled all six fires out of the boilers. We left the engine room. I went all the way up to the flying bridge because I wanted to make sure once again from the captain that they were totally abandoning the vessel."

As the sounds of the engines began to die out, the *Badger State* gradually lost headway in the sea. Wilson then focused on the lifeboat, placing Cobbs, the second-highest-ranking officer aboard ship, in charge. The mate had firsthand experience handling small boats, gained while sailing fishing vessels out of Newport, Oregon. With the mate in charge, Wilson did not anticipate any problems once the boat was in the water. Launching the boat in the sea conditions surrounding the ship would be the tough part.

Despite his concerns, the men were orderly and did not panic. With the davits out, crew members stepped gingerly into the boat swinging precariously on lines strung overhead. Once aboard, they grabbed the nearest seat and hung on. The boat filled rapidly, with Second Mate Bob Ziehm the last man to try to get on board.

Wilson watched anxiously as the heavyset officer climbed gingerly over the rail. As the boat swung in, Ziehm, still holding onto the rail, tentatively extended one foot toward the lifeboat, trying to judge the moment when he might safely jump in. But the boat unexpectedly accelerated its swing back toward the ship. Seeing the movement, Ziehm withdrew his foot, but he was a fraction of a second too late. He screamed in pain as the heavy lifeboat crushed his foot against the side of the *Badger State.*

"Help him!" Wilson yelled. One of the men grabbed the second mate and wrestled him back over the rail. Ziehm crumpled to the deck in agony, his foot stuck out awkwardly. He had no choice then but to stay aboard and throw his lot in with the captain and his volunteer helpers: Third Mate Willie Burnette, Able Seaman Ed Hottendorf, and Fireman-Watertender Sam Kaneao. Their help was needed to get the lifeboat down and safely into the water. Ziehm's injury was worrisome; the group would have to shepherd him along the way as best they could.

For the moment, Wilson's major concern was getting the lifeboat into the water. "Lower away!" he shouted.

Hottendorf, manning the winch brake, released the pressure. The boat began to drop, then stopped, swaying erratically on the davits. As the ship rolled from side to side, the boat swung out, the seamen braced within her, then back, crashing against the side of the *Badger State*. The frapping lines—designed to hold the boat close to the ship while being lowered—were largely ineffective due to the steep rolling of the ship.

"Release the brake all the way!" Wilson yelled. As Hottendorf complied, the boat dropped quickly into the surging sea.

"Keep the brake open," Wilson shouted. He wanted no strain on the falls which might jerk the boat clear of the water as she bobbed up and down in the swells. The curses of the seamen, a response to events beyond their control, filled the air as the waves carried the boat back up, banging against the ship's hull and then down and back again in a single swift movement. Two of the sailors in the boat struggled to trip the release on the davits, finally working them loose.

Third Engineer Richard Pattershall remembered the boat hitting the water. "Seas were high," he said. "Lifeboat was being thrown around like it was just a twig. A couple of waves took us and swept us back up, way up by the boat deck, and it was throwing the lifeboat all around. At this time, we were starting to drift aft, and we hadn't released the falls. When we did, they swung through the boat. We were a good way aft when the falls were released."

"First time the boat went down," Steve Bordash said, "a heavy sea caught her and brought her all the way back up to the boat deck because there was no chance to loosen the two falls. She hung up on the boat deck for some reason and slammed pretty hard against the rails. The second time she went down, I saw Pattershall loosen the after fall of the boat, and someone else loosen the other fall."

The boat was finally free of its ties to the ship, but remained locked in her embrace. It could not get away. The strong winds and surging seas were forcing it up against the now equally powerless *Badger State*. The boat's painter—the line attached to the ship to allow the boat to get clear—had ripped loose in the struggle.

Wilson watched helplessly as the lifeboat weaved and bobbed before crashing against the ship once more. Gradually it began drifting aft of the larger vessel, past No. 4 hold, and out of sight at last. He breathed a sigh of relief. The better part of his crew was out of danger. The boat should be able to reach the *Khian Star*. He could even glimpse the rescue vessel sporadically on the horizon, a mere few miles away.

Now the captain and his volunteers had to make their own way to the rescue ship, helping the badly injured Bob Ziehm as best they could. There were no lifeboats or rafts to help them. They would have to bridge the miles of raging seas, high winds, and freezing cold that separated them from the *Khian Star*, and do so entirely on their own.

CHAPTER 13

An Unforgettable Hell

Thank God we got the lifeboat safely away," Wilson muttered to no one in particular. He turned to the four men who had thrown their lot in with him. Ziehm slouched on the steel deck, his back braced against a wet bulkhead, grimacing as he wrapped both hands around a badly bruised leg. The others braced their feet against the unsteady deck and waited for orders. Someone had scrounged up a first-aid kit and handed it to Wilson.

Concerned that a seaman may have been injured in the explosion and then overlooked, Wilson ordered the men to check rooms and passageways to make sure no one was still aboard. With the men gone, Wilson tried to reassure a distraught Bob Ziehm.

"Should've known better," Ziehm said, grunting, continuing to massage his leg. "There's no way I can make it to that ship, Charlie. No way in God's name."

Wilson grabbed Ziehm roughly by the shoulders, trying to reassure him. "We'll get you home," he told him, removing an Ace bandage from the kit. He twisted it around the injured mate's leg. "Rest, while I give the guys a hand," he said.

Wilson hurriedly climbed down to the main deck, tension building in his chest. He poked his head into the nearest passageway. "Anybody here?" he shouted, "anybody?" He paused, listening intently for human sounds rising above the creaking and groaning of the ship and the banging of loose bombs in No. 5. There was no response, only an occasional echo from the shouts of the others.

He speedily checked other nearby compartments, his mind a maze of conflicting thoughts. It seemed possible that his men in the lifeboat, having reached the rescue ship, might still be able to return and take all of them off the *Badger State*. Conceivably, the *Khian Star* might launch its own lifeboat for that purpose.

But then reality checked in as a sharp roll caught him unawares and knocked him against a bulkhead. He grabbed a nearby railing with both hands and hung on until he could catch his balance, his body shaking. *A pipe dream,* he said to himself, discarding both scenarios. *The high seas and rough weather were giving the* Badger State *all it could handle, never mind trying to maneuver a small boat. They were just plain lucky to get their own lifeboat over the side without more people getting seriously hurt.*

He hurried back on deck, holding tightly to every handhold along the way. All the sights, sounds, and smells seemed suddenly overpowering: the nerve-wracking din from the holds; pontoons and booms askew on deck; the dangling lifeboat beating against the hull; the fire and smoke. Reluctantly, he admitted to himself that the ship was a floating time bomb.

The men returned. There were no stragglers aboard.

"Okay, let's go!" Wilson said, his voice sharp.

Extra life rings were stored on deck. "Put 'em on," Wilson told his crew, "they're not doing any good on the ship." Placing the rings over the life jackets would increase buoyancy. The men clumsily fumbled with straps and buckles, helping each other in the process.

Wilson paused, glancing up at the flag flapping wildly from the main mast, seeking out the lee side—winds blowing *away* from the ship, the better to help them escape the *Badger State* as quickly as possible. "We'll go in from the port side, near Number Three hatch," he shouted. The decision meant that the men would jump overboard from the side opposite where the lifeboat had been launched.

Worried about Ziehm's injured leg, Wilson turned to Hottendorf, the youngest man there, and directed him to keep an eye on the second mate. The seaman nodded.

The group moved quickly over to the port side, Hottendorf and the others helping Ziehm along the way. They gathered at the railing, looking like visitors from another planet, their heads seeming to swell out of bodies made huge by the combination of life jackets and rings.

Time was of the essence, and yet the men hesitated briefly as though weighing the merits of staying aboard the hazardous ship, their seagoing home, or leaping into the cold and raging sea to face unknown dangers. Grim-faced, somber, each with his own thoughts, they seemed mesmerized by the high waves pounding the ship, reaching up over the rail as if to fetch them in. There was a strange faraway look about them. Wilson had seen that thousand-yard stare before—in the eyes of a crew dealing with death.

It was on the SS *Steel Rover*. Wilson's officers, in dress khakis, had lined up on deck. Opposite them in single file stood a row of seamen, trim in white shirts and clean trousers. Separating the two ranks was a newly built platform fresh with the scent of pine. Bedded down on it was the lifeless body of a sailor about to be buried at sea. The ship's carpenter had sewn him tight in canvas and weighed him down with two links of anchor chain carefully placed at his feet. An American flag covered the body in a splash of red, white, and blue.

The ship slowed, wallowing gently in the blue waters of the Pacific Ocean off Guam. Under a bright sun, Wilson recited a passage from every captain's bible at sea, *The Book of Common Prayer*. He concluded with the solemn words "We commit his body to the deep." The ship's whistle sounded a mournful requiem as the men raised one end of the platform. The shrouded body slid off the platform, the canvas rasping down the wood as though reluctant to take its leave. The canvas cloak picked up speed and plunged into the water, a string of bubbles marking its descent into the deep. The dead mariner gone, there was a somberness about the ship, a stillness in the air marked only by the slight rustling caress of an ocean breeze—intimations of mortality.

Wilson shivered, more from the brief recollection than from the wet and cold that enveloped the *Badger State*. "God help us," he prayed, half to himself, as he strived to contain his own feelings. He turned to the crew. "Let's get a move on!" he shouted, trying to be heard above the wind. "Once in the water, try to get away from the ship as fast as you can," he counseled, fearful that more explosions would rack the *Badger State*.

Wilson motioned to the injured second mate and Hottendorf to go first. "Time the roll of the ship," he added. "When the deck is closest to the water, jump! And then get the hell away from the ship!"

Hottendorf nodded, a blank look on his face. He quickly placed an arm around Ziehm's shoulder and helped him to the rail. The others lent a hand, eyes watching intently as the two prepared to jump in.

Once over the rail, the men faced inboard and waited, both hanging on tightly to the railing of the ship. Their faces turned sideways, the two men tried to gauge the safest moment to jump in, staring intently at the ocean water that periodically swept up to deck level as the ship rolled in one direction, and then as quickly receded as the ship rolled back.

"Get ready!" Wilson shouted, as the water receded and then began to rise again. "Get ready!" he repeated, and then "Go! Go! Go!" The two men jumped, a brief flash of form and darkness as they hurtled into the ocean. The water swallowed them up briefly and then spit them back up to the surface, sputtering and struggling for breath. "Christ, this is freezing!" Hottendorf shouted, teeth chattering.

"Get away from the damn ship!" Wilson hollered. "Get away!" The men, arms flailing, struggled to swim away from the side of the ship.

Wilson stared at Third Mate Burnette, motioning him to go next, trying to hurry the men along.

Burnette, pausing only long enough to get his bearings, quickly followed suit. Wilson and Fireman-Watertender Sam Kaneao were the only ones left.

"Your turn. Jump!" Wilson ordered the fireman. Kaneao stared at the turbulent waters. "I can't, I can't," he muttered, his voice quavering. "I can't do it!"

"You don't have any choice, dammit!"

The sixty-year-old Kaneao hesitated, as if uncertain which was the worst situation: staying aboard the disabled and dangerous *Badger State,* or jumping into the surging ocean. "No, no, I can't!" he repeated.

We can't wait; maybe he'll follow me if I go first, Wilson reasoned, sensing the fear in the old man. He grabbed Kaneao by the shoulders, and stared into his eyes. "I will go first," he shouted, striving to be heard above the chorus of the wind. "Then you follow! Understand?"

The fireman looked blankly at Wilson, saying nothing. "Line up next to me," Wilson told him.

Wilson shivered as he wrapped his hands around the wet, ice-cold metal railing. He swung his legs over, his movements awkward in the life jacket and life ring that encircled his body. He turned to face inboard, hands still clutching the railing. He hunched over and extended a hand to Kaneao, to help guide him over the rail. The two men stood side by side, the last of the crew still aboard the *Badger State.*

Wilson tried to clear his mind, summoning the will to jump over the side. The water was freezing cold, and subconsciously he hunched up his shoulders in an effort to conserve his body heat. He hung on, the seconds feeling like minutes as he waited for the right moment to jump. He watched several cycles of water rise and fall to gauge the rhythm of the ship's movements. Then, with the water appearing to be near deck level, he took a quick breath, held it, and with every bit of strength he could summon, hurled his body backward, as far away from the ship as he could.

Almost immediately Wilson realized he had misjudged the water level. He was in a free fall dropping quickly down, down, the scarred gray presence of the hull of the ship moving rapidly upward before his eyes. And then the shock: freezing cold water washing over him as his body was submerged.

Propelled upward by the buoyant jacket and life ring, Wilson shot to the surface. Salt water filled his mouth and burned his eyes. He coughed, spat, and clumsily tried to clear both eyes with his hands. Facing away from the ship, he twisted and turned his body around, struggling, and spotted Kaneao still on the ship.

"Jump!" Wilson bellowed. "For crissakes, jump!"

The seaman turned to face the ocean. "I heard Captain Wilson say 'jump,' and I hesitated a little bit," Kaneao recalled. "I considered my age. If I can make it, I can make it. I don't know which is the worst enemy. I jumped, and I swam. It was cold, and one minute you are up in the water and the next minute you are down. Seemed like the waves came in a bunch. After a while, it tapered off. It was cold. I was swimming any which way I could, mainly backstroke so the water didn't hit me in the face."

Satisfied that all his men were safely in the water, Wilson struggled to propel himself away from the ship. The chill of the cold water swept through every part of his body. He saw Kaneao struggling in the water, also trying to distance himself from the ship.

From the safety of the ship's main deck, the waves had seemed high, at times dwarfing the ship, but now, caught up in the midst of them, they loomed like skyscrapers, and were dangerous in every direction. He struggled to swim on his back, his arms burdened by the life jacket. Moving clumsily, he willed himself with all the resolve he could muster to get away from the ship, but the seas were too strong, keeping him uncomfortably close to it.

And then, unexpectedly, a wave swept under him. Gathering force, it catapulted him up on a torrent of water above the deck of the *Badger State*. A series of disconnected watery images flickered before his eyes as he was tossed in the air: the ship's rolling hull; her deck crisscrossed with the collapsed booms; fire and smoke pouring out of her insides; and streams of water cascading in all directions. He thrashed about, trying to get away. Just as quickly, the water dropped out from under him, bringing him down sickeningly into the trough of the wave. A quick fleeting thought told him this was the end, crushed on the deck of his own ship. But he missed it by a matter of inches.

Adrenaline powered his arms and legs as instinct took over. *Get away*, he commanded himself, *swim for it before it's too late*. Gradually, stroke by stroke, he put open water between himself and the ship.

Throughout his ordeal, Wilson remained fearful of the possibility of the bombs exploding and killing them all. The fear was justified. According to Dr. P. G. Landsberg, an explosion of equal force is more dangerous in water than on land. The reason is that a shock wave in air dissipates much more rapidly. In water, that same wave travels faster and farther, and when it reaches a human body, it passes through it because it is of similar consistency to water. In doing so, it shreds and tears apart gas-filled cavities—lungs, intestines, ears, and sinus cavities. For those reasons, exploding a small bomb in an empty metal drum may not dent it, but add water and the same explosion will rupture the drum. Similarly, a hand grenade exploding in air might not harm a man, but the same explosion in water would kill him.

Wilson put as much distance between himself and the ship as he could. Finally, feeling safe, he paused to rest. He turned in the water to stare at the *Badger State*. The outline of the ship stood out boldly, and she seemed deceptively harmless and seaworthy. She was not listing and seemed to be on an even keel despite the continuous rolling. The only visible signs of damage on her port side were the pontoons and booms askew on the deck; the port lifeboat dangling awkwardly from a davit, swinging pendulum-like with every roll of the ship; and the black smoke spouting out from No. 5 hold. Serious damage must have been confined to the topside, he reasoned.

Slowly, painstakingly, he continued to swim away from the ship, forcing himself to keep his limbs moving. But it was hard work, riding a roller coaster of water that rocketed him high on a wave one moment, and the next, threw him on a nauseating ride down to the depths. In the trough of the waves, he was almost completely submerged in water, his view cut off in every direction. It was only in the brief moments when he soared high on the crest of a wave that he could see any signs of a human presence.

During one such movement, he spotted the *Khian Star*, far off, and set his course in its direction. He also caught glimpses of the other men who had remained aboard the ship with him, and had jumped overboard. Seeing them in the water, fighting as hard as he was to stay alive, bolstered his spirits.

The waves continued to sweep over him, filling his mouth with salt water. He tried to anticipate the movement of the water, shielding his nose and mouth with his hand when a wave seemed imminent. Swallowing too much water could lead to drowning.

The closest idea one can have to such a sensation was described by a Scottish doctor named James Lowson, a passenger aboard the British SS *Bokhara,* a three-masted steamer that departed Shanghai in October 1892. After a typhoon arose, the ship struck a reef and went down. Only two of the twenty-five passengers were saved, Dr. Lowson, one of them. He later recorded the sensations of near-drowning in an article published in the *Edinburgh Medical Journal* in 1903:

> I got clear under water, and immediately struck out to reach the surface as I thought, but evidently only to go further down. This exertion was a serious waste of breath, and, after what appeared to be ten or fifteen seconds the effort of inspiration could no longer be restrained, and pressure on the chest began to develop. Probably the most striking thing to remember at this period of time was the great pain produced in the chest, and which increased at every effort of expiration; it seemed as if one were in a vice, which was gradually being screwed up tight until it felt as if the sternum and spinal column must break.... The "gulping" efforts became more frequent for about ten efforts, and hope was then extinguished.... The pressure after these ten (*circa*) rapid "gulps" seemed unbearable, but gradually the pain seemed to ease up as the carbonic acid was accumulating in the blood. At the same time the efforts at inspiration with their accompanying "gulps" of water occurred at longer and longer intervals. My mental condition was now such that I appeared to be in a pleasant dream.... Before finally losing consciousness, the chest pain had completely disappeared, and sensation was actually pleasant.

But drowning was probably not Wilson's immediate enemy. Hypothermia—a drop in the temperature of the core organs of the brain, spinal cord, heart, and lungs—was.

Normal body temperature is 98.6 degrees Fahrenheit. Wilson was immersed in water colder by fifty degrees. Cold attacks from the outside, cooling skin and nearby tissues, but within ten to fifteen minutes, it affects the critical organs, heart, and brain. Once core temperatures dropped roughly ten degrees, to 86 degrees, Wilson would blank out, and death would rapidly follow. Someone once succinctly described it in another way as "the fifty-fifty rule": a fifty-year-old person in fifty-degree water has a fifty-fifty chance of surviving for fifty minutes.

Other critical factors enter the equation: the type of clothing worn; the amount of body fat; and most important of all, the movement of the person in the water. Surprisingly and paradoxically, the less exercise, the better. The reason: although any exercise pumps warm blood to the hands, and other extremities, making the person feel better, blood drawn to the extremities cools faster, and this, in turn, drastically cuts body temperature and thus one's ability to survive in the water. Hence, a person wearing a life jacket in frigid water should simply float.

Unfortunately, the strong impulse to survive may be overwhelming, and Wilson's body reacted accordingly. He continued to try to swim toward the *Khian Star*. His hands and feet were numb, but he kept moving them, and focused on reaching a ship that always seemed beyond arm's reach. Riding the crest of a wave at one point, Wilson saw the hazy outline of a lifeboat, capsized. It had to be from his ship, but he was uncertain. Physically and mentally exhausted, he seemed unable to grasp the meaning of anything that was happening around him. Then he spotted the stricken *Badger State*, rolling violently from side to side, riding broadside in the huge swells, seemingly as helpless as he was in the waters they shared. Seeing his ship out of control, at the whim of the waters that surrounded her, pained him. He tried to avert his eyes and, striving to keep his mind occupied, he wondered about the impact on the *Badger State* if he did not survive. A government inquiry was inevitable, that much was certain. Any maritime disaster of consequence automatically generated an investigation, and when the skipper did not survive or was otherwise unavailable to testify, panels usually found that the disaster was *his* fault. "Master's error," it's called. Or they might even find mistakes made by the crew.

The thought galvanized Wilson. *No way*, he said to himself, *are they going to blame me or my crew for the loss of the* Badger State. *I have to live,* he said to himself, *I must live!* He continued to repeat the words, a mantra seemingly more powerful with each repetition. The simple repetition intensified his determination to survive.

As time passed, it felt as if the water had lost its cold edge. That was deceptive, he realized. His limbs must be freezing. He pushed himself to move his arms and legs, to keep them constantly moving.

On the crest of a wave, he again spotted the *Khian Star.* The ship looked like it was moving toward him. A glimmer of hope sprung up, mixed with gratitude for this mystery rescue ship and her crew. When it was near enough for him to see a figure on the bridge of the ship, a man waved at him. Wilson felt his heart jump—they had seen him! He waved back frantically.

Sporadically, the ship came into view, looming larger as it neared him. Rescue seemed at hand. Riding a wave high in the water, he glimpsed the ship moving broadside to him. *They must be getting ready to take me aboard,* he reasoned. Spurred by that thought, he tried to move his limbs faster to get closer. But then he saw the ship circling away from him, making a 180-degree turn as if to retrace her course. It slowly dawned on him: the ship was going away from him.

Bitter feelings of dejection and loneliness swept through him. He could not understand why the ship had turned about. Had he lost his best chance of being rescued? Wilson realized he had to dispel the negative thoughts that now consumed him, and tried to understand what had happened. *Don't lose it,* he told himself. *Hold tight. The ship must be backtracking to pick up other seamen. That must be it. They would return!*

With that thought held strongly in mind, Wilson moved his numbed arms and legs with renewed vigor, and tried to swim in what he thought was the direction of the *Khian Star.* He tried to focus as he prayed for the ship to return. It seemed to help settle his mind. *The ship was going to pick up others,* he kept reassuring himself. *They had seen him. The ship would return.* He began to calm down.

Wilson realized that to survive he had to force himself to direct his thoughts elsewhere. Random memories and pictures of his family filtered through his mind. His folks working hard to raise him right by their old-school standards; his younger sisters looking up to their big brother. Parents and siblings were his family. And he knew, with a sudden fierce protectiveness that seemed part of the hostile environment he was caught up in, that he would kill anyone who harmed them. It was an unexpectedly strong emotion that swept over him, bolstering his will to live.

Other thoughts crowded in, but memories of his family kept cropping up. He wanted to take them to some remote place of peace and quiet. *Just to get reacquainted,* he thought, *and renew the bonds that tied them together.*

He continued struggling in the water, tossed about by the high-riding waves. Minutes or hours flashed by—he had lost all sense of time. And then he saw, like a distant mirage on the ocean, a blur on the horizon. His spirits rose as the image became clearer. He was looking at the *Khian Star.* And it was heading dead center for him. It must have rescued some of the others, he reasoned, and was now coming back to get him.

The ship closed rapidly, one moment appearing to be in the distance, and the next at arm's length. It loomed above him so unexpectedly close that Wilson felt he might be carried beyond the ship's bow. He tried to swim parallel to the ship, but he had lost most sensation in his hands and feet. The distance narrowed. Suddenly, the ship was *too* close, rearing up above him like some strange monster from the deep.

Heart pumping, Wilson tried to lunge away from the ship, but his movements were sluggish, as if in slow motion. He could not get away. The huge ship crashed down almost on top of him, the flare of the side of the vessel driving him deep underwater. Rising, he felt the rough metal hull of the ship brushing against his body.

The ship's screw, he thought, panic-stricken. He pushed with numbed hands against the metal of the ship, struggling, trying to push himself away. Rising to the surface, he looked up. "Help! Help!" he shouted as loud as he could, waving hands he could not feel. Two dark-faced seamen poked their heads over the rail, and stared briefly at him.

"Help!" Wilson repeated. One of the men quickly heaved toward him a life ring with a line attached. The ring sailed overhead, but the line fell close by. He lunged desperately for it, finally grabbing it with numbed hands. He hung on desperately, trying to wrap the line around his body. A feeling of exhilaration filled him as he realized he was connected to the rescue ship. He looked up at the two men, trying to make them out through water-filled eyes. They had the lifeline in hand, and were pointing toward the stern of the ship as they moved to carry the line aft. Wilson realized they wanted to haul him aboard at the stern, where the water rose closer to deck level.

He struggled to wrap the line around his body while the seamen towed him aft. Wilson suddenly noticed that the ship was rolling steeply toward him. A wave had broken over the *Khian Star*, washing across her deck, reaching to the waist of the two seamen above who were also hanging on to save their own lives. Simultaneously, a wave picked Wilson up bodily and catapulted him upward in a heart-stopping arc high above the deck of the ship. He instinctively dropped the lifeline and reached out frantically toward the railing, but his numbed fingers could not grab it, and he fell back into the trough of the wave. Thrashing about, he glimpsed the line floating close by. Frantic, he threw himself toward it and grabbed it again with both hands. He wrapped unfeeling hands and arms about the line and hung on with all the strength he could muster.

The two seamen retained their footing on deck. They continued to tow him aft. Reaching the stern, Wilson spotted a pilot ladder lowered from the ship. The seamen gestured with their hands, signaling for him to get on the ladder. Wilson grabbed a rung with hands and arms, and tried to put his feet and legs through it. But he could not move his limbs.

It's now or never, he realized grimly. Gathering his strength about him in one massive exercise of will, he lunged at the rung of the ladder with numbed hands. He poked his arms through, and hung on. The seamen pulled the ladder up, grabbed him by his hair, his life jacket, his clothes, and heaved him up on deck, where he collapsed. As if in a dream, he was finally, safely on the deck of the *Khian Star*.

The Greek sailors half pulled and half carried him to a room below deck, stripped him down, and placed him on a bunk. Regaining consciousness, he saw two men rubbing him down with a liquid. They grinned, and spoke to him in a language he did not recognize. But he understood the universal language of care and kindness they showed in looking after him.

All feeling had left his limbs. Purple splotches dotted his body. Violent spasms ran through him as sensation began to return. He struggled to sit up. The men reached down with strong arms and pulled him up, and then put whiskey to his lips. He dutifully swallowed, feeling the liquid burning its way down his throat. He vomited, coughing as he did so, until there was nothing left in his stomach. As his body continued to heave convulsively, intense pain stabbed both legs. The cramps were excruciating, and he could hardly move. The seamen continued massaging his limbs. Gradually, the pain subsided. Feeling returned to his hands and fingers first, then to his legs and calves.

He stood, shaking, and with the seamen supporting him, he tried to walk, gradually feeling his way around. They helped him put on dry trousers too large and slippers too small, but they felt warm and comfortable.

"I am the captain of the *Badger State*," he said to the seamen, his speech halting and breaking up. He repeated the words slowly. "I want to see my crew, the survivors . . . who they are, how many, their condition." Wilson gestured, pointing toward the overhead, toward the bridge, trying to communicate with words and signs.

The two seamen talked to one another in their own language, smiled at him, and then escorted him to the wheelhouse. There stood a short, dark-eyed man, wearing blue trousers and matching shirt, who unmistakably was in charge of the ship. It was Captain Niros, the master of the *Khian Star*.

There, for the first time, Wilson learned the fate of the men who had shared with him the unforgettable hell of the past few hours.

CHAPTER 14

Drop Me Deep

But me they'll lash in hammock, drop me deep.
Fathoms down, fathoms down, how I'll dream fast asleep.
—Herman Melville, "Billy in the Darbies," from *Billy Budd*

While Captain Wilson and the volunteers struggled to reach the rescue ship, the crewmen in the lifeboat waged their own fight for survival. The boat, thirty-five frightened souls huddled aboard her, rocked and pitched in the waters alongside the *Badger State*. "Get the boat away from the ship as fast as you can!" Wilson ordered the mate, concerned that more bombs might explode. But fate determined otherwise.

Lifeboat and ship were hooked together by the painter. In theory, it would allow the boat to veer away on its own by taking advantage of the larger vessel's headway and the boat's rudder and hand-propelled gear. However, in the confusion and commotion that ensued, the crew could not push or pull the levers designed to turn the boat's propeller. And even if that propulsion system had worked, the outcome would have still been in doubt. The painter itself had somehow parted or broken loose.

Failure of the painter, plus the power and direction of wind and waves, forced the small boat into the iron embrace of the mother ship. It was a fearsome coupling. At a length of 441 feet, the *Badger State* reared high over the lifeboat in one moment, and in the next, it plunged ominously down on it as the men clustered fearfully together. Destruction appeared imminent, but the weight of the ship as it descended in the water pushed the smaller boat violently aside.

The out-of-control lifeboat with seamen hanging on to seats, sides, and each other, drifted slowly aft. The small craft pitched, rolled, and banged against the side of the *Badger State*. Frigid waters, squeezed between the two, flooded into the boat, drenching the seamen. As the boat lurched aft, one of the men screamed, "Good God! Look! There's a fuckin' hole in the hull!" All heads turned as one toward the side of the ship, at the metal skin that separated the ocean from the interior of No. 5 upper tween deck hold.

The explosion in No. 5 had blown a huge, gaping, eight-by-ten-foot hole through the hull, an area not visible from the deck of the ship. Long curving fingers of steel, ripped out by the force of the explosion, ringed the hole.

As the men watched helplessly, a 2,000-pound bomb shot out of the hole into the water directly ahead of the boat as it drifted near. Seeing this, a few of the panic-stricken seamen, reacting instinctively, dove into the water. Others held tight, frozen in uncertainty.

The boat quickly came dead abreast of the hole where it seemed to pause for an eternity. A wave suddenly swept the boat up, banging against the ship, throwing the men about in all directions. As boat and ship crashed against each other again, the steel ridges around the opening in the hull raked the scalp of one of the men, slicing skin to the bone. His shipmates, scrambling to stay in the boat, stared helplessly as the seaman screamed in pain and collapsed. A river of blood gushed out on those close by.

The lifeboat dropped back into the water. The ship, banging alongside in this macabre dance, rolled violently toward the boat. Those inside, near the boat's center, stared directly into No. 5 hold.

A mass of flames burned intensely inside—wood, mattresses, beef providing fuel. The hold glowed red with an eerie light, splashing shadowy figures across the dark interior. In a split second, out of the fire and the shadows emerged a dark form headed directly toward the boat. As the shape of a round cone began to materialize, the men realized it was a blockbuster one-ton bomb careening wildly across the deck of the hold, burning debris scattered along its path. It had a bead on the lifeboat, dead center.

Fireman Jim Beatty recalled the moment:

This bomb came right for us! Just before the bomb left the ship, the ship had started to roll the other way. When the bomb came out of the ship, it was like coming over a ski jump because it started to tilt back the other way, but the momentum was so great, and the speed of the bomb at that time so great, it came right into the lifeboat. It landed on the men aft of me, and it started to capsize us.

Chaos followed as the men scrambled in every direction, stumbling, screaming for help. "Let's get the hell out of here!" Beatty heard himself holler as he dove into the sea. Surfacing, he struggled to swim away, fearing that the edge of the boat, if it capsized in his direction, would break his back. The huge weight of the bomb cartwheeled the boat over, throwing the seamen overboard.

Beatty paused in his struggles to look back. Shipmates thrashed about in the water, most trying to stay near the capsized boat. Dick Hughes and several others had climbed on top of it, while others struggled alongside holding onto the boat's rail. The capsized boat, with a necklace of seamen strung around it, gradually drifted toward the stern of the *Badger State*.

The forty-three-year-old Beatty owed his swimming ability to his mother, who had insisted that he learn how to swim. He spent most of his younger years in and around water, and that training now gave him some assurance that he would be able to survive.

Only a few hours earlier, Beatty had looked down into No. 5 hold.

"The bombs were rolling and skidding around. It was the most awesome sight I had ever seen. It looked like a big pit of deadly, dangerous snakes!" In the water, Beatty had reason to recall the bosun's words which seemed to capture everybody's feelings: "We have nothing left. All we can do is pray to God."

Struggling to keep his head above water, the passport and cigarettes he had earlier taken from the ship now pulp, Beatty heard Jim McLure cry out in a voice tinged with excitement, "There's a ship! There's a ship!" Beatty looked in every direction, but could see nothing in the towering seas. Then a wave carried him high. On its crest, he spotted what appeared to be the tip of a mast miles off in the distance. Reasoning that it had to be the rescue ship, Beatty began swimming in the direction of the mast. The ship might not be able to see them, he reasoned, submerged as they were in the rough seas. They needed to get closer.

By his own reckoning, he swam out a mile. The outline of the ship began to take shape under its mast. He continued his efforts, occasionally losing sight of the ship, only to regain it as he was thrown up on a crest. Gradually, Beatty began to realize he was not gaining; he was falling behind. "I had a bad angle on the ship and I missed it," he recalled. "I came in on the stern. It was the most lonesome thing I ever saw in my life, to see that ship go away in the distance, and me out there in the middle of that ocean!"

He stopped struggling, and quit fighting the waves. Moments later, he decided he had better get back to the lifeboat and to the men drifting near it. Logically, the rescue ship should zero in on the lifeboat. Time passed slowly and Beatty estimated that it took him about an hour to return to the area of the boat.

Nearing the lifeboat, and exhausted from his efforts, Beatty glimpsed a scurrying form out of the corner of his eye. He then felt a sharp rapping blow to the back of his head. The unexpected hit stunned him. He instinctively raised a protective arm near his face. He turned, thrashing around with his other hand, and found himself face to face with a "big, old, gray bird," he recalled. "It looked like it was going to peck at my eyes. I took a swing at him with my right hand and missed him. Then I tried to grab his feet, but he got away. I could see other men in the water and the birds seemed to be pecking at their heads."

They were albatrosses, those giants among flying creatures, with wingspans exceeding six feet, the huge birds that spend their lives at sea, eternal mariners, returning to isolated islands only to breed. At a distance, their grace and dexterity have fascinated seamen over the millennia. Close up and in their "territory," the birds presented a terrifying spectacle, a danger to anyone crippled or helpless in the water.

Looking around him, Beatty noticed that some of his shipmates near the lifeboat were surrounded by the albatrosses that appeared to have materialized out of nowhere.

Briefly resting, Beatty spotted a raft apparently dropped by a plane. It was unopened, still in its pod. He swam over to the raft. Almost within reach, a wave carried him high. On its crest, his eyes sweeping the horizon, he again spotted the *Khian Star*. It seemed tantalizingly close by, and it was heading directly toward him.

He struck out toward the ship with renewed strength. The ship came on fast and he quickly and unexpectedly found himself near the bow. A seaman threw a life ring to him, but the wind carried it spinning away. A second life ring fell within reach and he grabbed the line. The seaman motioned aft to Beatty and began towing him toward the stern of the *Khian Star*.

As he was being hauled aft, Beatty looked up and saw two shipmates, engineers Kinnie Woods and Richard Pattershall, hanging on to the side of the rolling ship. "All of a sudden, they dropped like rocks and disappeared in the water," Beatty said. "Then Pattershall flopped up in the water and said, 'Jim, give me a life ring, give me a life ring.' I said okay, and I gave him my life ring."

When he reached the stern of the *Khian Star*, the men on deck dropped Beatty a rope ladder. He tried to climb, but he could not work his feet, numbed by the cold water, through the rungs. One seaman motioned to him to grab the ladder. Beatty managed to work one arm through a rung, encircled the rung with his other arm, and held on. The men began to pull the ladder up the side of the ship.

Halfway up, Beatty felt the ship beginning to roll, putting added pressure on his arms. His hands started to slip. Realizing that this might be his final shot, he mustered all his strength to hold on. "Finally," he recalled, "they got me up to the top, and they grabbed me by the hair, by the life jacket, by the pants, by the legs, and they jerked me out on the deck. Two young men grabbed me and took me into an apprentice engineer's room. They tore off my clothes, put me in bed, wrapped my legs with blankets, and massaged them with alcohol. They gave me hot coffee, hot tea, a couple of drinks of whiskey, and cigarettes. About this time, they brought Mr. Pattershall into the same room and he looked terrible, but I guess I looked the same as he did."

AB George Henderson dove over the side of the lifeboat shortly after it dropped down from the ship. He surfaced in time to see the blockbuster bomb smash into the boat. Struggling to get away from the capsizing boat as well as from the ship, he recalled passing near the stern of the *Badger State*. The tremendously high seas and the strong winds carried him off the port quarter.

"The lifeboat came around the end of the ship," Henderson said. "There was a large mass of sea birds, twenty-five or thirty of them, in a tight group floating aft of the ship. They kept flying around and landing by you, and trying to sit on you or get at you, and I kept wanting to swing at them so they would go away."

Drifting further away from the boat, Henderson met Third Mate Sam Bondy. "Let's stay together," Bondy said, gasping, "Let's just keep moving and stay warm."

Thinking they were drifting faster than the boat, the two men decided to swim back to it, where they were able to talk to their shipmates and try to encourage each other. The boat was riding roughly, and everyone was swallowing water. Henderson spotted a line floating close by. He yelled at the engine cadet to secure the line, figuring that the capsized boat would be the most likely target for the rescue ship to focus on. The line would help the crew to stay in the same general area.

"I was in the water hanging on to the line and surging with the boat," Henderson continued. "The boat was riding very rough and the guys that were hanging on were taking a lot of water. We were trying to stay as close as we could to the boat without actually having to get on it. A lot of guys were trying to hang on. Someone on the lifeboat could see the *Khian Star* and so we knew there was a ship in the area."

Gradually, the ship came into view, the lifeboat then being on the ship's starboard quarter. The captain maneuvered the huge rolling ship closer, and managed to bring it alongside the lifeboat. At that point, there were seamen riding the top of the boat, and others struggling in the water between boat and ship. Seamen aboard the rescue ship threw lines down to these men. As Henderson looked on helplessly, the capsized boat rose up on a wave and slammed against the side of the rescue ship, crushing the hapless seamen trapped between the two.

The capsized boat, with seamen still on top of it, then began to drift around the stern of the rescue ship. "I swam over to it, and I got up on it," Henderson said. "I remember there was the electrician, the third cook, and the day man. There were other men, but I can't remember because it was going so deep in the water that you would be hanging on, and then you would be completely submerged. So I let go of it and I got back off." The rescue ship meanwhile began maneuvering for another try at rescuing the men.

The life jackets were proving troublesome. They had lost some buoyancy and tended to ride up on the men, forcing their heads forward into the water. Henderson untied one of the straps of his jacket, and then retied it tightly under his chin to keep his head back. As he did so, he heard the droning sound of a plane overhead. A package dropped from the plane, a raft with a trailing line that fell across the lifeboat. Third Cook Donald Byrd grabbed it, enabling Henderson to swim over to the raft and pull himself aboard.

Others began to swim to the raft. Henderson pulled Florencio Serafino aboard and then Sam Bondy, Jim McLure, and Donald Byrd.

Bosun Dick Hughes, weak from the back injury he had suffered aboard ship as well as his struggles in the water, managed to swim over. Henderson helped him aboard, saying to him—as he later told the bosun's wife—"Get your ass on board or your old lady will never forgive me!" Others held on to the side of the raft.

Most of the surviving seamen were gathered in the same general area close to the rescue ship. They were either in the raft, on top of the capsized lifeboat, or floating close by.

The *Khian Star,* sporting a costume of manila lines, life rings, and ladders draped over her side, slowed to within a hundred yards of the raft. Maneuvering the ship in such close quarters called for expert seamanship. Aside from the obvious challenge of cozying up alongside a midget-sized raft, the flimsy smaller craft pitched and swayed to the lopsided rhythm of wind and seas. In a tantalizing game of now-you-do-now-you-don't, waves would float the raft high and pitch it toward the ship. Then, when rescue seemed tantalizingly close, the waves would quickly recede and snatch the raft away.

During this interplay in close quarters between raft and ship, Henderson saw that he was below the ship's waterline. In an instant, carried high on a wave, he found himself looking down at the seamen on the deck of the rescue ship. If it happened again, he told himself, he would be within reach of the deck. When a wave carried him up to the ship's rail, he jumped and, arms outstretched, caught the ladder. Rescuers hauled him aboard the *Khian Star*.

After being resuscitated, Henderson remembered going down a passageway and seeing other shipmates who had also been rescued. "I ran into the captain, and he had a list to see who had got aboard. I went on up to the bridge, and I remember seeing the third mate being brought aboard. Then the ship circled, looking for others. There were a lot of men in the water, floating face down."

All the crew members of the *Badger State* experienced similar problems: huge waves, frigid waters, attacking albatrosses, and the struggle to get aboard the *Khian Star*. Some men were able to grab a line thrown over, or latch onto the rung of a ladder. But getting connected to the ship was only half the battle. Once connected, the men had to hang on. A number of them passed out while maintaining a grip on line or ladder, and managed to be saved. Others, too cold, weak, or exhausted from their struggles, were unable to hold on and fell back into the sea.

After the boat capsized, First Engineer Steven Bordash and others tried to hang on to the capsized boat. But Bordash soon realized that his arms could not take the strain of the boat bobbing in the water. He floated free, going with the seas. Cadet Engineer Neal Kirkwood had rigged a line out from the boat and called to him to grab it. But Bordash was too exhausted to swim to it. Engineer Kinnie Woods floated nearby in the trough of one of the waves. Albatrosses were encircling the men and Woods hit the water with his hands, yelling, "Watch your eyes! They'll peck your eyes out if you're not careful!"

"I was attempting to keep my back to the seas all the time," Bordash said. "Maybe that is why I didn't have such a range of visibility. But when I turned again, it seemed like the *Khian Star* had come out of nowhere. She was in front of me. I turned to Woods and said, 'Woody, don't worry. We've got it made now. There's a ship.'"

The ship came about in a 90-degree turn, and the sea swept Bordash almost to amidship. "She looked about a mile high," he recalled. "They threw a ladder down. I missed it the first time, but the second time I locked my arms around it. I must have passed out as soon as I left the water because I don't remember leaving it until they were pulling me over the rail."

Engineer Richard Pattershall, seeing a bomb come out of the hold ahead of the boat, dove into the water. Surfacing, he swam back and grabbed the railing of the boat. "It was taking a terrific amount of strength to hold on. I couldn't do it," he said. "So I just let go and drifted off the boat. We all stayed around in the general vicinity. As far as I was concerned, there was no way to swim in those seas. I was bobbing around like a cork, laying there, taking it easy, trying to keep my life jacket tight around me. And someone yelled behind me, 'There's a ship!' I turned around and the *Khian Star* was perhaps fifty to seventy-five yards behind me and closing."

Kinnie Woods and a few others from the engine room floated nearby. A wave swept Pattershall and Woods up near the main deck where they grabbed onto the fish plate—a steel plate lapping over two other plates butted together. The plate edge was sharp, and they were unable to hold to it. They dropped back into the sea, Pattershall falling first, Woods coming down on top of him. Woods turned around and laughed, saying, "Sorry; too bad about that." It was the last time Pattershall saw Kinnie Woods.

A wave carried Pattershall over to a ladder. He grabbed it, hung on, and was hauled aboard the *Khian Star*.

With the lifeboat in the water abreast of No. 5, Neal Kirkwood dove into the water just before the bomb dropped into the boat. Surfacing, he swam over and grabbed the rail of the capsized boat.

Third Mate Sam Bondy, nearby, was one of several men who told Kirkwood to tie a line to the boat and string it out so other seamen would have something to hold on to. The cadet secured the line and then released his grip on the boat and drifted away, letting the line pay out to where Bondy and Richard Pattershall were. Looking around, Kirkwood noticed Steve Bordash some distance away. Concerned that Bordash might be missed by the rescue ship, he swam over to him with the line in tow.

At a distance of some ten to twenty feet away from Bordash, Kirkwood spotted the *Khian Star*. In the space of minutes, he watched Bordash being picked up on a ladder. The ladder was then lowered to him. A wave carried him up and he was able to put his feet on a rung of the ladder. He climbed up a few steps but, cold and exhausted, he could not move higher. It was enough. Seamen on the rescue ship hauled him to safety.

Ordinary Seaman James McLure was in the boat sitting next to the bosun, facing aft. "I looked at the ship and all I could see was the ship coming down on us. I thought, my God, we're gone! I heard somebody

yell, 'Watch out for the bomb.' The bomb hit the boat and it went sideways, and it slowly capsized us. The bomb had been on the port side of
the boat and I was yelling for somebody to get the bilge pump. I thought
to myself we've got to get this bomb out of here, but it was too late. Half
the boat filled with salt water, and it was capsizing."

Surfacing, McLure swam to the capsized boat and climbed on top of
it, joining Dick Hughes. Many of his shipmates were scattered some
thirty to forty feet away. McLure saw the rescue ship and yelled to everyone that it was headed their way. "I looked up in the sky, and I guess I
just started praying while I was hanging on for dear life," he remembered. "The waves would come over our heads and bury us underneath
anywhere from thirty-five to forty seconds. We would come up for a
breath of air, and then another one would hit us. Most of the men were
barely hanging on."

The boat was too unstable, and McLure swam to the raft dropped by
the plane. Henderson pulled him aboard. Exhausted, McLure lay down
on top of Serafino on the floor of the raft. He felt overcome with the
need to sleep. Henderson, concerned for his safety, ordered him several
times to get up. When McLure refused, Henderson slapped him, forcing
him awake.

Henderson, a tough sailor, told the men in the raft to stay close
together for warmth and to exercise their limbs. He encouraged them to
hold tight, and assured them they would all be rescued. McLure saw
Henderson pull five or six men into the raft, lifting them up and drag-
ging their legs over the side.

Although the rescue ship had arrived, McLure could not reach the
ladder. Someone threw a line down, and Henderson tied it around
McLure's waist so that he could be hauled aboard.

Wiper Florencio Serafino recalled swimming back to the capsized boat.
"I grabbed a line," he said, "but I couldn't hold on too long because every
time a wave came, I was afraid my arm might come out. A plane dropped
a float and I swam to it. George picked me up and put me inside. Some-

body from the ship threw us lines. I grabbed one and tied it around my waist and they pulled me up."

Third Cook Donald Byrd had stuffed his bible and his wallet in his pocket before leaving the *Badger State*. He did this before the Abandon Ship signal sounded because, as he remembered, "We took tremendous rolls and I couldn't sleep; I got knocked out of my bunk, that's how rough it was. I saw that the other fellows walking around were nervous. The bosun came and said, 'This is an emergency'."

In the lifeboat alongside the *Badger State*, Byrd recalled someone hollering that a bomb was headed their way and he dove over the side. Surfacing, he attempted to put as much distance as possible between himself and the ship. "I was trying to get away, as far away as I possibly could," Byrd said. "And every time I looked back, I figured I wasn't getting far enough away from the ship."

Carried upward on a wave, Byrd saw the rescue ship. "Here comes a ship," he hollered to the others, "we can make it!" A plane flew over about the same time, dropping a raft with a line attached to it. The line dropped across Byrd's shoulder. He grabbed the line and held it while six other men climbed into the raft, and then joined them himself.

"Every man I saw had their heads down in the water," Byrd remembered. "I did see one man on his back, and the gooney birds were pecking his eyes out. I wanted to assist, but I was weak and I couldn't do it."

When the *Khian Star* maneuvered alongside the capsized lifeboat, it trapped a handful of men between ship and lifeboat. "About six guys got hurt," Byrd says. "I heard the guys screaming so I jumped at the ladder and caught it three steps from the top of the main deck. I just froze; I had a death grip on it, and they grabbed my hands." Byrd was pulled to safety.

After the signal to Abandon Ship sounded, Third Mate Willie Burnette rushed to his room to get his Coast Guard license. He then climbed to the wheelhouse to get the ship's sextant, binoculars, and the log, which he handed to someone in the lifeboat. After helping to launch the boat, he jumped overboard with Captain Wilson and the other volunteers. Burnette recalled seeing the injured Bob Ziehm and AB Hottendorf floating near by.

Later, he saw the *Khian Star* heading directly toward him. "I was afraid of being run down," he recalled, "and so I swam to get out of the way and I went down the port side. There was a ladder in the water and I saw men on deck. But I could not get to the ladder. Then the *Khian Star* came alongside. They threw lines in the water and twice I dropped back in the water as I was unable to hold on to them. Then there was a life ring in the water and they were telling me to put my feet in it. And that is all I remember until I was on deck of the *Khian Star*."

Deck Utility Lawrence McHugh was the last man to board the lifeboat. "It was the worst weather I have ever seen in my life," he recalled. "There were thirty-to-forty-foot swells, and the boat took a terrific beating when we finally got in the water."

McHugh recalled seeing the bomb shoot into the boat and crushing two seamen. After the boat capsized, he joined the other men clustered around it "This was the first time something like this ever happened to me," he said. "I hope to God it never happens again, believe me." McHugh was eventually pulled aboard the rescue ship.

Messman Charles McCullar was facing the stern of the lifeboat when the bomb fell behind him, crushing one of the men. Someone hollered "Jump!" and he went over the side. Upon surfacing, he swam to the boat and climbed on top of it. When the *Khian Star* came alongside, there were more than ten crewmembers on or around the lifeboat. Someone pitched a line to him. He grabbed it and was pulled aboard the rescue ship.

Samuel Kaneao, one of the volunteers who leaped into the ocean from the ship, recalled the approach of the *Khian Star*. "When I was forty or fifty feet away from the ship, they threw a line. It just barely reached me. I grabbed it and hung on. When they pulled me halfway up the ship,

I let go. I couldn't hold on anymore and fell back into the water. The Jacob's ladder was about six or seven feet away from me down the ship's side. I caught it with my right arm and I hung on. This time I didn't let go. They pulled me up, ladder and all."

Bosun Dick Hughes was last seen clinging to the rung of a ladder being pulled up to the deck of the *Khian Star*. Exhausted, he could not hold on, and fell back into the sea.

CHAPTER 15

Rescue

Captain Niros of the *Khian Star* first sighted the *Badger State* early on the morning of December 26 from a distance of four to five miles. Shortly afterwards, he observed a flash of light, followed by a thick column of smoke pouring from the stern of the stricken vessel. He guessed correctly that a bomb had exploded in the ship's cargo hold.

Maneuvering to within a mile or two, looking for survivors, Niros noticed booms scattered about the deck on the stern of the ship. In the same general area, the capsized lifeboat surged in rough seas. Seamen perched atop of it, while others were clustered close by, either holding on or strung out holding lines attached to the boat. A life raft presented the same picture of anxious seamen awaiting rescue.

The *Khian Star* continued to roll steeply, occasionally shipping high waves over her bow. Under these conditions, the ship could not launch its own lifeboats, the move that would have offered the best chance for success. Captain Niros would have to maneuver the 466-foot-long, 10,000-ton ship as near to the boat and raft as was safely possible. When close enough, the seamen could be hauled aboard by means of lines and life preservers. Those able to do so would climb the cargo nets and ladders lowered over the side.

Beset by high seas and confused swells, the *Khian Star* itself would be in considerable danger. The process of turning and maneuvering the vessel to pick up survivors placed the ship broadside to the swells, causing it to roll severely. Her crew, manning their rescue stations on deck, were continually at risk of being washed overboard by the huge waves

crashing over the ship's bow. Worse perhaps for the captain and his officers, armed with the knowledge of the *Badger State*'s cargo, was the possibility of a massive explosion from the bombs it carried.

Setting aside the risks involved, Captain Niros headed his ship
toward the boat first. "I had all the crew make ready to rescue the men
by lowering over the side three pilot ladders, three or four Jacob's ladders, net slings, and lines," he recalled.

> I first approached the lifeboat where most of the men were. When we
> were about fifty feet away, the men left the lifeboat to swim toward
> our ship. Some, however, were carried away from the ship by the
> waves. On the first approach, we picked up five or six men. While we
> were circling to make the second approach, the men tried to get back
> to the lifeboat. Three times we approached the lifeboat, which many
> times touched the side of our ship. On the second approach, we
> picked up three or four men; on the third, two or three. And then
> we maneuvered towards those scattered about in the water. When
> we first approached the lifeboat, I did not notice anyone dead in the
> water, but after about an hour, many were dead, floating face down
> in the water.

The ocean temperature at the time was roughly 48 degrees Fahrenheit;
the air temperature was 53 degrees.

The three approaches proved difficult. In each instance, the ship had
to slow or stop her engines, back down or speed ahead as circumstances
warranted, and circle around in a wide sweeping turn. The ship rolled
40 to 50 degrees during these maneuvers. It needed good seamanship and
skill by the captain to keep the ship from running down the seamen they
were trying to rescue. The maneuvers were not only difficult but time-
consuming. And time had become a critical factor as men in the water
began to succumb to cold and exhaustion. Worse, albatrosses were sighted
attacking the dead, as well as live seamen too weak to fend them off.

Following the rescue of the men on and near the boat, Captain Niros
focused his efforts on the life raft and those seamen in the water showing
signs of life. Most seemed too weak to grip and hold on to a line. However, some were able to hang onto a ladder that was then pulled up on

deck. One seaman was hauled up upside down—he had been able to place his foot inside the loop of a line that had been thrown over the side before lapsing into unconsciousness.

Able Seaman Ioannis Kantziakis, a crewmember on the rescue ship known by the nickname "John Texas," went over the side to try to rescue a seaman who had washed off a ladder. The seaman was dead by the time Kantziakis reached him. The body could not be recovered.

As soon as a man was brought up on the deck of the *Khian Star*, he was taken to one of the spare rooms, stripped of wet clothing, massaged, and given dry clothes and spirits. All the men showed the same signs of distress: uncontrollable shivering, severe cramps, and exhaustion. Many had rope burns and scratches.

Several Air Force rescue planes appeared on the scene. The first appeared shortly after mid-morning and dropped rafts containing food and medicine, and walkie-talkies to establish communication. Once in the water, however, strong winds blew the rafts away, skipping and spinning like cartwheels in the open water. The planes also searched the area for seamen afloat and passed their findings on to the *Khian Star* to aid in the search.

The *Khian Star* rescued the first man at nine A.M., and the last at about noon. It continued to search for survivors for the rest of the day and night. Short on fuel and with further search deemed hopeless, the ship departed the area on December 27, bound for Yokohama. On board were the master and thirteen crewmembers of the *Badger State*.

While aboard the *Khian Star,* Captain Wilson sent the following message to Naval Headquarters:

1. ALL HOPE FOR FURTHER SURVIVORS NOW NONE.

2. BADGER STATE VERY DANGEROUS DERELICT AND MAY EXPLODE AT ANY TIME.

3. SITUATION AT TIME OF ABANDONING SHIP: NO. 5 HATCH HOLED AT UPPER TWEEN DECK LEVEL FROM LOOSE 2,000-POUND BOMB. TRIED TO RESECURE USING ALL SHIP MAT-TRESSES, HATCH BOARDS, SPARE LIFE JACKETS, CHAIRS,

LINE, STEWARD STORES, FROZEN MEAT, MOORING LINES, BEDS, FIRE HOSES, ANYTHING WE COULD USE TO TRY AND STOP THEM FROM ROLLING AROUND. LANDED PONTOONS ON TOP OF EVERYTHING TO TRY AND STOP THEM. AT THIS TIME WE CAME ABOUT IN AN ATTEMPT TO HEAD FOR MIDWAY AND SOME OF THE BOMBS EXPLODED IN NO. 5 HATCH AND NO. 5 HATCH WAS ON FIRE AT THAT TIME. THE ABANDON-SHIP SIGNAL WAS IMMEDIATELY SOUNDED.

4. THIRTY-THREE MEN WERE LOWERED TO THE SEA IN NO. 1 LIFEBOAT. NO. 2 LIFEBOAT DISABLED FROM HEAVY SEAS AND UNABLE TO LOWER IT. ALL HANDS AT THIS TIME WERE ALIVE. AS NO. 1 LIFEBOAT DRIFTED AFT THE PAINTER PARTED AND SHE SMASHED AGAINST SIDE OF SHIP WITH NO DAMAGE. WHEN SHE WAS ABEAM NO. 5 HATCH ONE 2,000-POUND BOMB FELL IN LIFEBOAT, CAPSIZING IT. SURVIVORS FROM LIFEBOAT SAW HOLD ON FIRE THRU APPROX. TEN-FT HOLE IN SIDE OF NO. 5 UPPER TWEEN DECK FORWARD AND OTHER BOMBS STILL ROLLING AROUND. ALL BOMBS OFF OF THEIR STEEL CASES.

5. TWO RUBBER LIFERAFTS WERE LAUNCHED AND SECURED IN WATER AT SIDE SHIP BUT SEA PARTED LINES AND CARRIED THEM AWAY. NO SURVIVORS FOUND IN EITHER RAFT.

6. FIVE MEN STAYED ON BOARD WITH ME: CHIEF MATE LEONARD COBBS, SECOND MATE ROBERT ZIEHM, THIRD MATE WILLIE BURNETTE, ABLE SEAMAN ED HOTTENDORF, AND FWT SAM KANEAO, ASSISTING LAUNCHING LIFEBOAT AND SEEING THAT ALL HANDS WERE OFF THE SHIP. AFTER ALL WERE CLEAR, WE TOOK TO THE SEA SWIMMING IN AN ATTEMPT TO MAKE THE RESCUE SHIP. THREE OF US MADE IT. MYSELF, THIRD MATE, AND FWT.

7. RESCUE SHIP KHIAN STAR DID AN OUTSTANDING JOB PICKING UP SURVIVORS AS SEAS WERE OVER TWENTY-FIVE TO THIRTY FEET IN WINDS OVER FORTY KNOTS.

8. I DO NOT HAVE THE AUTHORITY TO DESTROY MY OWN

SHIP OR I WOULD ORDER IT SUNK NOW. IT IS A FLOATING
TIME BOMB FOR THE FOLLOWING REASONS:

NO. 1 HATCH: CLAYMORE MINES AND DETONATORS ARE
   ADRIFT.

NO. 2 HATCH: 500-POUND BOMBS ARE ADRIFT.

NO. 3 HATCH: SMALL ARMS AMMO AND 500-POUND
   BOMBS ARE ADRIFT.

NO. 4 HATCH WAS SECURE, BUT PROBABLY HAS CARGO
   ADRIFT DUE TO EXPLOSION FWD END NO. 5 TWEEN
   DECK.

NO. 5 HATCH STILL HAS LOOSE 2,000-POUND BOMBS
   ROLLING AROUND AND SOME HAVE DROPPED DOWN
   INTO THE LOWER HOLD WHERE 750-POUND BOMBS
   ARE STOWED.

9. FOURTEEN SURVIVORS.

10. STOCK OF SPARE SHORING MATERIAL WHICH WAS TAKEN
    OFF IN BANGOR AGAINST WISHES OF SHIP TO A GREAT
    EXTENT CAUSED LOSS OF BADGER STATE.

11. ARE ANY U.S. NAVAL OR COAST GUARD VESSELS COMING
    TO SCENE TO EITHER DESTROY THE DERELICT OR TRY TO
    SALVAGE IT? MASTER, BADGER STATE, ABOARD KHIAN
    STAR.

There are two errors in the message attributable to the shock and
distress experienced by the survivors of the tragedy. Chief Mate Leonard
Cobbs did not remain aboard the *Badger State* to help launch the lifeboat,
as indicated. Rather, in accordance with Wilson's orders, he was aboard
the lifeboat as officer-in-charge when it was launched from the ship.
Also, as determined by the U. S. Coast Guard Marine Board of Investigation, thirty-five seamen left the ship in the lifeboat.

According to Captain Niros, all survivors were disturbed by their
experience, but none needed special medical attention. He also reported
that "all survivors said that Captain Wilson had done all he could on the
Badger State, and that he was a very good man. They all liked him."

*   *   *

The SS *Flying Dragon*, a U.S. vessel enroute from Sasebo, Japan, to Long Beach, California, also diverted to the scene early on the morning of December 25. The Navy had requested that the ship meet the *Badger State* and escort her to Midway. While en route to the area, the *Flying Dragon* received word that the stricken ship had been abandoned and was dead in the water.

Upon arrival on scene on December 27, the *Flying Dragon* closed to within a mile of the *Badger State*. Captain Richard F. Toomey observed the evidence of an explosion aboard the ship. The *Badger State* lay broadside to the swells, rolling severely. As it did so, water entered the hole blasted in the hull of the ship, and then poured out as the ship rolled in the opposite direction.

Preparing for rescue, all hands except watch standers were mustered on deck to serve as lookouts and to help in rescuing any survivors. Some debris was spotted in the water. Closer inspection showed that it was the *Badger State*'s capsized lifeboat. Captain Toomey maneuvered his ship alongside, bumping against the boat, flipping it over on its side. There were no bodies in or under it.

The *Flying Dragon* cruised through the area searching for signs of life, but there were none. Several men in lifejackets, floating head down, were all that remained of the crew of the *Badger State*. One body was recovered, using grappling hooks. Sea conditions were too dangerous to permit the recovery of any other bodies.

The *Flying Dragon* remained on scene until relieved by a Navy ship, the USS *Abnaki*, on December 30.

CHAPTER 16

The Will of God

The room was small and sparsely furnished with a bunk, a miniature table with a reading lamp bolted to it, and a wash basin. But it was private, courtesy of the skipper of the *Khian Star*. Wilson desperately needed the privacy, and time to be alone with his thoughts.

Exhausted, he lay uncomfortably on his back in the dimly lit room, eyes bloodshot, face deeply furrowed, staring blankly at the overhead. Every part of his body ached from the strain of the day, and an uncomfortable queasiness in his stomach threatened to spill over. He closed his eyes tightly, but sleep would not come. His mind, supercharged with images, would not allow him the luxury of forgetting.

Earlier, a seaman had ushered him into the wheelhouse of the *Khian Star*. One of the crew had given up a pair of oversized trousers and a shirt to match which Wilson gratefully wore under an ill-fitting overcoat. His legs felt terribly weak, but a Greek seaman had walked by his side, steadying him. The seaman spoke to Captain Niros who then turned to him, extending his hand.

"Captain Wilson, how do you do," he had said politely with a friendly smile and barely a trace of an accent in his voice.

Wilson grasped the hand he was offered. "I would hope for better circumstances . . ." He paused, feeling sick to his stomach. And then the words tumbled out. "My men? How many—"

"Last count, Captain, we have taken on board twelve of your crew. We are still searching. You are welcome to help me here, if you are able to."

Wilson caught his breath, feeling as though he had been punched hard in the pit of his stomach. "Thank you," he managed to say in a low voice. The captain's words echoed in his ears. *Only twelve of his crew saved . . . twelve out of thirty-nine of his crew!* He shook his head, recalling his own desperate fight for survival. But only twelve saved. He closed his eyes, and his head fell forward, overcome with the enormity of the loss.

"Captain, Captain, are you all right?" Niros asked, a look of concern crossing his face. Sensing Wilson's thoughts and feelings, he added, "Do not worry, we will continue all efforts to save your men."

Wilson could only nod, tears welling up in his eyes. He didn't have to say anything. Both men understood.

The two captains, the rescued and the rescuer, had much in common. The sea had shaped their lives. They risked its dangers, and shared an immense responsibility for the safety of countless crews, ships, and cargoes. As both knew, the ocean was a fanciful adversary. One could never know when their respective roles might be reversed.

Wilson had accepted the captain's invitation and remained in the wheelhouse, holding to the slender hope that more of his men might still be found. He watched with professional admiration as Captain Niros expertly maneuvered his ship in the raging seas looking for signs of life. And finally there had been such a sign, a weak gesture by a seaman in the water. Niros brought his ship about in close proximity to the man. Seamen on deck, themselves hanging on in the face of waves that sometimes washed over them, hauled someone up from the water.

Wilson's face lit up as he recognized one of his officers, Willie Burnette. A thirteenth survivor! He felt his emotions bubbling to the surface, and he went below to greet him. But Burnette was in wretched shape and unable to talk.

The *Khian Star* continued her search. Wilson spotted another man feebly struggling in the water. His heart leaped as he recognized the unmistakably bulky frame of his good friend, Bob Ziehm. Bad leg and all, he had managed to make it to the ship. Wilson limped out to the open wing of the bridge and waved excitedly, shouting encouragement.

Ziehm, making little movement in the rampaging waters, seemed to be trying to raise an arm in response, but appeared exhausted and too weak to manage the effort.

Wilson watched anxiously as Captain Niros attempted to maneuver his ship close to Ziehm. It took precious moments for Niros to bring the huge ship about. Wilson lost sight of the officer as the ship turned. On the return approach, they found only an empty life ring. No sign of the second mate could be seen anywhere. Wilson's hopes and good spirits were dashed.

As it turned out, Willie Burnette, one of thirteen crewmembers to survive, was the last survivor taken aboard. The others, including the bosun, the mate, the chief engineer, Ed Hottendorf, and Bob Ziehm, had not made it. They had succumbed to the cold, to exhaustion, and to injuries.

Wilson first learned from George Henderson what happened to the men in the lifeboat—the bomb, the boat capsizing, the birds. To Wilson, the loss was extraordinarily personal. He had lost the best of a crew of good and brave men under his command. Such an immense loss felt like more than he could bear.

The inevitable questions, which had plagued him and the crew from day one, tortured him, tumbling out in his mind one after the other: the loading at Bangor; the ship's routing north; the inability to break out south; the unpredicted and violent storms over Christmas; the inadequate shoring; the loss of the port lifeboat which forced launching on the starboard side where the hull had been holed; the delays from the engine room casualties; and many other matters. All were critical events. A change in any one might have enabled them to reach their destination without harm.

And then came the second-guessing. Would any of the numerous decisions he had been forced to make have made a difference if he had chosen differently? In raising these issues, he knew there could never be answers.

It was not only the questions that bedeviled him, but other circumstances and coincidences: the sinking of the *Badger State*'s sister ship in the same waters a few years earlier; the demoralizing presence of the scavenging seabirds, compounding the fear of men trapped in the frigid waters; even the number of his crew saved—thirteen.

But most tragic and unaccountable of all was the blockbuster bomb hurtling into the lifeboat at the precise moment the boat was directly abreast of No. 5 tween deck. Had that not happened, the lifeboat and all of the seamen aboard would have reached the *Khian Star*. It would have been possible to rig a line between boat and ship, and the men could have been hauled aboard, one by one, probably without any loss of life. That single bomb out of the belly of the *Badger* had been a killer.

As Wilson's mind began to wander, it seemed to him that the difference between living and dying was incredibly fragile. Grabbing a line or the rung of a ladder, or being unable to wrap limbs around them. Summoning the strength needed at the very last critical moment, or succumbing to hours of struggling in unforgiving waters. The line between life and death was fragile indeed.

Wilson simply did not know what to make of it. The questions about what might have been always returned to the reality of the present, the loss of ship and crew. *Maybe if I had stayed on board,* he thought. *Let the damn bombs roll out. What the hell, maybe I could have tried to roll them out.*

Even considering such questions seemed somehow ridiculous. *God,* he thought, *I'm losing it! The best thing I did was to get everybody off the damn ship! Rest easy with that, Wilson.* But he couldn't. He tossed and turned, and could not rid himself of the torrent of pictures flooding through his head.

As his torment subsided, Wilson knew that he and his crew had been severely tested by a series of major events that had come unbidden into the ordinary routine of their daily lives. The challenge had been laid down. And the men of the *Badger State* had given every part of themselves—their strength, their endless work day and night, their hearts and souls—to the battle. No bitching, no griping, no excuses. They dealt with the hand the Dealer gave them and did the best they could with what they had. No more could be expected or demanded of anyone.

He pondered over these thoughts for a long time. *Yes,* he thought, *his men were true heroes. The ones that survived would somehow have to pick up the pieces of their lives and move on.*

Death is no stranger in the hostile environment of the sea. It cultivates a largely unspoken belief in a higher power. Wilson, as did many of his crew, shared a rough-hewn faith in a supreme being. Most, if put to it, would probably find comfort in the simple creed expressed by Melville's Ishmael in *Moby-Dick*: "But what is worship?—to do the will of God—*that* is worship. And what is the will of God?—to do to my fellowman what I would have my fellowman do to me—*that* is the will of God."

Wilson turned on his side, staring at the bulkhead, eyes wide open, seeing nothing. A thousand-yard stare. He slowly slipped the lines to consciousness, and drifted off into oblivion.

Epilogue

SS *Badger State*

The armed forces began a massive effort to rescue survivors and to salvage the *Badger State* and her military cargo. Seven ships were deployed, among them the Navy's USS *Abnaki* from Pearl Harbor, which relieved the *Flying Dragon* on scene. Coast Guard and Air Force planes from Hawaii also pitched in, covering roughly eight thousand miles of ocean in a search that continued until the end of December. No other survivors were found.

Abandoned, the *Badger State* drifted aimlessly, too dangerous to board, too risky to salvage. She was a stubborn old lady to the very end, reluctant to take leave of the seas she had sailed on for so many years. Gradually, the ocean savaged her compartments and holds, weighing her down by the stern. The *Abnaki* told the story in a report filed with Navy headquarters:

> Recommend *Badger State* be considered a total loss due to fire on board, potential hazard to navigation, and extreme danger to any boarding personnel.

The response:

> In view of the dangerous conditions of the SS *Badger State* as reported by USS *Abnaki*, Commander Service Force Pacific Fleet considers that any further attempt to salvage the SS *Badger State* are not justified due to the unwarranted risks involved. Signed, Captain James Cook

In her last moments, as though making a last-gasp plea for help, the *Badger State* emitted mysterious red, white, and orange flashes of light before disappearing forever. The *Abnaki* dared not approach her close up, and tracked her as a pulsating blip on a radar screen. Eventually, that slender contact was lost. Captain Wilson's gallant ship went down in the deep waters of the north Pacific. There she joined her sister ship, the *Panoceanic Faith*, which sank almost within heaving distance in the same general area.

The ship left a few mementos recovered by the *Abnaki*: scraps of dunnage and sheet plywood; a few broken wooden chairs; pieces of Styrofoam; a dilapidated board bearing the ship's name; and, fittingly, a "tombstone"—a tattered life ring buoy imprinted with the ship's name and bearing a Coast Guard inspection plate dated May 3, 1968.

The *Badger State* was one of ten C-2 cargo ships operated by States Marine Lines. Following her loss, States Marine scrapped or sold all its C-2s and replaced them with the larger and faster C-3 and C-4 models.

Captain Charles T. Wilson

Following his return to the States and the inevitable government inquiry, Wilson felt the need to get away for a spell. He saddled up "Old Blue," an ancient Jeep Wagoneer, and struck out into southern California's Anza-Borrego Desert for a breather. Extending his road trip along the Colorado River, he sought solitude. It was a time for rest and reflection—to sit back and absorb the desolate beauty of the area and listen to the silence.

The break was short-lived. States Marine Lines showed their confidence in the young skipper by assigning him as master of another one of their ships, the SS *Gopher State*. "It was the right medicine administered at the right time," Wilson said, "the get-back-on-your-horse-when-it-throws-you approach. And it worked."

Sometime afterward, Wilson started seriously courting his lovely Mary. The planets were in their proper orbit, and the chemistry was right. She became that special person in his life, and they married. Dropping anchor ashore is always a momentous move for a skipper devoted to his profession, but this was the right move at the right time for these two.

A few other details in his life demanded attention. He bought that Honda cycle, and later added a second one. While he was at sea, baby sisters came along and he decided the motorcycles would do nicely to transport them around the college campus.

Between voyages at sea, he got acquainted with a nifty Cessna. Eventually, he earned a commercial pilot's license and the right to ferry planes and cargo. He did that for a spell, a love affair that continues.

Not the least of his acquisitions, a baby grand piano graces the beautiful home shared by Mary and Charles Wilson.

Of memories, Wilson has many. But always hovering close to the surface is the tragedy of the *Badger State*, and the loss of so many outstanding seamen. Tears brim over unexpectedly at times when he chances to think of them. "They were all heroes!" he says sadly.

Bosun Richard D. Hughes

Jennifer Miller has only hazy memories of her dad, Bosun Dick Hughes. She looks for closure that never quite seems to come. It is the same dilemma faced by Theresa Anderson, the daughter of Kinnie Woods, and by many other kin to those who did not return. Dad is there one day, and the next, he is gone. No body, no grave, no place to mourn, nothing to hang on to. The feelings recall those described by Richard Dana in *Two Years Before the Mast*, when he describes the aching loss of a shipmate:

> Death is at all times solemn, but never so much so as at sea. A man dies on shore; his body remains with his friends, and "the mourners go about the streets"; but when a man falls overboard at sea and is lost, there is a suddenness in the event, and a difficulty in realizing it, which give to it an air of awful mystery. A man dies on shore— you follow his body to the grave, and a stone marks the spot. You

are often prepared for the event. There is always something which helps you to realize it when it happens, and to recall it when it has passed. . . . but at sea, the man is near you—at your side—you hear his voice, and in an instant he is gone, and nothing but a vacancy shows his loss.

Jennifer does remember vaguely her sojourn to Washington, D.C. She was three years old at the time, unable to fathom the significance of being a guest of the President of the United States. It was 12:15 P.M. on August 13, 1970. She had escaped the guiding hand of her mother and, pretty-as-you-please, traipsed across a squeaky-clean room in the White House in a breach of West Wing protocol. Minor Executive Office underlings gasped as she wended her way innocently toward President Richard M. Nixon.

President Nixon, surrounded by his aides and other important-looking dignitaries, was expressing the nation's appreciation for the bravery of her dad, Richard D. Hughes, the bosun aboard the SS *Badger State*. Jennifer could not understand the words, or the loss that prompted them. The President paused as she approached, bent down, kindly patted her on the head, and gave her a pen. She smiled somewhat precociously, and then looked back at her mom who motioned for her to return. She slowly meandered back to stand by her mother's side.

The occasion was the presentation of the American Merchant Marine Seamanship Trophy Award. An honor established in 1962 to recognize acts of extraordinary seamanship and maritime skill by American citizens, this occasion marked the first time that the award had been given posthumously.

Bosun Hughes was cited for his organizational ability in supervising the attempts to resecure the bombs, working without rest, and for improvising solutions to the increasingly dangerous situation aboard the *Badger State*, despite severe back injuries and exhaustion. The citation on the trophy paid tribute to his "distinguished seamanship under great stress displayed during the fire and explosion which cost him his life." The Maritime Administration's press release, issued June 8, 1970, read in part:

Mr. Hughes was chosen to receive the Award because of his self-less courage, skill, and devotion to duty. He lost his life when the *Badger State* exploded, caught fire, and sank on December 26, 1969, while carrying materiel to support our forces in Vietnam.

For little Jennifer, the loss would be temporarily forgotten in the rhythm of early childhood, only to resurface in later life. For Hughes's widow, Nancy Hughes (now Keys), there has been no such relief. As it is for most of the widows and mothers seamen leave behind, the loss was a major tragedy. It aroused emotions which years later still hover close, spilling over when triggered by a photo, a song, or any number of treasures of a shared life suddenly no more.

Able Seaman George D. Henderson

Henderson proved to be a strong force throughout the voyage in resecuring the cargo. Beyond that, however, he helped some half-dozen of his shipmates, including Dick Hughes, to board a liferaft dropped by an airplane, and then encouraged them not to give up and to stay alert while awaiting rescue. For his heroic actions in helping save his shipmates, he was awarded one of the Coast Guard's top awards, its Silver Lifesaving Medal. The citation "for heroic action" read in part:

Mr. Henderson's courageous performance is in keeping with the highest traditions of the sea and reflect great credit upon himself and the United States Merchant Marine Service.

The Survivors

On January 9, 1970, at sea aboard the *Khian Star*, Captain Wilson drafted a letter of appreciation to the captain and crew of the ship. It summed up the sentiments of those who survived, each of whom signed the letter. The letter read as follows:

We, the survivors of the SS *Badger State*, give to you our deepest thanks and most profound gratitude for saving our lives. Your rescue efforts, under extremely adverse conditions of high winds and seas, were truly outstanding. Even after seeing the explosion and fire on board the *Badger State*, and knowing we had extremely dangerous explosives on board, you ventured nearer our stricken ship, without thought for your own safety, in an effort to save all hands.

Again, we thank you for our lives; and may God bless and keep every one of you.

Captain C. T. Wilson, Master
Steven Bordash, First Engineer
Willie L. Burnette, Third Mate
Lawrence O. McHugh, Deck
   Utility
George Henderson, Able
   Seaman
James McLure, Ordinary
   Seaman
Naji Saiban, Chief Cook

Donald D. Byrd, Third Cook
Charles McCullar, Messman
Richard Pattershall, Third
   Assistant Engineer
Neal Kirkwood, Cadet Engineer
James H. Beatty, Fireman-
   Watertender
Samuel Kaneao, Fireman-
   Watertender
Florencio Serafino, Wiper

Those Who Did Not Survive

The body of one seaman was recovered: John S. Kaleiwahea, Ordinary Seaman.

The roll call of those missing and presumed dead in a mission undertaken on behalf of their country:

Mohamed T. Al-Muwallad,
   Wiper
Gilbert F. Baker, Chief
   Engineer
Nick Barbieri, Oiler
Sam A. Bondy, Jr., Third Mate
Bennie L. Brown, Steward
Joseph Candos, Able Seaman

Leonard Cobbs, Chief Mate
Charles E. Coe, Messman
Nelson Fabre, Able Seaman
Ali A. Gazaly, Messman
Edward C. Hottendorf, Able
   Seaman
Richard D. Hughes, Bosun
John H. Jenkins, Galleyman

Edwin L. Jones, Messman
William K. LaFayette, Radio
  Officer
Konstantinos Mpountalis,
  Electrician
Richard C. Murray, Ordinary
  Seaman
Francisco C. Nunez, Oiler
Raymond W. Reiche, Second
  Assistant Engineer

Floyd K. Rilling, Able Seaman
Jose A. Rodriguez, Second
  Electrician
Leonard J. Scypion, Fireman-
  Watertender
Calvin R. Smith, Oiler
Kinnie Woods, Third Assistant
  Engineer
Robert A. Ziehm, Second
  Mate

The Coast Guard, in its investigation of the sinking of the *Badger State*, was unstinting in its praise of the master and crew: "Throughout this ordeal the actions of the master and crewmembers of the *Badger State* were in the best traditions of the sea. Although their untiring efforts failed to save the vessel, the calmness and devotion to duty which they exhibited undoubtedly prevented an even more extensive loss of life."

Aside from the heroics, a dark side followed a few of the men, the memory of the voyage weighing heavily on their lives. Some sought escape in heavy drinking; one seaman reportedly experienced severe mental stress on a later voyage and had to be put ashore for treatment; and some stopped sailing completely, perhaps fearful of a similar voyage. One seaman changed his name as though that act alone would somehow wipe clean a memory that could not be forgotten.

MV *Khian Star*

The *Khian Star* carried the surviving seamen to Yokohama, Japan, whence they were subsequently repatriated back to the States.

The survivors of the *Badger State* uniformly praised the efforts and the generosity of the crew of the *Khian Star* in seeing to their comfort and general welfare. "We were treated the finest that I have ever been treated in my life," James Beatty said. "They saw to our comfort, our happiness, our well-being. They risked their lives to stay out with the seas breaking over their own decks to pull us out of the water. Their captain had the greatest courage in the world to bring his ship around in those seas. Sometimes the ship seemed to almost disappear under the water with only the smokestack showing. I don't know how he ever stayed up in those seas. They deserve all the credit in the world."

Captain Evangelos Niros, master of the *Khian Star*, was later awarded the American Bureau of Shipping Valor Medal, only the fifth such award made since its creation forty years earlier. It carried the following citation:

> With a display of great seamanship and courage, Captain Niros maneuvered the *Khian Star* off the disabled vessel, and he and his men rescued fourteen survivors of the *Badger State*.

The Coast Guard Lifesaving Medal was awarded to Greek seaman Ioannis "John Texas" Kantziakis for bravery. The citation read in part:

> For heroic action on the morning of 26 December 1969 when he attempted to rescue a seaman from the American merchant vessel SS *Badger State*. . . . Mr. Kantziakis displayed outstanding courage, initiative and fortitude while jeopardizing his own life in this valiant attempt to save the life of a fellow man. His courageous act is in keeping with the highest traditions of the sea.

Coast Guard Marine Board of Investigation

Federal law requires the U.S. Coast Guard to inquire into casualties at sea in order to determine the cause of a casualty and then recommend ways to prevent it from recurring. The procedure is similar to that followed after airplane disasters.

A Board of Investigation was convened in Seattle, Washington, on January 14, 1970, to hear testimony from the survivors of the *Badger State*, and to hear from other persons of interest. The Board's findings were submitted to Coast Guard headquarters in Washington, D.C., and ultimately to the National Transportation Safety Board for final approval.

The National Board concluded that the casualty was probably due to the way the bombs were stowed and packaged. The techniques used at Bangor could not contain the bombs when the ship rolled during bad weather. In the case of the extreme roll to 52 degrees, a total load of 14,000 pounds was estimated to have been placed on the support sheathing and blocking. That load could not be sustained. Once the bombs started moving, kinetic energy came into play, resulting in more breakage of the supports.

The Board cited certain contributing factors: lack of a stowage design criteria; the method of stowage, which created a "chain series" of possible failure points so that a break in the chain inevitably caused other links in the chain to fail. The Board also faulted the design of the pallet bands; the distribution of cargo and fuel; the ship's sailing light on cargo; lack of bilge keels; the unpredicted storms of December 25 and 26, and the severity of the storm on the 26th.

Looking at factors which may have contributed to the loss of life after abandoning ship, the Board noted the following, among others: failure of the life rafts to remain close so that crewmembers could board them; the failure of the lifeboat painter, which deprived the crew of a means of shearing the lifeboat away from the ship; the falling of the 2,000-pound bomb into the boat; the lack of better techniques to detect and rescue persons in stormy seas; and the tendency of the life jackets to slide upward, pushing the head of a person forward into the water.

The testimony of the survivors relating to technical issues figured largely in the findings of the Marine Board. But there was also a personal side to their statements. Donald Byrd commented, "If it wasn't for the captain, none of us would be here. If I ever go back to sea, if I saw his name, I would go just because he was the skipper, and we all feel the same way." James Beatty added, "I would be proud to be the first man to sail with Captain Wilson again, and I sincerely mean that. He did everything he could for us. Certainly, his consideration was for his crew and

for his ship at all times. I am very proud to know the man." The sentiments of the crew may have been summed up best by Samuel Kaneao,
who displayed considerable emotion as he testified under oath, "My captain is brilliant and my ship is tough!"

The U.S. Merchant Marine

New techniques have revolutionized the carrying of goods at sea since
World War II. Ships like the *Badger State*, with its break-bulk cargoes—
loading and unloading cargo piece by piece as distinguished from bulk
cargoes such as grain, coal, and oil—continued to operate for years after
the war, but they were gradually replaced by a new breed of ships.

The container ship, for one, proved to be a major advance. A shipper
simply packaged his goods in twenty- to forty-foot-long steel and aluminum boxes at the plant, sealed them, and trucked them to the dock
where special lifts loaded them aboard specially built ships. The containers eventually reached the shipper's ultimate customer unopened. The
results were dramatic: container ships can carry four times more cargo
than the C-2 *Badger State*; sail at twice the speed; and load and unload in
a fourth of the time.

"Roll-on, roll-off" was a further refinement of that concept. The
containers were trucked directly into the ship through openings in her
sides and stern, the cab then returning ashore, leaving the container on
wheels aboard the ship. At destination, cabs wheeled the containers off
the ship and delivered them. LASH (Lighter Aboard Ship), which
employs a similar principle, carries lighters or barges loaded with goods
moved by the ship's own crane, a system particularly useful in ports
served by river systems.

In spite of such developments, the U.S. merchant marine remains
what it has largely been throughout this past century: a high-cost operation. Government subsidies help build and operate merchant ships under
the American flag, but that help has been uncertain, subject to political
whims and largely dependent on foreign military needs. A Vietnam or

Gulf War invariably dramatizes the need for the merchant marine, but interest flags with the passing of the emergency that precipitated it.

Checking ships' arrivals and departures in most newspapers, readers are usually amazed to find that Liberia, or perhaps Panama, or even the Marshall Islands may boast what seems to be ownership of the largest fleets of merchant ships in the world. How can such small countries, so far out of the mainstream of international trade, have so many ships flying their flag? Flags of convenience, the arrangement is called. Registry in these countries needs only a fee paid upfront, and an annual payment based on tonnage. In exchange, owners pay no income tax, can hire seamen from wherever they wish, and can build and operate their ships anywhere without restriction. The U.S. government has confused feelings about the arrangement, but says that U.S. owners still control foreign-flagged ships, and those ships can still be made available to the military in times of emergencies.

Whatever the future may hold, the past and present are perhaps best summed up in the words of a presidential proclamation issued on May 21, 2003, that recited a litany of contributions made by the U.S. merchant marine: more than 6,000 merchant mariners and 700 U.S. merchant ships lost during World War II; additional sacrifices of men and ships during Korea, Vietnam, and the Persian Gulf; and, most recently, over 5,000 merchant mariners sailing on 157 ships to supply U.S. troops in Iraq.

"Today, as in the past," the proclamation reads, "America depends on our maritime services to help ensure our security, promote our prosperity, and advance the universal hope of freedom. We honor the service and proud history of our merchant mariners."

Bibliography

Books

Albion, Robert Greenhalgh, and Jennie Barnes Pope. *Sea Lanes in Wartime: The American Experience, 1775–1945*. 2nd ed. Hamden, CT: Archon Books, 1968.

Baarslag, Karl. *Famous Sea Rescues* (formerly titled *SOS to the Rescue*). New York: Grossett & Dunlap, 1935.

Bunker, John. *Liberty Ships: The Ugly Ducklings of World War II*. Annapolis, MD: Naval Institute Press, 1972.

Burton, Hal. *The Morro Castle*. New York: Viking Press, 1973.

Cornell, Felix M., and Allan C. Hoffman, *American Merchant Seaman's Manual*. New York: Cornell Maritime Press, 1946.

Crowell, Benedict, and Robert Forest Wilson. *How America Went to War: An Account from Official Sources of the Nation's War Activities, 1917–1920*. New Haven, CT: Yale University Press, 1921.

Dalzell, George W. *The Flight from the Flag: The Continuing Effect of the Civil War Upon the American Carrying Trade*. Chapel Hill, NC: University of North Carolina Press, 1940.

Dana, Richard H., Jr. *Two Years Before the Mast*. New York: P.F. Collier & Son, 1909.

De La Pedraja, Rene. *A Historical Dictionary of the U. S. Merchant Marine and Shipping Industry Since the Introduction of Steam*. Westport, CT: Greenwood Press, 1994.

Dunmore, Walter T. *Ship Subsidies: An Economic Study of the Policy of Subsidizing Merchant Marines*. New York: Houghton Mifflin, 1907.

Felknor, Bruce L., ed. *The U. S. Merchant Marine at War, 1775–1945*. Annapolis, MD: Naval Institute Press, 1998.

Gannon, Michael. *Operation Drumbeat: Germany's First U-Boat Attacks Along the American Coast in World War II*. New York: Harper & Row, 1990.

Garitee, Jerome R. *The Republic's Private Navy: The American Privateering Business as Practiced by Baltimore during the War of 1812*. Middletown, CT: Wesleyan University Press, 1977.

Gibson, Andrew, and Arthur Donovan. *The Abandoned Ocean*. Columbia, SC: University of South Carolina Press, 2000.

Gibson, Charles Dana. *Merchantman? Or Ship of War: A Synopsis of Laws, U.S. State Department Positions, and Practices which Alter the Peaceful Character of U.S. Merchant Vessels in Time of War*. Camden, ME: Ensign Press, 1986.

Hagan, Kenneth J. *This People's Navy*. New York: Free Press, 1991.

Hayler, William B., John M. Keever and Paul M. Seiler. *The Cornell Manual for Lifeboatmen, Able Seamen, and Qualified Members of Engine Department*. Centreville, MD: Cornell Maritime Press, Inc., 1984.

Healey, James C. *Foc'sle and Glory Hole: A Study of the Merchant Seaman and His Occupation*. New York: Merchant Marine Publishers Association, 1936.

Hilton, George W. *Eastland, Legacy of the Titanic*. Stanford, CA: Stanford University Press, 1995.

Junger, Sebastian. *The Perfect Storm*. New York: HarperCollins, 1998.

Kell, John McIntosh. *Recollections of a Naval Life, Including the Cruises of the Confederate States' Steamers "Sumter" and "Alabama"*. Washington, D.C.: Neale, 1900.

Lawrence, Samuel A. *U.S. Merchant Marine Shipping Policies and Politics*. Washington, D.C.: Brookings Institution, 1966.

Ludins, George H. *Seamanship for New Skippers*. Miami: Banyan Books, 1980.

Maclay, Edgar Stanton. *A History of American Privateers*. New York: D. Appleton and Co., 1895.

Marvin, Winthrop L. *The American Merchant Marine: Its History and Romance from 1620 to 1902*. New Haven, CT: Yale University Press, 1919.

McCunn, Ruthanne Lum. *Sole Survivor: A Story of Record Endurance at Sea*. Boston: Beacon Press, 1999.

Melville, Herman. *Moby-Dick, or The Whale*. 1851.

Moore, Arthur R. *A Careless Word ... A Needless Sinking*. Kings Point, NY: American Merchant Marine Museum, 1983.

Nevins, Allan. *Sail On: The Story of the American Merchant Marine*. New York: United States Lines Company, 1946.

Norris, Martin J. *The Law of Seamen*, Vol. 1. New York: Baker, Voorhis & Co., 1951.

Paine, Ralph D. *The Old Merchant Marine: A Chronicle of American Ships and Sailors*. New Haven, CT: Yale University Press, 1921.

Rachlis, Eugene. *The Story of the U.S. Coast Guard*. New York: Random House, 1961.

Riesenberg, Felix, Jr. *Sea War*. New York: Rinehart, 1956.

——. *Standard Seamanship for the Merchant Marine*. New York: D. Van Nostrand Company, 1936.

Sherman, Rev. Andrew M. *Life of Captain Jeremiah O'Brien, Machias, Maine.* Morristown, NJ: George W. Sherman, 1902.

Spears, John R. *The History of Our Navy: From its Origins to the End of the War with Spain 1775–1898*, Vol. 1. New York: Charles Scribner's Sons, 1902.

———. *The Story of the American Merchant Marine.* New York: The Macmillan Company, 1919.

Standard Oil Company (New Jersey). *Ships of the Esso Fleet in World War II.* New York: Standard Oil Company, 1946.

Summersell, Charles Grayson. *CSS Alabama: Builder, Captain, and Plans.* University, AL: University of Alabama Press, 1985.

Thomas, Gordon, and Max M. Witts. *Shipwreck: The Strange Fate of the Morro Castle.* New York: Viking Press, 1973.

Turpin, Edward A., and William A. MacEwen. *Merchant Marine Officers' Handbook.* Cambridge, MD: Cornell Maritime Press, 1950.

Wentworth, Commodore Ralph S., and Commander John V. Noel, Jr. *Knight's Modern Seamanship.* 12th ed. New York: D. Van Nostrand Company, 1953.

West, Wallace. *Down to the Sea in Ships: The Story of the U. S. Merchant Marine.* New York: Noble and Noble, 1947.

Periodicals, Magazines, Internet Sources

Ambrose, Stephen. "Remembering Sultana." *National Geographic Society.* 2001. www.news.nationalgeographic.com/news/2001/05/0501_river5.html

Bunker, John. "The Seafarers in World War II." Detroit: SIUNA, 1951.

Cameron, John S. "The Sea Wolf's Prey." *Sunset*, August-November 1918.

Doolin, Ralph. Marine Net, Inc. "RogueWaves." October 14, 2000. www.sailnet.com

Encyclopaedia Britannica, s.v. "Ship"; "Dynamic stability." www.britannica.com

Federation of American Scientists. "Bombs for Beginners." June 11, 2003. www.fas.org

Fleming, Douglas K. "Reflections on the History of US Cargo Liner Service [Part II]." *Maritime Economics & Logistics*, 2003.

Gale Encyclopedia of Medicine, 2nd ed., s.v. "Near Drowning"; "Hypothermia."

Hong Kong Cricket Association. "History of Cricket in Hong Kong—Sinking of the SS *Bokhara*," 2003. www.cricket.org/link_to_database/NATIONAL/ICC_MEMBERS/HKG/HISTORY/BOKHARA.html

International Commission on Shipping. "Ships, Slaves and Competition." Media Release, 2003. www.icons.org.au/operations.html

Landsberg, P. G., "Underwater Blast Injuries," *Trauma & Emergency Medicine*. Vol. 17, No. 2, July 2000.

Lawton, Graham. "Monsters of the Deep." *New Scientist*, Vol. 170, issue 2297. June 30, 2001.

Levine, David, and Sara Ann Platt. "The Contribution of U.S. Shipbuilding and the Merchant Marine in the Second World War." In *America's Maritime Legacy*, Robert A. Kilmarx, ed. Boulder, CO: Westview Press, 1979.

Lind, James. "A Treatise of the Scurvy." London: A. Millar, 1753.

Lowson, James A. "Sensations in Drowning." *Edinburgh Medical Journal*. 13:41–45. 1903.

Mapes, Harold T. "Wireless Man Tells of Silver Shell's Fight." *New York Times Magazine*, July 8, 1917.

McKie, Robin, and Mark Townsend. "Danger on the seas as walls of water sink tankers." *The Observer* (United Kingdom). November 10, 2002.

Muldoon, Tony. "Classic Casualties." *Professional Mariner*. June–July, 2003.

National Archives, College Park, MD. "SS *Brilliant*, Torpedoed on November 18, 1942." U. S. Navy Memorandum for File, February 4, 1943.

———. "Loss of USA Transport *Jack* by Enemy Action May 27, 1942." Record Group 38. Zone Public Relations Office, Tampa. "How heroes are made . . ." August 21, 1942.

———. "Loss of M/V *Kattegat* by Enemy Action," May 20, 1942. Record Group 24. U. S. Navy Memorandum for File, February 28, 1943.

———. Naval Armed Guard Reports. Record Group 38. Voyage Report of SS *Nathaniel Greene*. Lt. (jg) R. M. Billings, USNR.

———. Naval Armed Guard Reports. Record Group 38. Voyage Report of SS *St. Olaf*. Lt. (jg) Wesley Norton Miller, USNR.

Nova Scotia Museum, Department of Tourism and Culture. "The Halifax Explosion." www.museum.gov.ns.ca/mma/AtoZ/HalExpl.html

Pendick, Daniel. "Death of the *Britannic*: An Autopsy." Public Broadcasting Service, 2002. www.pbs.org/wnet/savageseas/captain-side-brittanic.html

Svitil, Kathy. "Freak Waves." 2003. Public Broadcasting Service. www.pbs.org/wnet/savageseas/neptune-side-waves.html

Texas State Historical Association. "Texas City Disaster." www.tsha.utexas.edu/handbook/online/articles

United Nations International Maritime Organization, Marine Safety Committee. "Advice on the Dangers of Flooding of Forward Compartments." Circular No. 995, June 11, 2001.

————. Marine Accident Investigation Branch. "Review of Lifeboat Launching Systems' Accidents." Safety Study 1/2001.

U. S. Department of Commerce, Maritime Administration. "A Veteran Returns." Publicity Release, October 30, 1966.

U. S. Department of Transportation. Coast Guard. "Coast Guard History." GPO, 1973.

————. "Marine Casualty Report, SS *Badger State*, Explosion Aboard and Eventual Sinking in the North Pacific Ocean, December 26, 1969."

————. "Marine Casualty Report, SS *Panoceanic Faith*, Foundering with Loss of Life, north Pacific Ocean October 9, 1967."

————. "Scotch Cap Light, General Information." www.uscg.mil/hq/ g-cp/history/weblighthouses/lhak.html

U. S. Maritime Administration. C-2 Ship Design.

U. S. Maritime Service Veterans. "Privateers and Mariners in the Revolutionary War". www.usmm.org/revolution.html

U. S. Naval Historical Center. "By Sea, Air, and Land". www.history.navy. mil/seaairland/chap4.htm

————. "Port Chicago Naval Magazine Explosion. Court of Inquiry: Findings of Facts, Opinion, and Recommendations." www.history.navy.mil/ faqs

Westcott, Alan. "Sinkings of American Merchantmen." *Current History*, October, 1918.

Whitemarsh, R. P. "Great Sea Waves." *U. S. Naval Institute Proceedings*, Vol. 60. August, 1934.

Court Decisions

Butler v. McClellan, Fed Cas 2242 (DC Me 1831)

Candee v. Sixty-eight Bales Cotton, 48 F 479 (DC Ala 1891)

Fisher v. Fisher, 250 NY 313, l65 NE 460 (1929)

F. I. Merryman, The, 27 F 313 (DC ED NY 1886)

Harden v. Gordon, Fed Cas 6047 (CC Me 1823)

Healy v. Cox, 45 F 119 (DC SC 1891)

Morris v. United States, 3 F2d 588 (CCA 2d, 1924)

Robertson v. Baldwin, 165 U.S. 275 (1897)

Shorey v. Rennell, Fed Cas 12806 (DC Mass 1858)

Stacey Clarke, The, 54 F 533 (DC Ala 1892)

Index